DIRECTORY

EAT-LONDON

London's restaurants, hotels, shops, arts and entertainment

2001-2002
VOL. 5

Cross Media Ltd.
13 Berners Street
London W1T 3LH
Tel: 020-7436-1960
Fax: 020-7436-1930

How to use RED

The RED Directory lists some 650 great restaurants, shops, sights and essential visitor services. Carefully selected for their quality and interest, all our entries are accurately marked on RED's easy-to-use maps – setting London at your feet.

To get the most out of your Eat-London, take a few moments to get acquainted with our new look – including a special feature on what's in vogue on the London restaurant scene and the Eat-London reviews.

Sections

Dining: *Eat-Global London:* The culinary world tour featuring a selection of top London restaurants listed by country.

Hotels: Recommended places to stay.

Shopping: Designer fashion, street fashion, markets and auction houses, herbalists, organic & gourmet foods, showcase of contemporary arts, & traditional British products, many awarded the Royal Warrant.

West End Theatre & Musicals: Long-running West-End successes, including listings and synopses.

Places of Interest: London's Arts & Places of Interest, a wealth of British heritage from science to Sherlock Holmes, historic houses to the latest in modern art & design.

Entertainment: Pubs, wine bars, tea rooms, internet cafes, jazz, opera, classical music, nightlife and cinema listings.

Other information: Essential contact information: airlines, embassies, tourist offices.

Features

What's in Vogue on the Food Front: Inscrutable, Japanese Cuisine.

Eat-London - The Reviews: *EAT-* Trendy, Posh, For Less, No Fuss, Authentic, Ambient, Pizza, Fish, Dim Sum, Veg, a selection of top London Eateries.

Maps

There are two maps of Central and Greater London and 14 area maps of London.

Use the entry map reference to refer to area maps and find your destination.

● numbered - indicates entries from the shopping, dining and musical sections.
○ numbered - indicates all other entries.

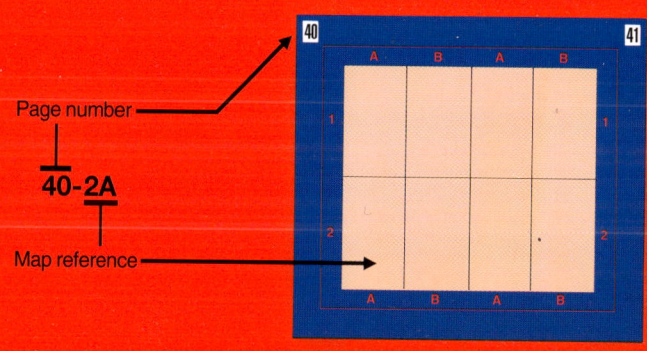

Page number

40-2A

Map reference

Key to Symbols

☎	Telephone Number	◎	Opening Hours	GN	Gatwick North Terminal
F	Fax Number	⊗	Holidays	GS	Gatwick South Terminal
E	E-mail Address	⊗No	Open 7 days	L	London Airport
H	Homepage Address	●	Opening days	C	Stansted Airport
T	Reservation Tel/Fax Number	Ex.	Except	Credit Cards:
↔	Underground/ Docklands Light Railway	Airport terminals:	VISA	VISA
≷	British Rail	H1	Heathrow terminal 1	M/C	Mastercard
₤	Admission ( )Child's Admission	H2	Heathrow terminal 2	AMEX	Amex
		H3	Heathrow terminal 3	D	Diners
		H4	Heathrow terminal 4	JCB	JCB

Restaurant closing hours indicates last orders time.
Restaurants - ₤ average cost of meal
Hotels - ₤ minimum rate
Details given in the embassies/consulates section refer to respective visa information desks.

CONTENTS

Special Feature – What's in Vogue –	8-13

Getting Around in London	17-19
Underground Map	17
Bus Routes	18-19

From the Centre to the Outskirts	22-53
Greater London	22-23
Central London & Environs	24-25
Mayfair/Bond St.(Central)	26-27
Piccadilly/Soho/Regent St./Bond St.(South)	28-29
Piccadilly/Regent St./Bond St.(Enlarged)	30-31
Oxford St.(West)/ Bond St.(North)/Baker St.(South)	32-33
Oxford St.(East)/ Hanover Sq./Tottenham Court Rd.	34-35
Covent Garden/Strand/Holborn	36-37
Blackfriars/St Paul's/ Mansion House/Barbican	38-39
Moorgate/Liverpool St.	40-41
Cannon St./Bank/ London Bridge/Tower Hill	42-43
High St. Kensington/Notting Hill Gate	44-45
Knightsbridge/Brompton Rd./ South Kensington/Sloane St.	46-47
Victoria/Hyde Park Corner/Belgravia	48-49
Westminster/Trafalgar Sq./ Charing Cross/Waterloo	50-51
Chelsea/Sloane Sq./King's Rd.	52-53

Eating London & Satisfying all the Sences	56-71
EAT-TRENDY	56-57
EAT-POSH	58-59
EAT-FOR LESS	60
EAT-NO FUSS	61
EAT-AUTHENTIC	62-63
EAT-AMBIENCE	65
EAT-PIZZA	00
WAT-FISH	67
EAT-DUM SUM	69
EAT-VEG.	70-71

Eating Global London & the Luxury of Choice	74-97
EAT BRITAIN	74-75
EAT-FRANCE	76-77
EAT-ITALY	78-79
EAT-SPAIN	80-81
EAT-EUROPE	82-83
EAT-INDIA	84-87
EAT-MID EAST & AFRICA	86-87
EAT-THAILAND	88-89
EAT-CHINA	90-93
EAT-ASIA	92-93
WAT-JAPAN	94-95
EAT-INTERNATIONAL	96-97

Eat & Sleep in London's Best Hotels	100-109

Eat & Shop in London's Shopping Paradise	112-131
Fashion	112-115
Tailoring/Knitwear/Shirts/Outdoor Clothing	116-117
Leather Goods/Shoes	118-119
Glass/China/Silverware	120-121
Jewellery/Watches	122-123
Antiques/Art Galleries/Auctioneers	124-125
Cosmetics/Toiletries/Linen/Other	126-127
Stationery/Gifts/Other	128-129
Gourmet Foods/Tea/Chocolate/Others	130-131

London Theatre & Musicals (data)	134-137

London Theatre & Musicals (synopses)	140-145
Buddy	140
Cats	141
Chicago	142
Les Misérables	143
The Phantom of the Opera	144
Art	145

London's Arts & Places of Interest	149-159
Places of Interest	149-153
Galleries, Museums	154-159

Entertainment	162-190
Cinemas	162-164
Art Centres	164
Classical Music	164-165
Opera, Ballet	165-166
Jazz	166-167
Rock	167-169
Nightclubs	169-172
Casinos	172-173
Department Stores	173-175
Shopping Centres & Arcades	175
Markets	175-177
Pubs	177-181
Wine Bars	181-184
Cafés	184-186
Internet Cafés	186-187
Tea Rooms	187-189
Sports	189-190
Exhibitions	190

Useful Information	192-199
Embassies, Consulates	192-194
Airlines	194-196
Tourist Boards	196-199
Useful Information	199

Index	202-208

JAPANESE IN LONDON

日本の味、欧風仕込み

● スコットランドの新鮮なサーモンのたたきに、わさびソースを添えて

MATSURI
St.James's

ランチ	£6.50～£40	12:00～14:30	(ラストオーダー)
ディナー	£15.50～£70	18:00～22:30	(ラストオーダー)

● ピカデリーサーカスより徒歩5分
● トラベラーズチェック、主要なクレジットカードがご利用いただけます
● お問い合わせは日本語でもどうぞ

欧風和食レストラン **MATSURI**
15 BURY STREET, LONDON SW1Y 6AL
TEL.020 7839 1101   FAX.020 7930 7010
matsuri@japanglobe.net   www.matsuri-restaurant.com

この広告をご持参の方に、もれなくグラスワイン1杯プレゼント

RED DIRECTORY 08.200

What's in Vogue on the Food Front

First it was Feng Shui, now it's Zen,
and London is seeking enlightenment for
its taste buds and health in Japanese cuisine.

8 WHAT'S IN VOGUE

Inscrutable Attraction
Japanese Cuisine

Whether it's raw fish, noodles or the fashionable bento boxes, Japanese restaurants are facing ever soaring popularity, but some of the more authentic ones remain illusive...

Shrouded in some mystery and written in exotic letters, the Japanese menu can be quite daunting, so lets step back inside the sushi bars and Japanese restaurants and discover how to get a real taste of - *Japan in London* - and see if there's anything we might still be missing, after all... no one's really *too sexy for Japan*.

Lotus Roots
in London

Despite being able to find Japanese restaurants all over the UK, 90% of them are located in London, and Japanese cuisine boasts more than thirty years history in the capital. One of the oldest of these restaurants is *Hiroko*, based inside the Kensington Hilton Hotel W11, and others such as *Saga*, *Kiku*, and *Suntory* have established themselves as leaders in Japanese cuisine over the past twenty-five years. Brewer Street in Soho is now fast becoming the Japanese equivalent of China Town on nearby Gerrard Street.

In Japan the restaurants specialise in particular cuisine, sushi at the *sushi-ya*, soba-noodles at the *soba-ya*, grilled chicken at a *yakitori-ya* and so on, but for the great unwashed, these foods can often be found under one roof in London.

Big Catch
in a Small Pond

Originally, the restaurants catered for Japanese businessmen seeking a taste of home, and this set the tone for the restaurants that came afterwards, many serving up a bountiful selection of Japanese dishes. You can therefore choose between sushi, noodles, soups, grilled meat and fish dishes, one-pot stews and deep fried vegetables or seafood at many of London's Japanese restaurants.

Japan-in-London

JAPANESE CUISINE 9

Virtual-Real

In London there are Japanese restaurants that cater mostly to international clientele and then there are the more authentic Japanese restaurants whose diners are predominantly Japanese. Indeed the measure of authenticity might well lie in the ratio of Japanese to non-Japanese customers and the number of Japanese waiting staff. The fusion-Japanese restaurants have a lot going for them, but the food and atmosphere is markedly different from their purist counterparts.

Western Chic or Modern Cheek

In recent years London has seen the rise of a new wave in Japanese restaurants. At the various *Wagamama*, *Moshi Moshi Sushi* & *Yo-Sushi*, *Nobu* and *Satsuma* the emphasis is on colourful fusion style Japanese menus, modern minimalist interiors and a very trendy, often noisy, but fun atmosphere.

Ultimate Zen

For most, the Japanese menu is still as imperceptible as the geisha, and the most authentic Japanese restaurants remain foreboding with their mannered, efficient service, enigmatic setting and beautiful if inaccessible language. But if you scratch beneath the surface just enough, you'll realise there's a whole world of dining open to anyone, and just a few guidelines will be enough to steer you through.

If you find yourself in a very formal Japanese setting, perhaps one with *tatami* mats, be sure to take your shoes off and leave them neatly at the entrance. It's then usual to kneel at the table, but let's face it, most of us can't do that for long without ending up with dead legs, so feel at ease to sit cross-legged. Some tatami rooms are designed with leg space beneath the table, in that case, you can relax and sit on the mats with you legs hanging comfortably under the table, and get on with the important matter of ordering the beer or sake. As far as the menu's concerned, it's best to read up on a few dishes (details p.13) or ask the staff what they recommend within a certain price range, most will be happy to advise. *Suntory*, *Asuka* and *Mitsukoshi Restaurant* have tatami rooms.

La rose et la noire
Japan's balance of contradictions

It is somehow inherently Japanese that their cooking, culture and indeed lifestyle contain many contrasting elements. The exacting proportions and subtle flavours of the rice and raw fish of sushi are placed next to the strength in taste in the hidden *wasabi* (Japanese horseradish) and a strong cold glass of beer. A full Japanese dinner will contain ingredients that both stimulate and surprise the palate - and perhaps that's the attraction. No one would argue at how well the ingredients work together, and this play of opposites seems to lie at the heart of Japanese dining.

10 WHAT'S IN VOGUE

Etiquette

If you are choosing items from the menu individually, it's usual to choose something like *tofu* or salad as an appetiser, followed by *sashimi* (raw fish), sushi or a main meat or fish course, and if you have a real appetite a bowl of rice, finishing off with *miso-shiru* (soup with fermented soybean paste) and perhaps dessert. A good way to sample a full Japanese meal is to try a lunchtime set menu, these are reasonably cheap; you will be served soup, rice and pickles alongside your main course.

When using chopsticks remember not to leave them sticking in the food whilst you rest, especially not in the rice, this may cause offence as it is part of Japanese funeral rites.

It is usual to drink the soups especially *miso-shiru* and *o-suimono* directly from the bowl.

Japanese cuisine doesn't have to be intimidating, a few pointers and you'll soon be calling *oishii!* (delicious!) with the best of them.

Artful dining

Selfish Bliss

In a culture dominated by group activity, the bento box might seem like something of an anomaly, but that's because they were originally made up for individuals working outdoors or travelling. The more sophisticated *shokado bento* (calligrapher's paint box) is the haute cuisine version of the bento and is a wonderful example of the balance of aesthetics, taste and atmosphere of Japanese dining. True to the origins of Japanese cuisine, bento are composed of healthy, attractive ingredients, and are readily available at many of the London restaurants whether your taste is for one of the trendy joints or the more traditional Japanese restaurants.

Calligrapher's paint box

Shared Fun

In contrast to bento, *nabe-mono* (one-pot dishes) developed as communal dishes. There are various kinds of *nabe* including *suki-yaki* and *shabu-shabu* (details p.13) and this food is cooked in a large pot over a burner at your table. You are served all the ingredients fresh, and add these to the pot yourselves. Fish, meat and longer cooking vegetables go in first, followed by more delicate ingredients like tofu or lighter vegetable leaves. As the ingredients appear to be cooked, people help themselves. Further ingredients might be added including noodles, which are served last and taste great cooked in the same broth. Other than that it's a mood of eat, drink, be merry and refill the pot! A brilliant, fun night out. *Aykoku-Kaku* and *Nakamura* both serve Nabe.

One-pot masterpiece

JAPANESE CUISINE 11

Drinks

Japanese dining is nothing if not sociable and despite a reputation for over-politeness and formality, there are many occasions when austerity and artistry are set aside in favour of a relaxed eating atmosphere, accompanied by copious drinking. Sake, beer and *ume-shu* (plum wine) are familiar to most of us, but if you're now ready for a bit more adventure, or if you've tried sake once and not been taken by it, the taste of another might just persuade you. And there are literally thousands of different sake.

Sake is served by the glass, or if it's hot, in a *tokkuri* (traditional ceramic bottle) which you pour into a tiny *ochoko* (ceramic cup), and it ranges in price by the same extremes that apply to wine, so be cautious about what you order. Some sake are served hot, others cold but generally speaking those served cold are better quality. In London a tumbler of fairly decent sake starts from £6 a glass. Here are a few of the sake as recommended by London's Japanese restaurant proprietors: *Oyama, Kubota, Ozeki, Koshino Cambai, Tsukasa Botan, Tamano Hikari* and *Hokkai San*.

Other drink favourites are the Japanese cocktails, *Chu-hai*, these consist of the Japanese spirit *shochu*, and are mixed with various fruit flavours, plum and lemon are popular. *Shochu* varies in strength from 36% to 50% proof, and sake from 16% to 32% + proof. Take it easy, but *Campai!* (Cheers!)

Curious Condiments

Soy Sauce...Tonkatsu Sauce

Soy Sauce is a must with Japanese cuisine as it is one of the few stronger tasting ingredients in cuisine dominated by subtle flavours. Soy sauce is an obvious accompaniment to *sashimi*, sushi, vegetable and grilled fish dishes, and Kikkoman is a popular brand. *Tonkatsu sauce* is a Japanese version of Worcestershire sauce but unlike the original, its consistency is very thick – more like that of tomato ketchup. Tonkatsu sauce is served with various fried dishes such as the fried pork cutlet dish called *Tonkatsu*.

Kikkoman

Yakumi

Yakumi are the herbs and spices used in Japanese cuisine, here are some of the most common ingredients. *Shichimi* can be added to the noodle dishes – *udon* and *soba*; *wasabi* and *shiso* come with sushi and *sashimi*, both for their taste and antiseptic, antibacterial properties; *beni-shoga* is served with *yaki-soba* (fried noodles), and *sansho* is served with eel dishes to spice them up.

Shichimi
Seven Spice Chilli Powder

Beni-shoga
Red Pickled Ginger

Wasabi
Green Condiment, like horseradish

Shiso
Beefsteak Plant, like peppery mint

WHAT'S IN VOGUE

Naked & Raw

Sushi

Sushi is the artful marriage of vinegared rice with a topping or filling of fish, vegetables, sweet omelette or a combination of such ingredients. The Japanese fusion-style restaurants experiment with lots of ingredients that wouldn't be used by a traditional Japanese sushi chef, but are nonetheless exciting and palatable. For those entering a traditional *Sushi-ya*, perhaps for the first time, here are a few pointers. At the counter you will first be offered a hot towel for your hands. You can choose and eat your sushi one by one, ask the chef's advice on what's the best catch and let him know your budget for the meal, it can get pricey. In terms of eating sushi, it's fine to eat it by hand, dipping the topping into the soy sauce first. *Wasabi* (Japanese horseradish) is usually added to the sushi by the chef, so ask for it to be left out if you don't have a taste for it, and if you *love* it, mix a little extra into the soy sauce before you begin dipping, give it that extra *bite*.

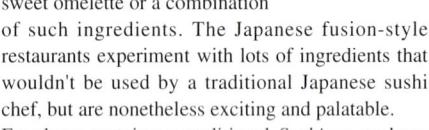
Tuna

Sushi counter

Salmon roe

Cucumber

If you're looking for an authentic *kaiten-zushi* (conveyor belt sushi), try out *Kulu Kulu Sushi*. Traditional style sushi counters can be found at *Kikuchi*, *Matsuri St. James's*, *Mitsukoshi Restaurant*, and the incredible *Dai-Chan* sushi bar, which seats a maximum of only seven at any one time, and can be found inside the *Karaoke Box* on Frith Street.

For the sushi connoisseur, *Tajima-tei* serves *Kansai-zushi* - specialising in particular types of sushi from the west of Japan. There are also plenty of Japanese restaurants with a cosmopolitan ambience that serve sushi, and these include the obvious *Yo-Sushi* restaurants and *Itsu*.

Eel

Salmon

Mixed roll

Prawn

Omelette

JAPANESE CUISINE 13

An Adventure in Japanese Cuisine

So for anyone seeking a wider take on the Japanese menu, here are some details on the kinds of dishes you can be served up in London.

Yaki-mono (Broiled dishes) include: **Yaki-tori** (1.) - skewers of grilled chicken, **Teppan-yaki** (2.) - griddled steak, fish or shellfish served with a selection of vegetables and **Okonomi-yaki** (3.) – a pancake/omelette usually cooked at the table. Age-mono (Fried dishes) include: **Tonkatsu** (4.) – a breaded pork cutlet served with shredded cabbage and tonkatsu sauce, and **Tempura** (5.) – vegetables or seafood in a crispy egg batter. Nabe-mono (One-pot stews) include: **Suki-yaki** (6.) - slices of browned beef simmered in a sauce (traditionally the beef slivers are dipped in beaten raw egg before eating), and **Shabu-shabu** (7.) - a beef fondue which you dip in sesame or ponzu (citrus and soy sauce). Domburi-mono (Rice bowl dishes) include: **Katsu-don** (8.) – deep fried pork soaked in egg, partly poached in broth with onions and served on rice, **Gyu-don** (9.) – slivers of simmered beef and onions on rice, **Oyako-don** (10.) – pieces of chicken in lightly beaten egg, cooked with onions and broth and served on rice, and **Una-ju** (11.) – charcoal-grilled eel served on rice in a lacquer box. Men-rui (Noodle dishes) include: **Zaru-soba** (12.) – buckwheat noodles served cold with stock combined with soy sauce, and **Ramen** (13.) – Chinese egg noodles in a meaty broth with a variety of ingredients such as pork, fish roll, bean sprouts and bamboo.

The official Internet site for probably the world's most popular city destination, and the "Coolest City in the World" *(Newsweek)*, LondonTown.com has become undoubtedly one of the top international destination sites on the Internet.

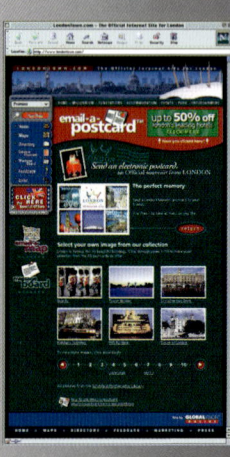

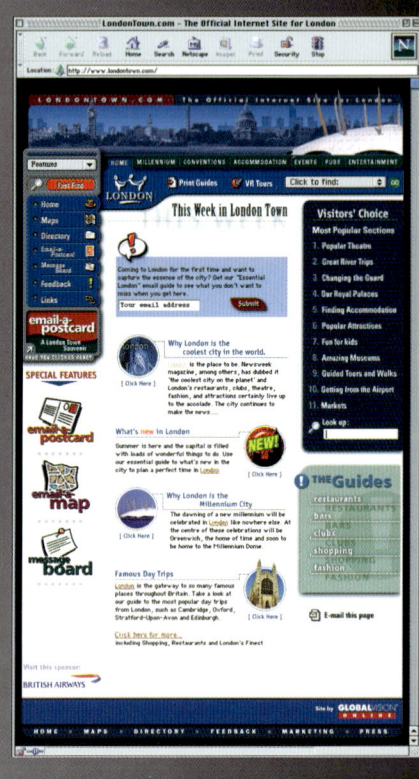

Events, hotel booking, special offers.

Detailed information on your favourite London days out.

160 postcards to personalise and email.

Getting Around in London

Underground Maps and Bus Routes.

JAPANESE FOOD IS THE IN THING!!

RED DIRECTORY

Price £4.99. Distribution in Europe and throughout the UK: bookshops - airports - hotels - restaurants.

SIZE : 117mm x 106mm
PAGES: 112pp/144pp

Each dish fully explained in **6 languages:**
English - French - Italian - German - Spanish - Portuguese

RED DIRECTORY MENU BOOKS
FIRST IN THE SERIES

1. THE SUSHI MENU   **2. THE JAPANESE MENU**

Cross Media Ltd.   4th Floor, 13 Berners Street, London W1T 3LH UK
Tel: 020-7436-1960   Fax: 020-7436-1930

UNDERGROUND MAP 17

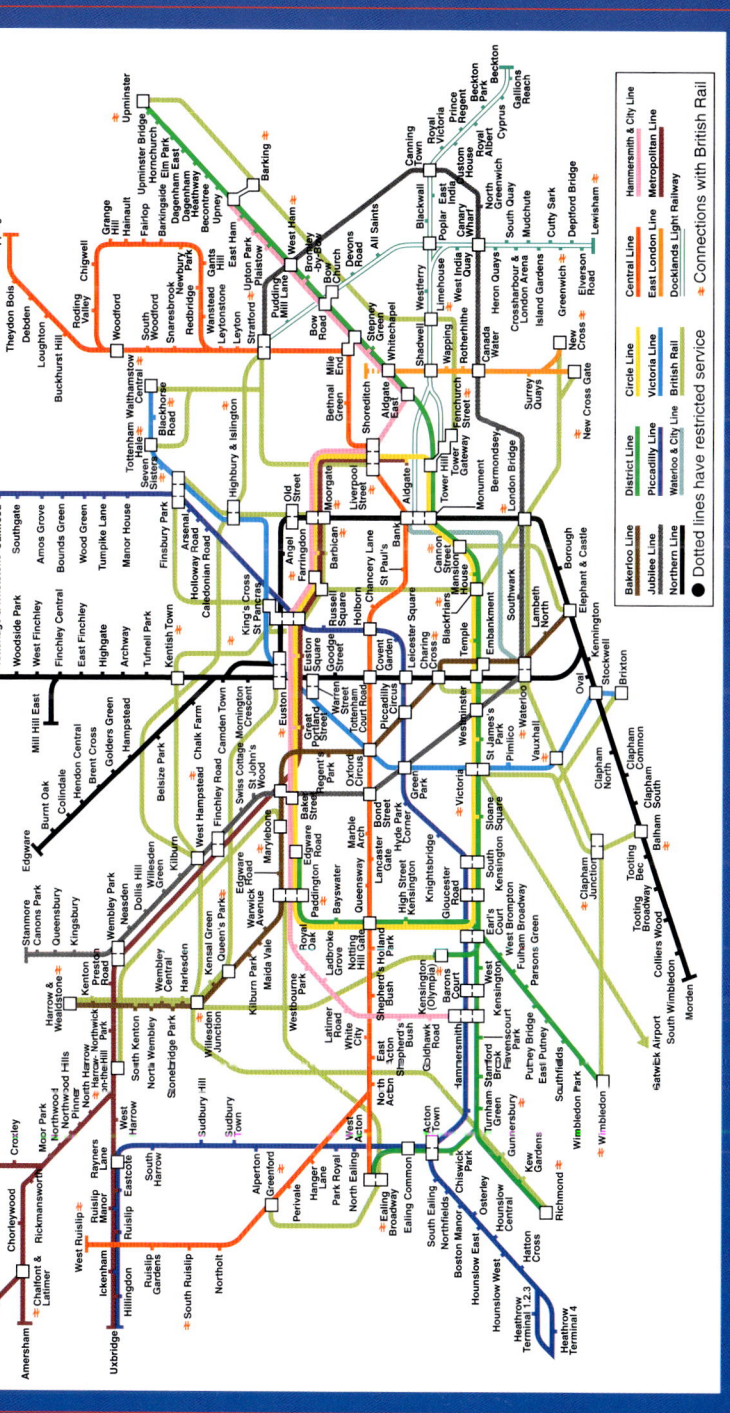

18 BUS ROUTES

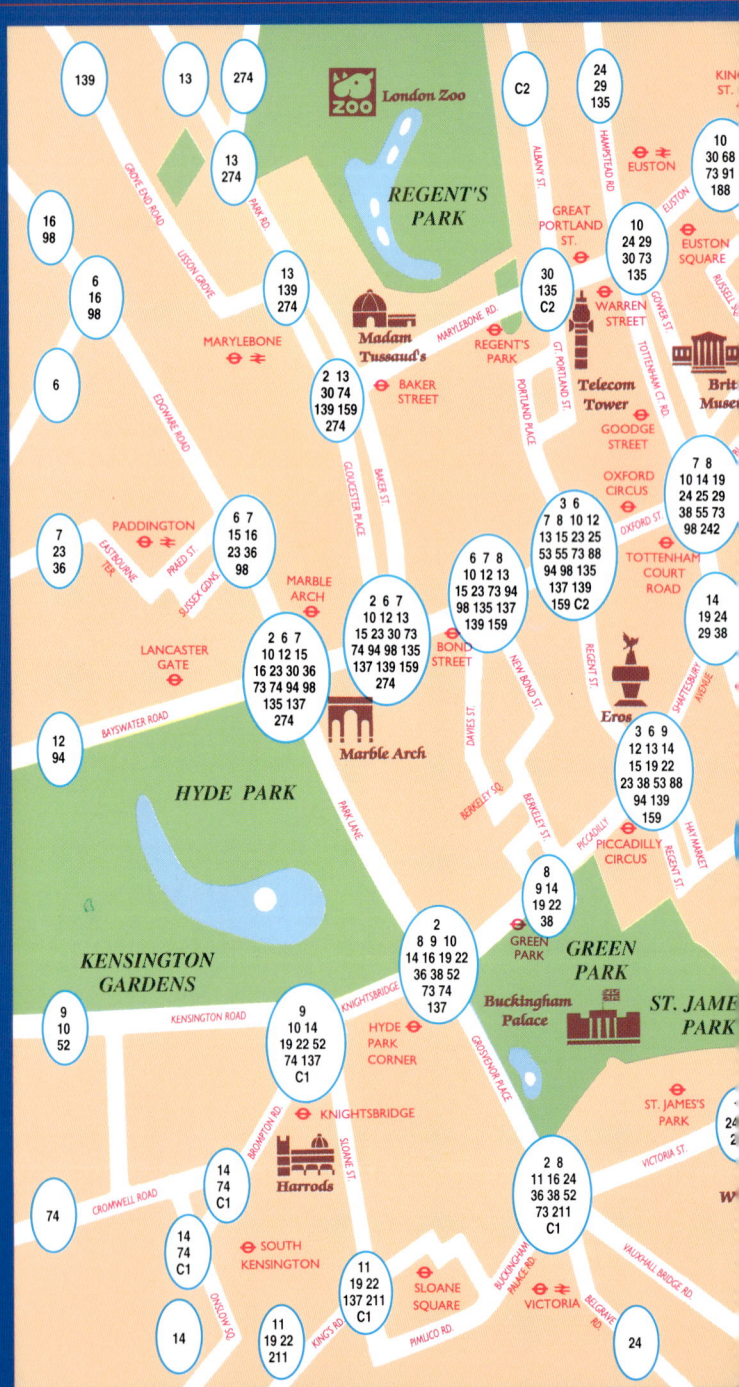

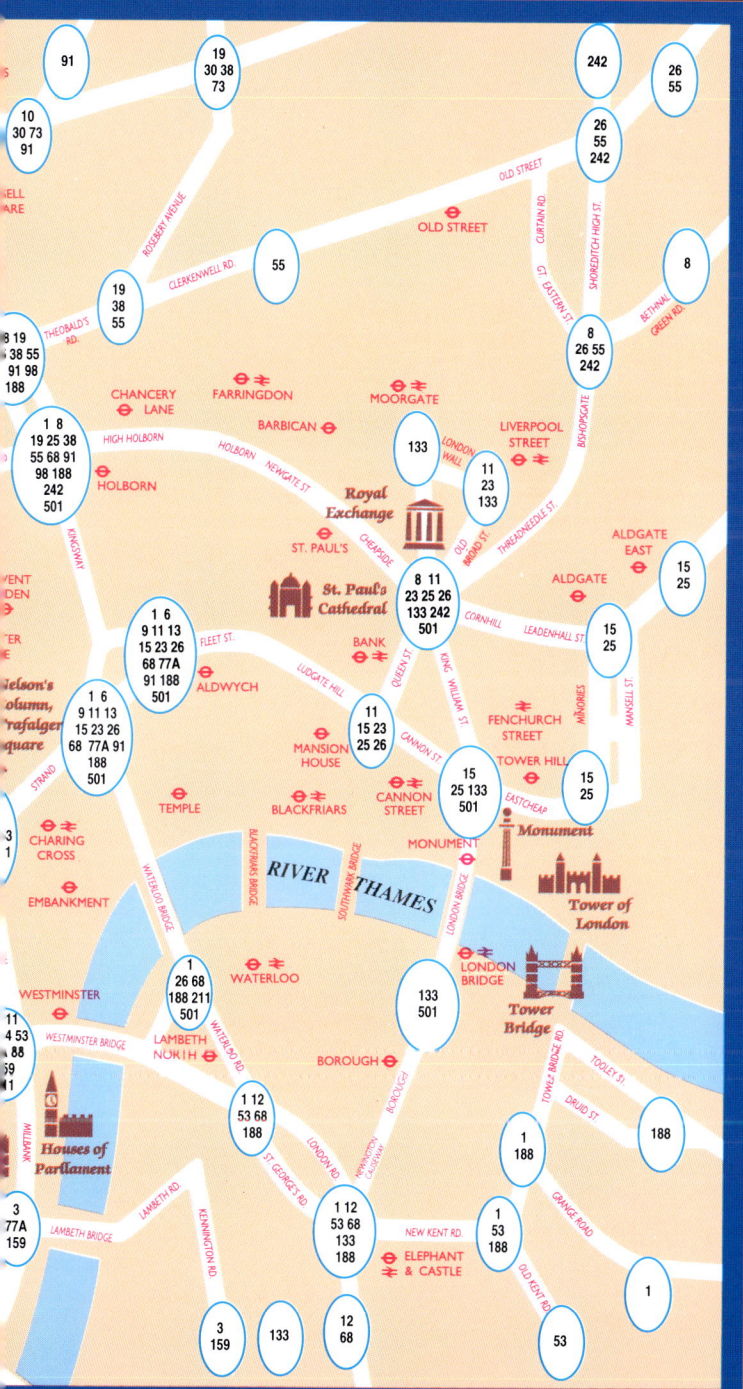

ロンドン・ブランドアウトレット

World's Famous Brands at Fabulous prices

House of Hanover is well known for its huge variety of the world's finest branded merchandise at fabulous low prices.

This is a store NOT TO MISS when you are in London

ハウス オブ ハノーバーでは、世界の名品を特別価格でお買い求め頂けます。ロンドンにお越しの際は是非一度ご来店下さい。

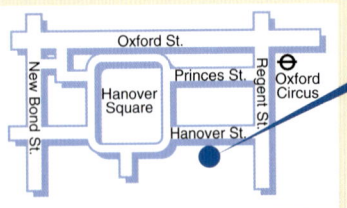

HOUSE of HANOVER

Opening Hours
Monday-Saturday
9:45-18:15
Sunday & BankHoliday
11:00-17:00

ツーリストの方には免税手続きを行います。
Tax Free shopping available for overseas visitors(Non EC customers)

HOUSE *of* HANOVER

ハウス オブ ハノーバー

13-14 Hanover Street, London W1R 9HG
Tel: 020 7629 1103   Fax:020 7491 1909

For reasons of supply, there may be changes to prices.
We cannot guarantee that all items will always be in stock.

From the Centre to the Outskirts

London Maps: Greater London,
Central London and Street Maps.

22 GREATER LONDON

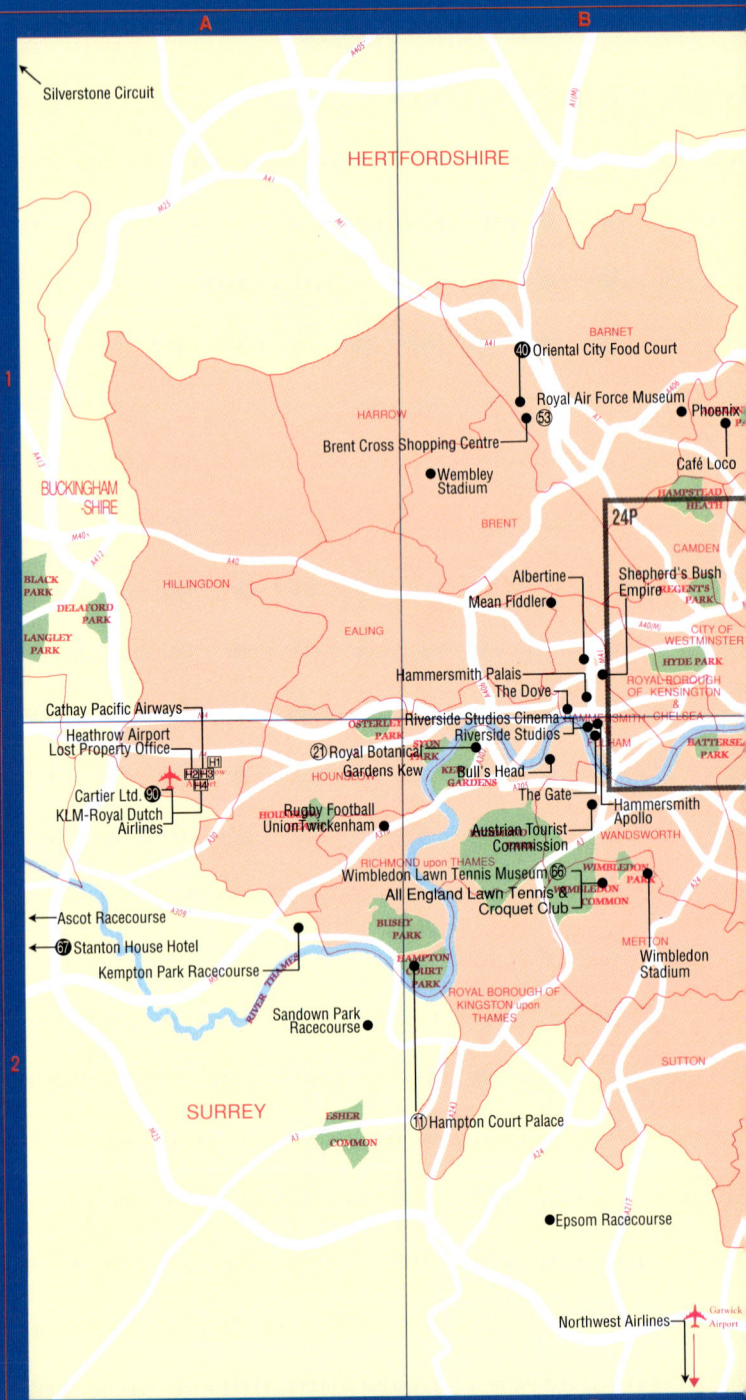

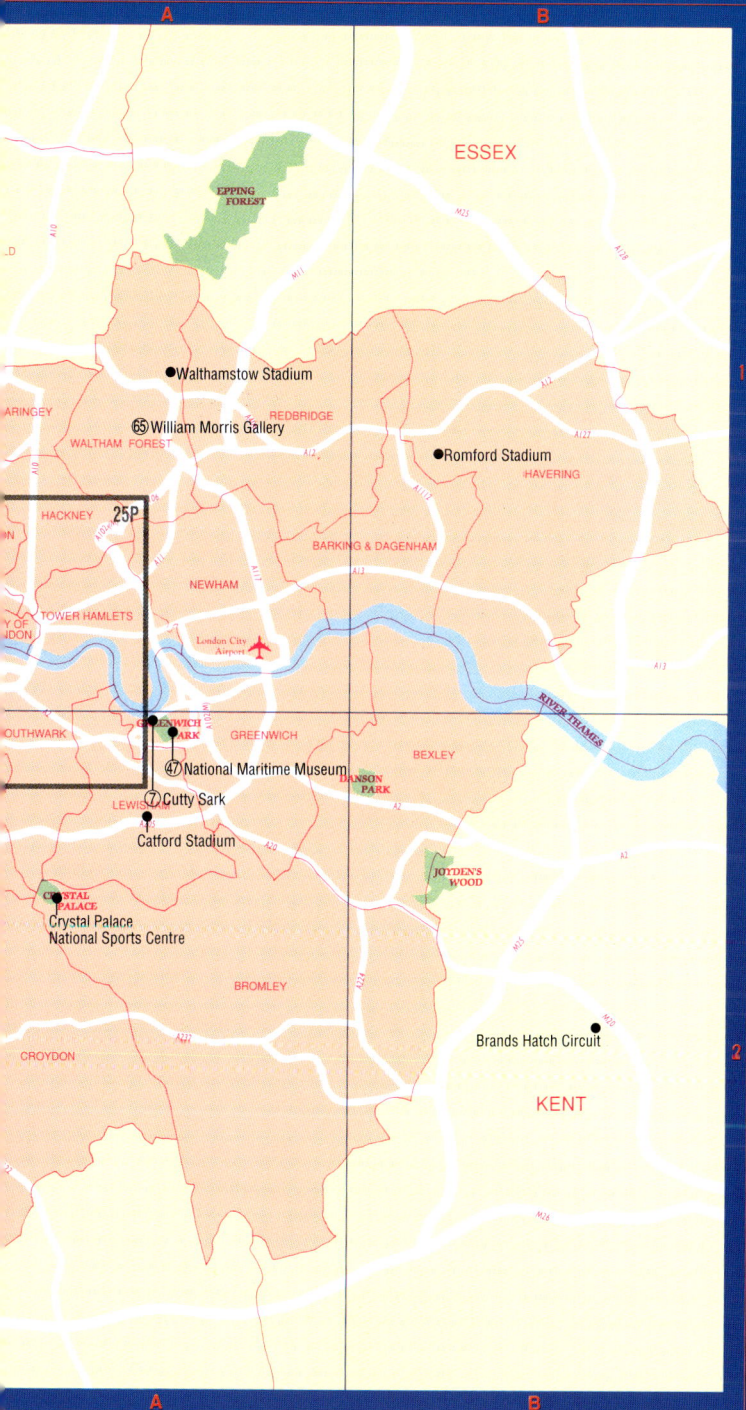

24 CENTRAL LONDON & ENVIRONS

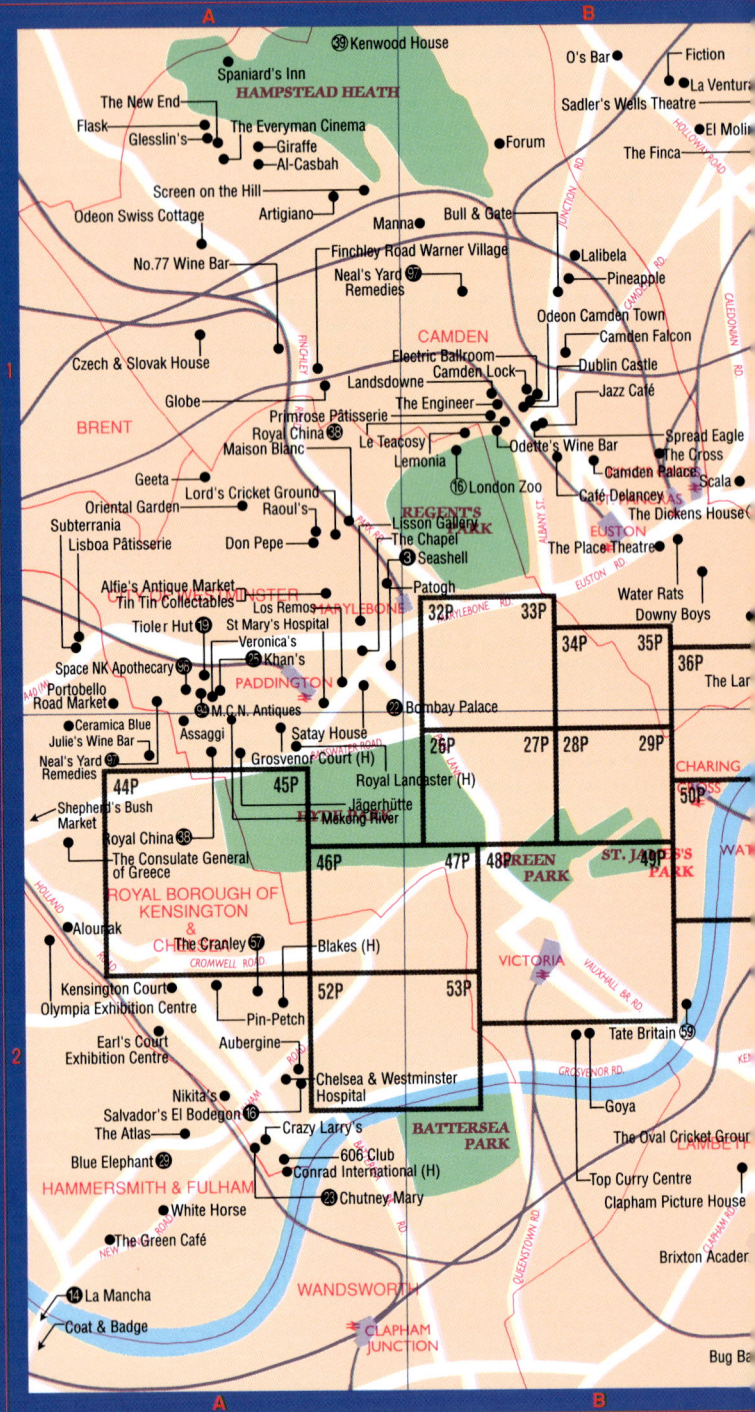

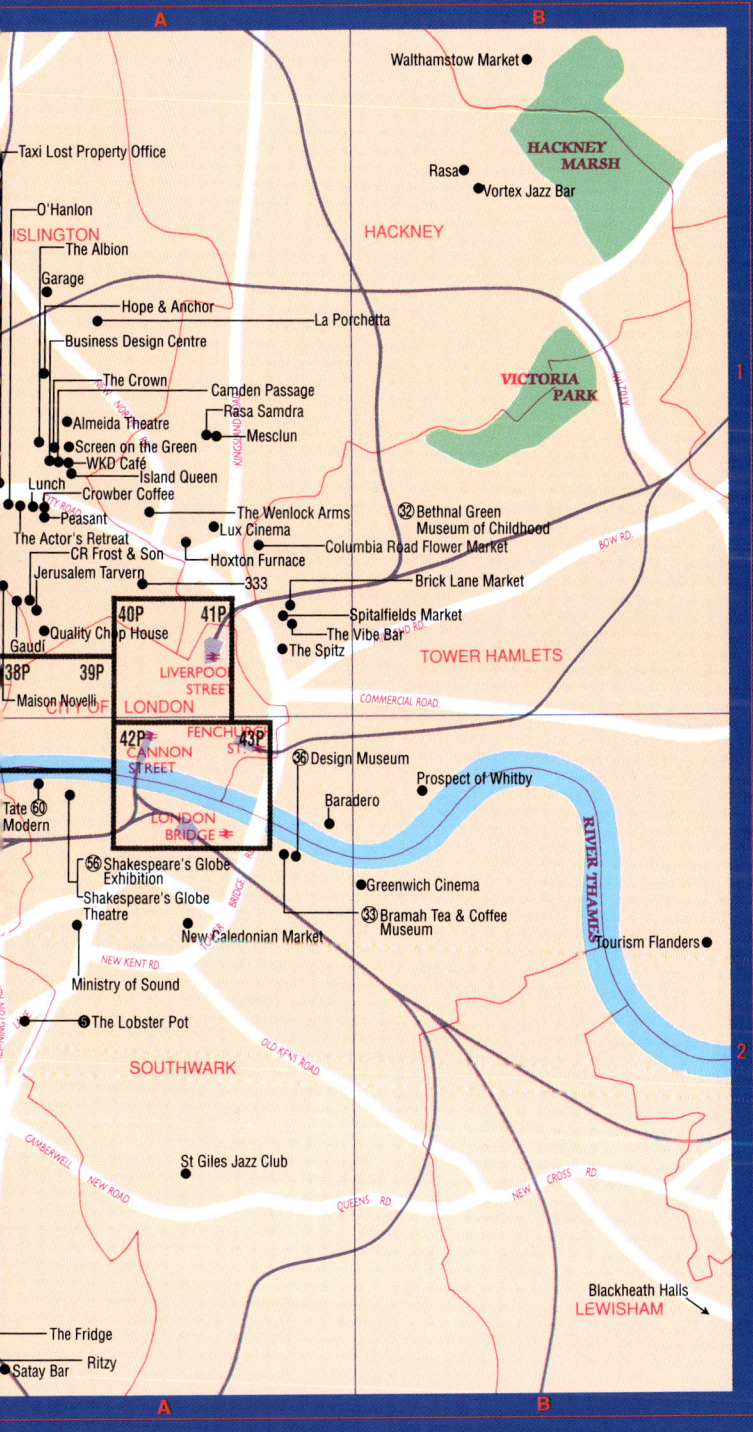

26 MAYFAIR, BOND ST. (MIDDLE)

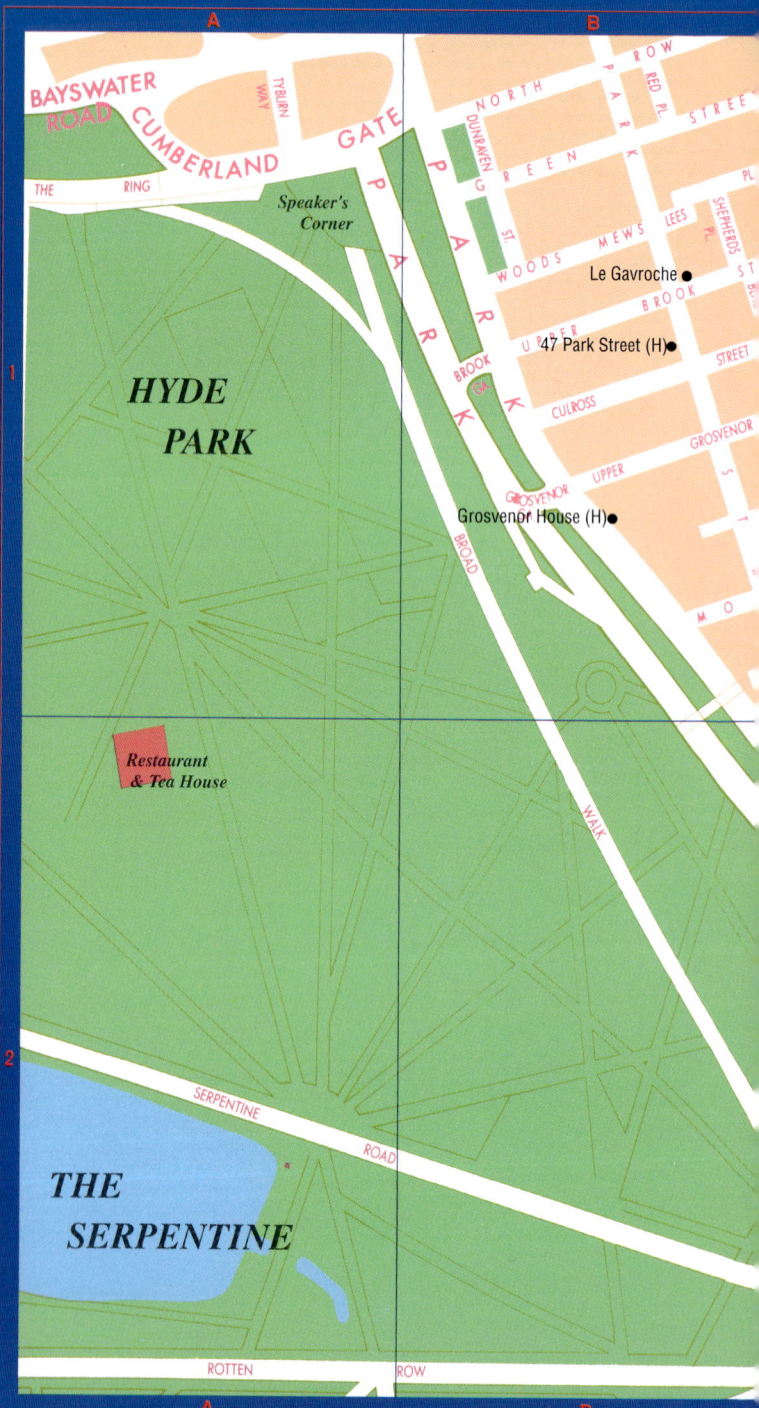

28 PICCADILLY, SOHO, REGENT ST., BOND ST. (SOUTH)

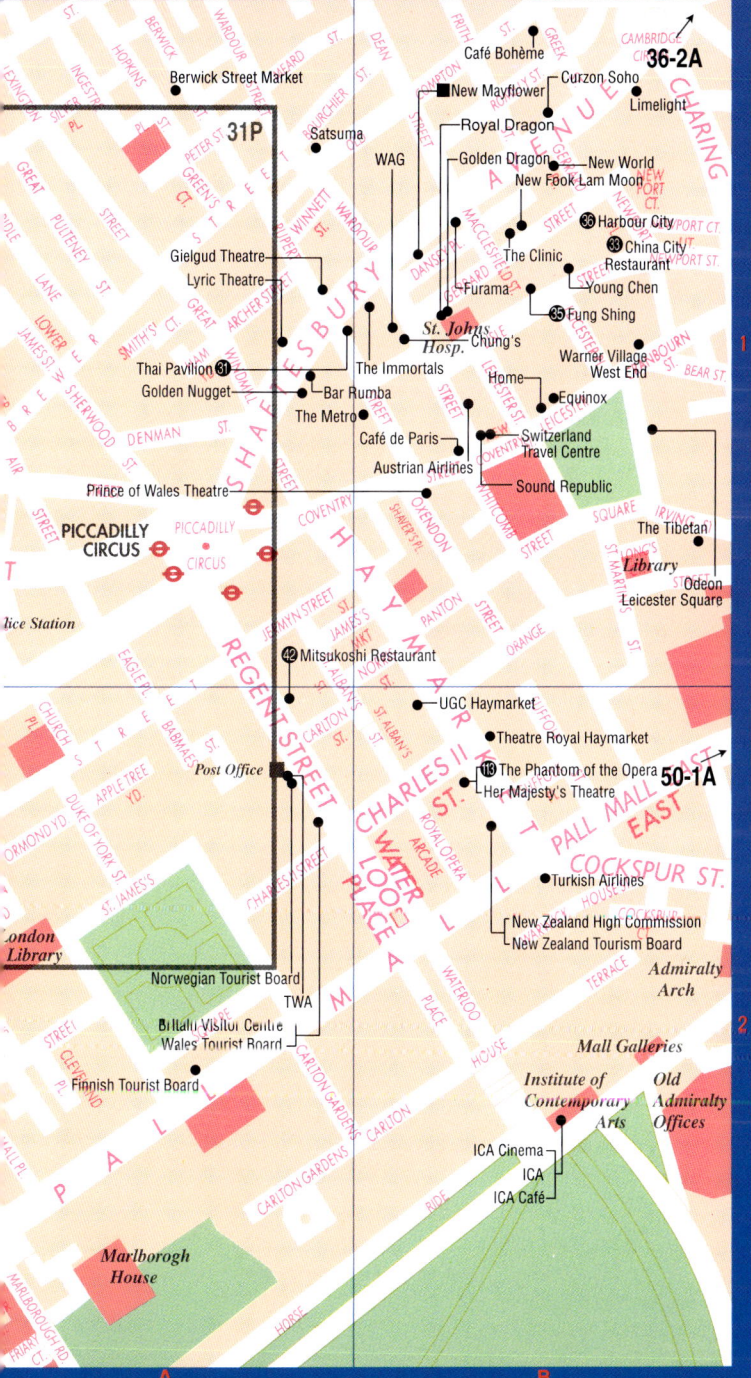

30 PICCADILLY, REGENT ST., BOND ST. (ENLARGED)

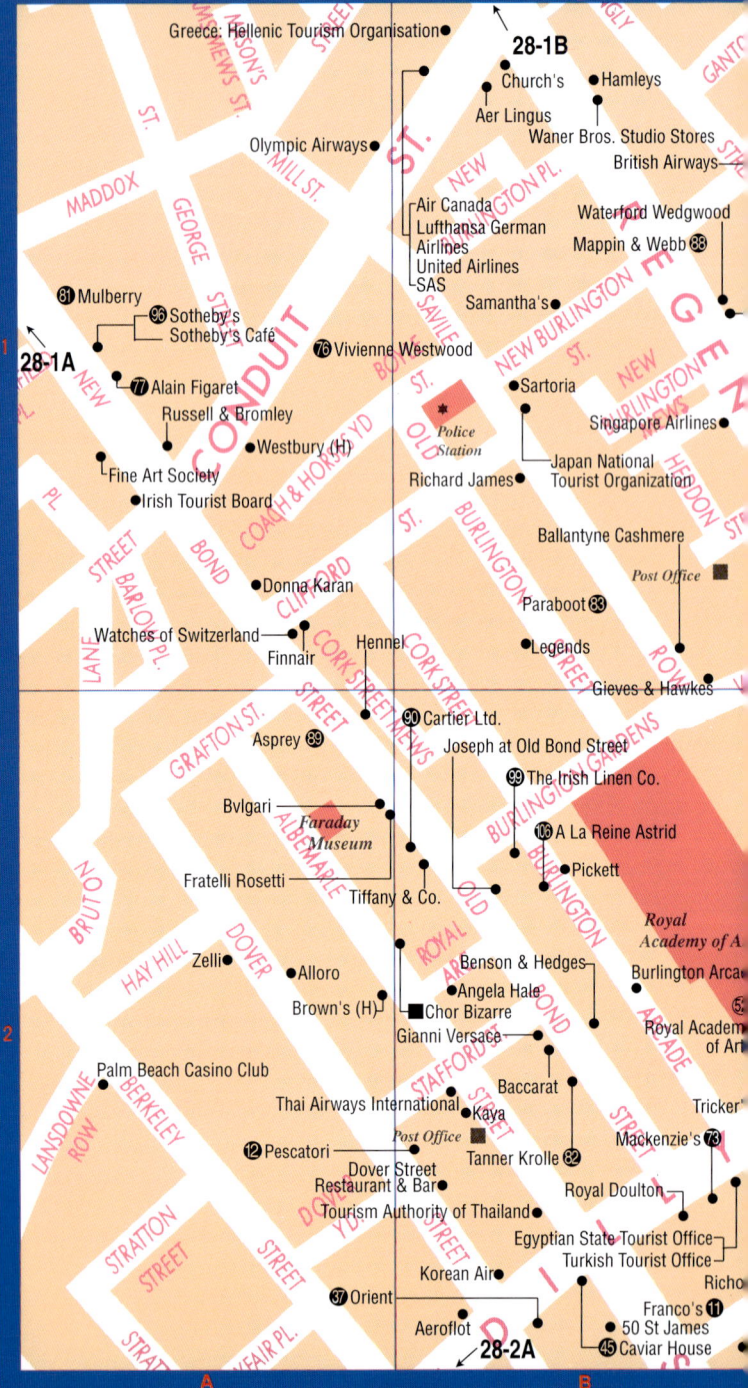

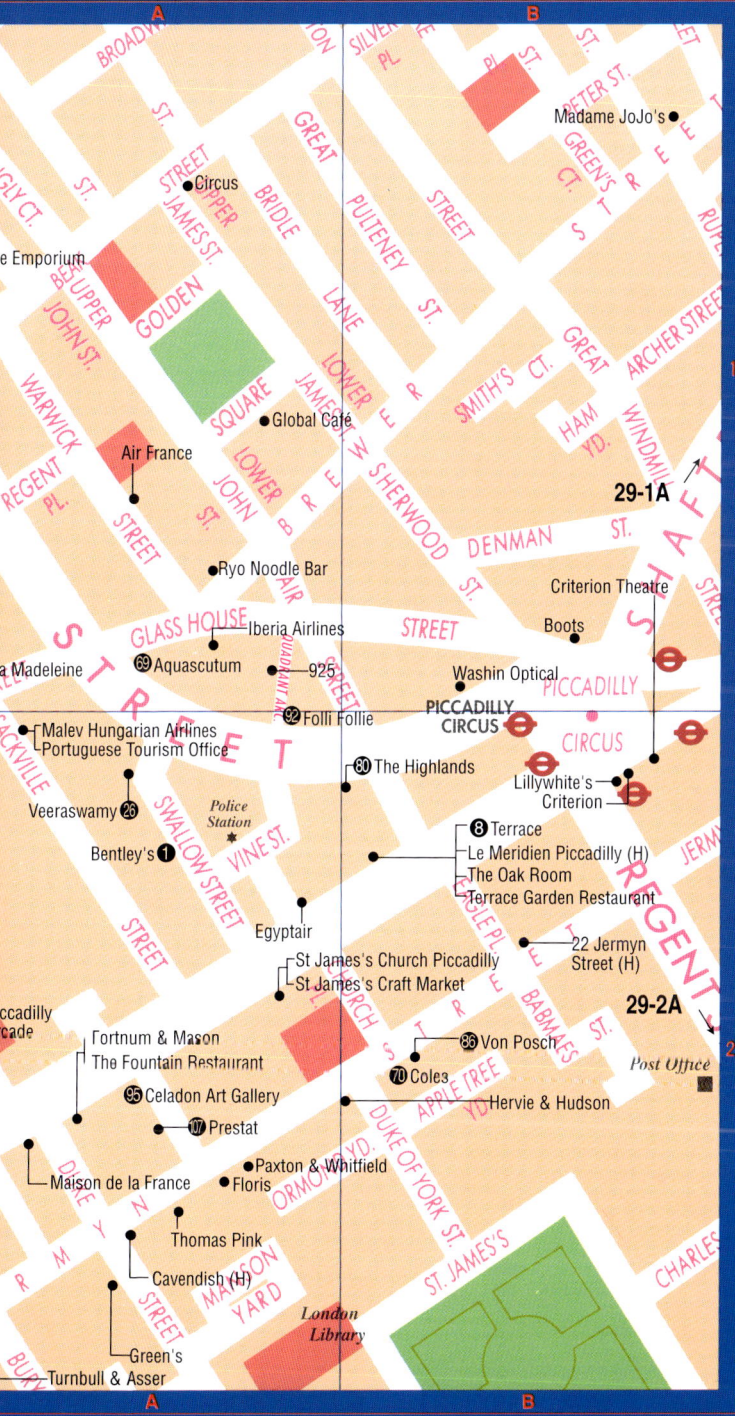

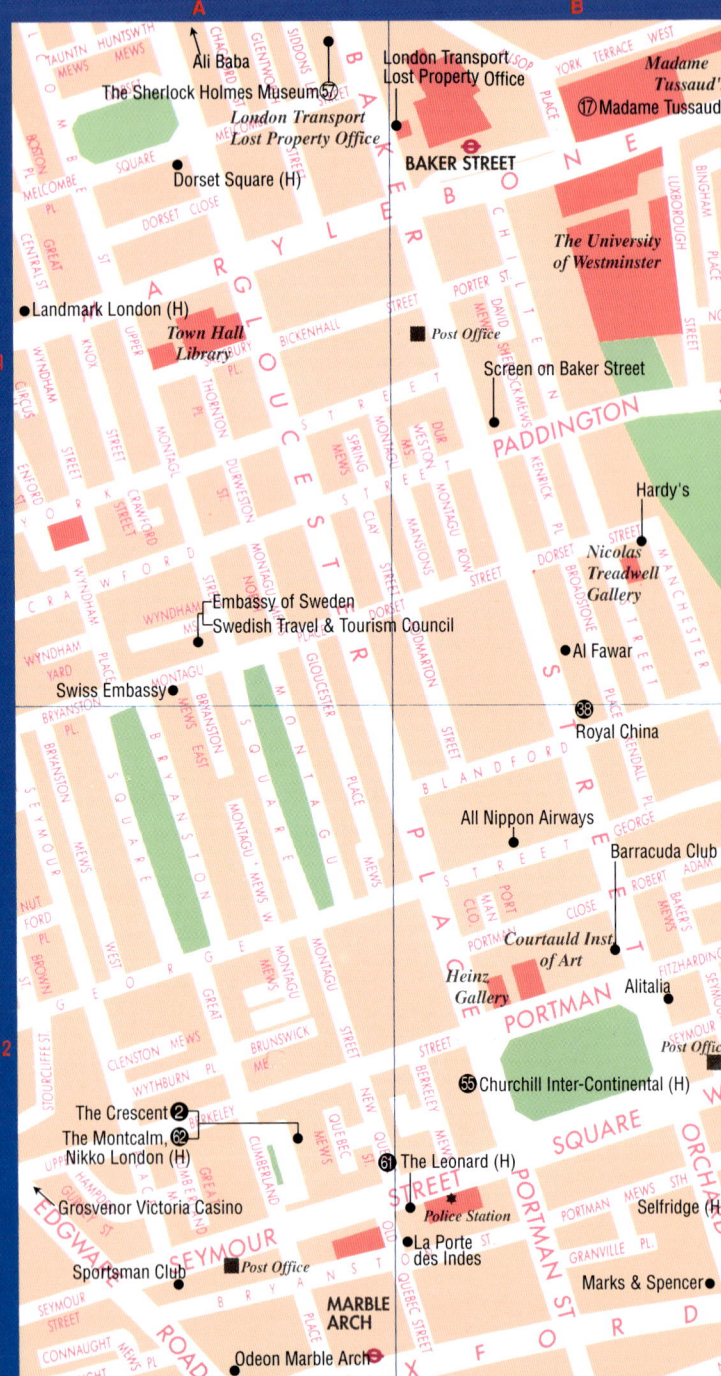

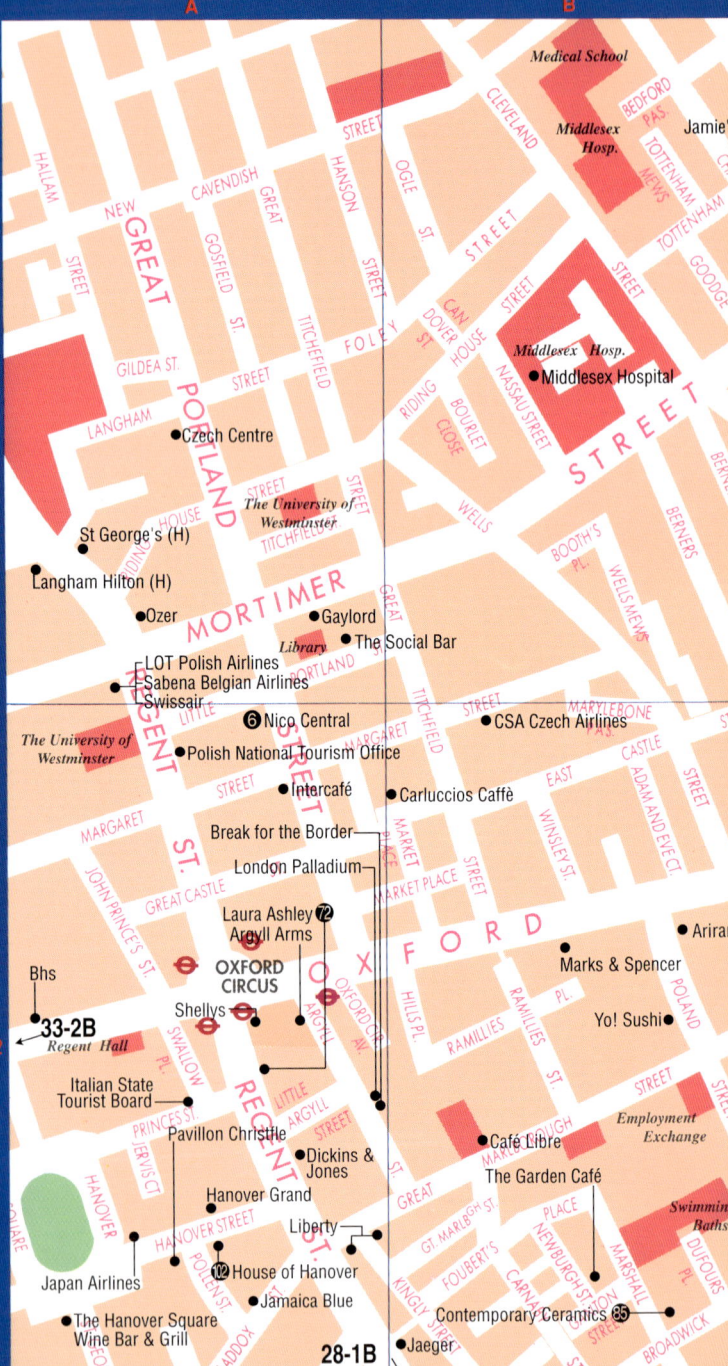

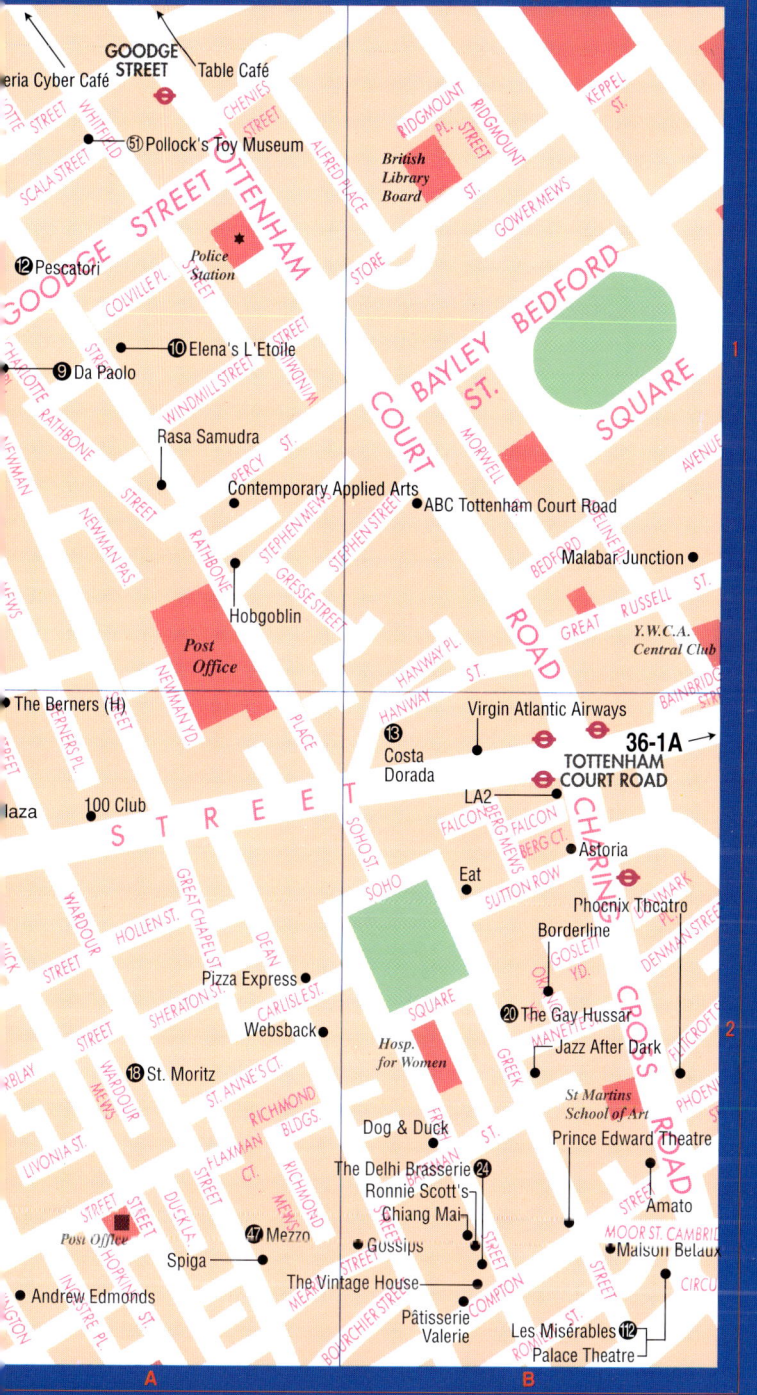

36 COVENT GARDEN, STRAND, HOLBORN

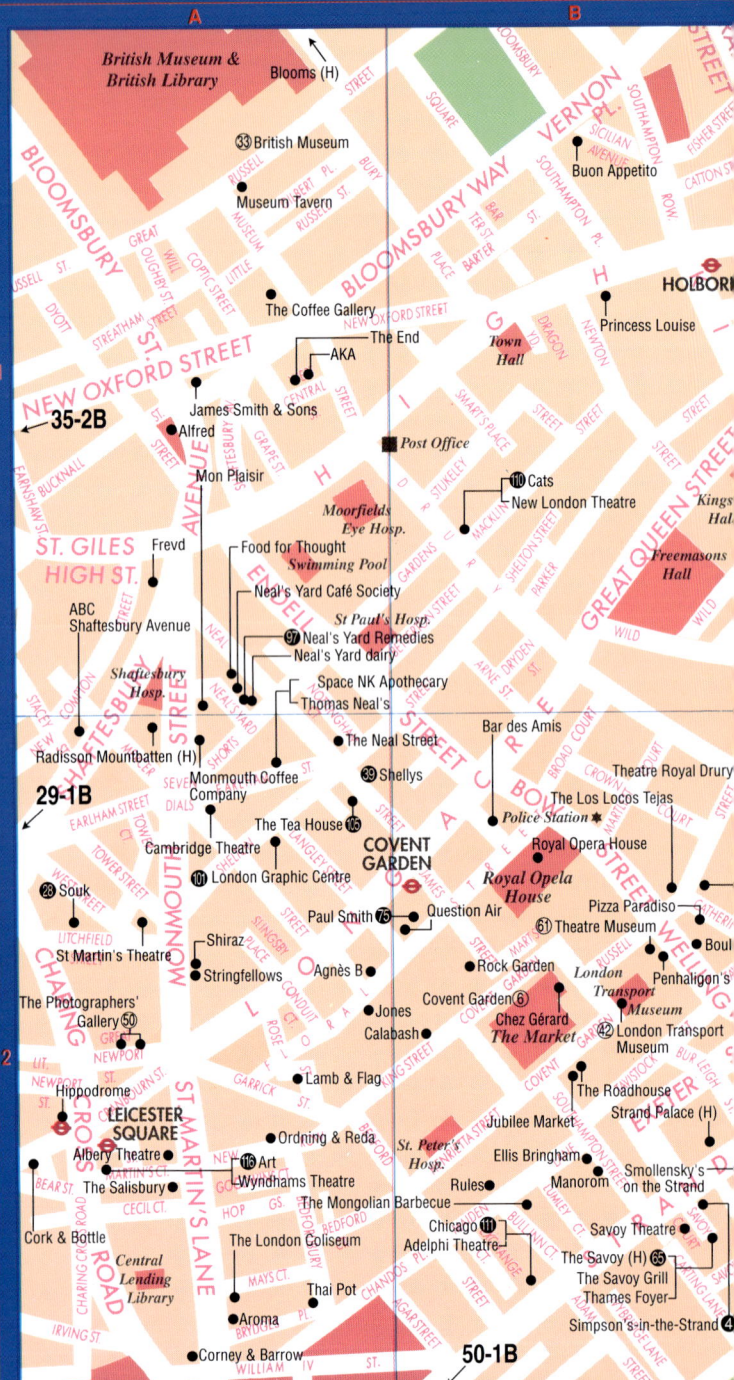

37

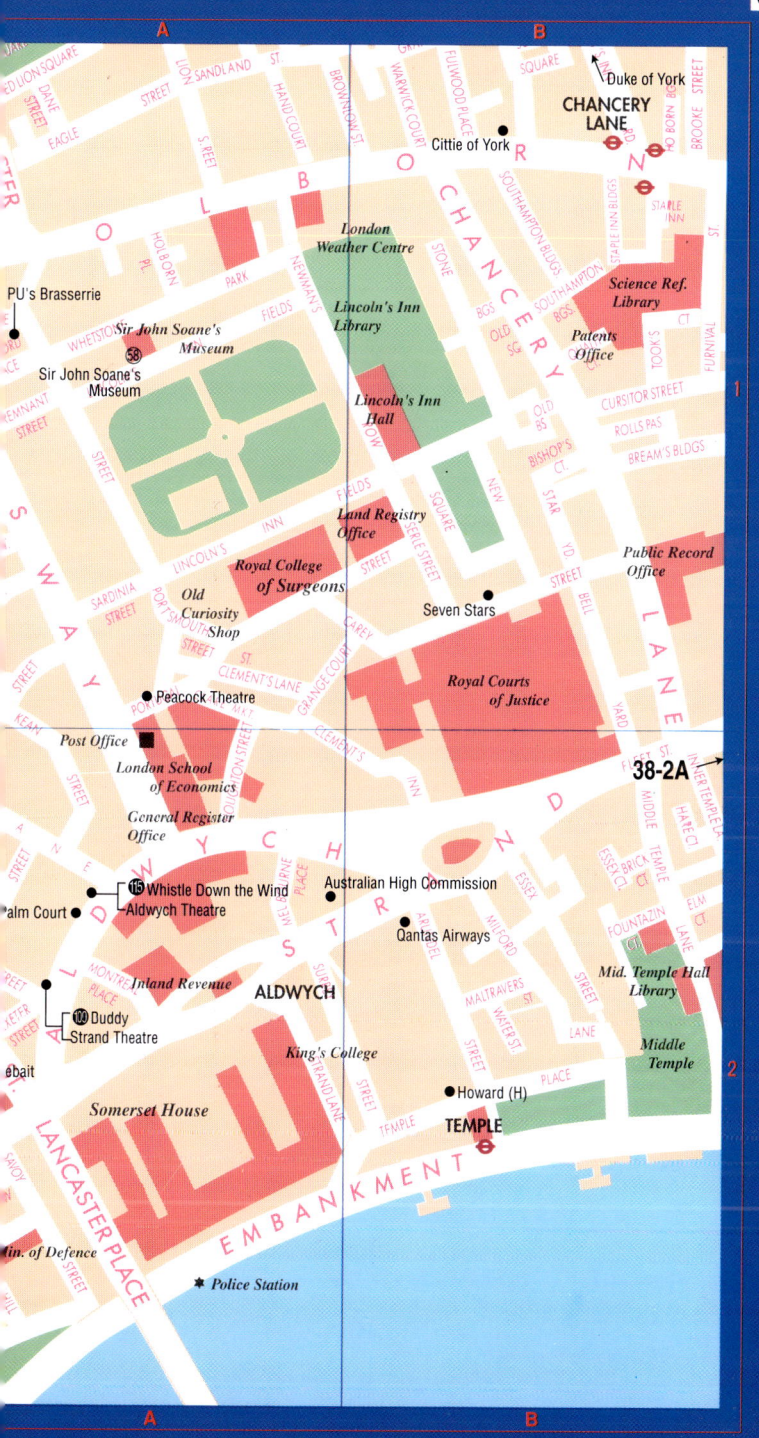

A / B

- Duke of York
- **CHANCERY LANE**
- Cittie of York
- London Weather Centre
- Lincoln's Inn Library
- Science Ref. Library
- PU's Brasserie
- Sir John Soane's Museum
- Sir John Soane's Museum
- Patents Office
- Lincoln's Inn Hall
- Land Registry Office
- Royal College of Surgeons
- Old Curiosity Shop
- Seven Stars
- Public Record Office
- Peacock Theatre
- Royal Courts of Justice
- Post Office
- London School of Economics
- General Register Office
- 38-2A
- Whistle Down the Wind / Aldwych Theatre
- Australian High Commission
- Palm Court
- Qantas Airways
- Mid. Temple Hall Library
- Inland Revenue
- **ALDWYCH**
- Duddy / Strand Theatre
- King's College
- Middle Temple
- Somerset House
- Howard (H)
- **TEMPLE**
- LANCASTER PLACE
- **EMBANKMENT**
- Min. of Defence
- Police Station

38 BLACKFRIARS, ST. PAUL'S, MANSION HOUSE, BARBICAN

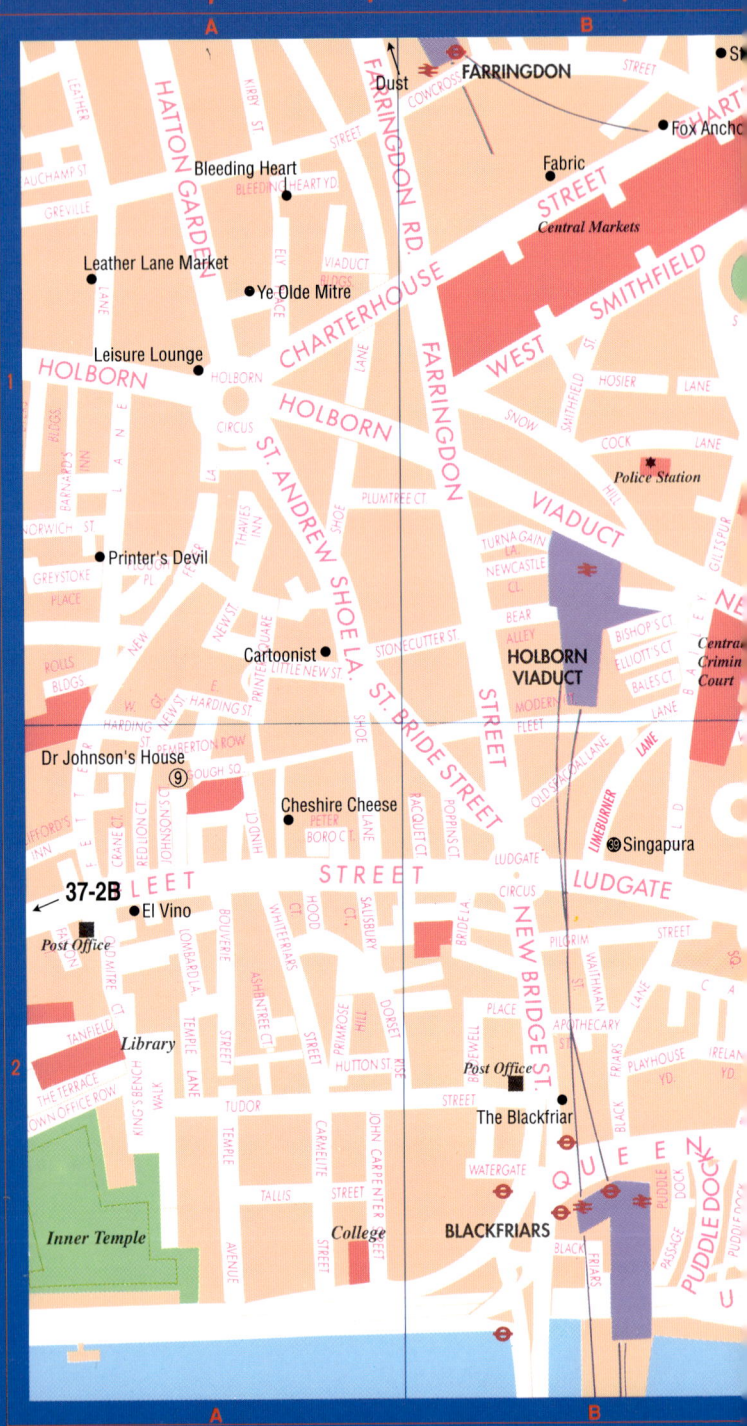

39

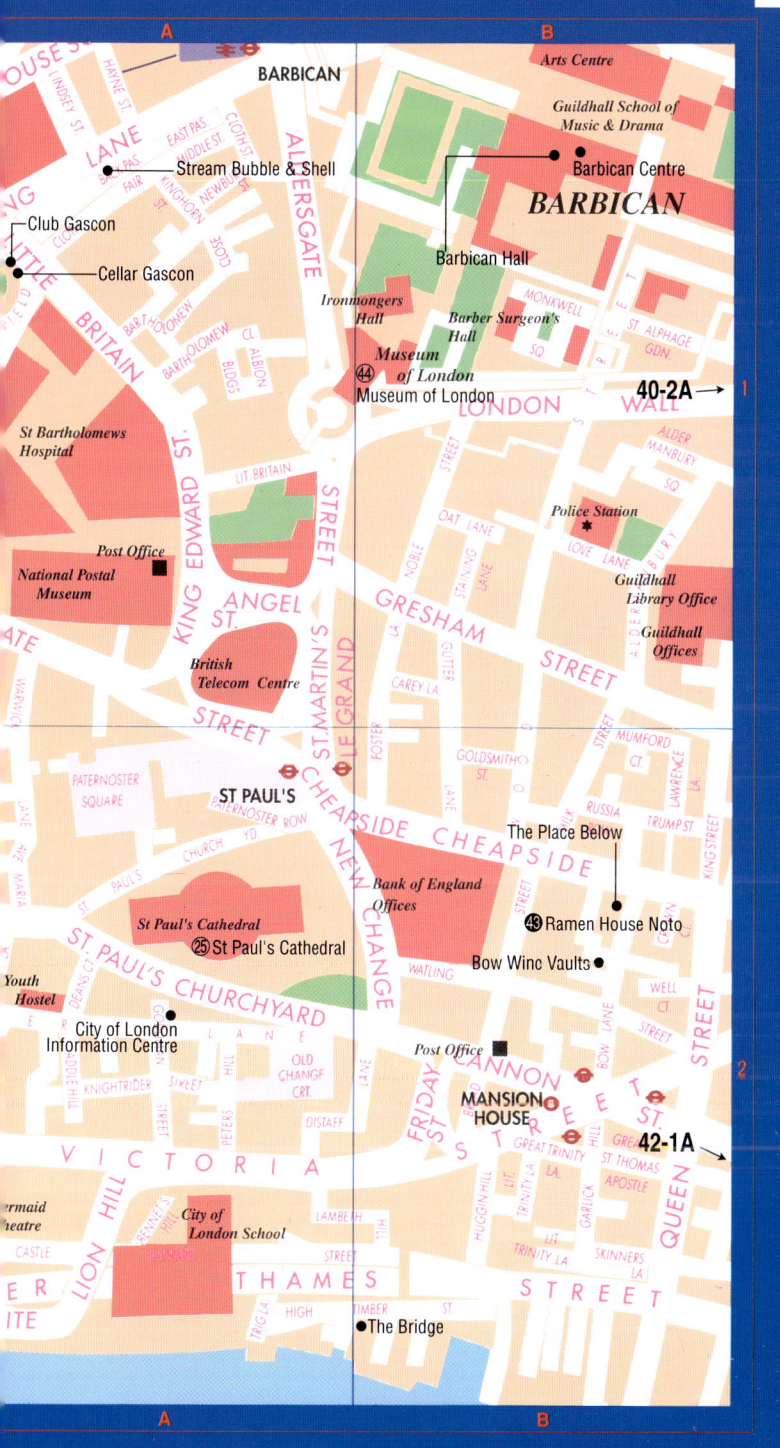

A | B

BARBICAN

Arts Centre

Guildhall School of Music & Drama

Stream Bubble & Shell

Barbican Centre

BARBICAN

Club Gascon

Cellar Gascon

Barbican Hall

Ironmongers Hall

Barber Surgeon's Hall

Museum of London
Museum of London

40-2A →

St Bartholomews Hospital

Police Station

Guildhall Library Office

Guildhall Offices

Post Office
National Postal Museum

British Telecom Centre

ST PAUL'S

CHEAPSIDE

The Place Below

Bank of England Offices

St Paul's Cathedral
St Paul's Cathedral

Ramen House Noto

Bow Wine Vaults

Youth Hostel

City of London Information Centre

Post Office

MANSION HOUSE

42-1A →

Mermaid Theatre

City of London School

The Bridge

A | B

40 MOORGATE, LIVERPOOL ST.

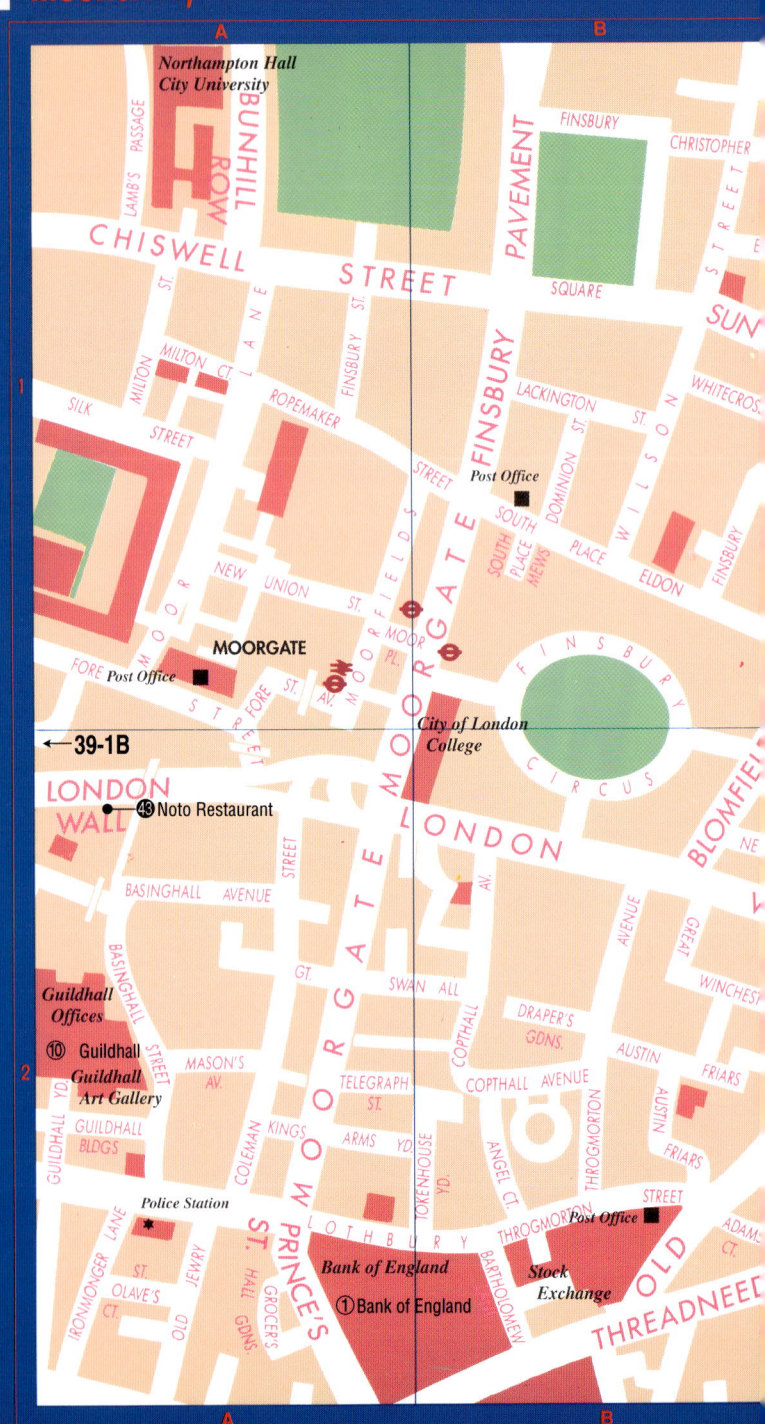

41

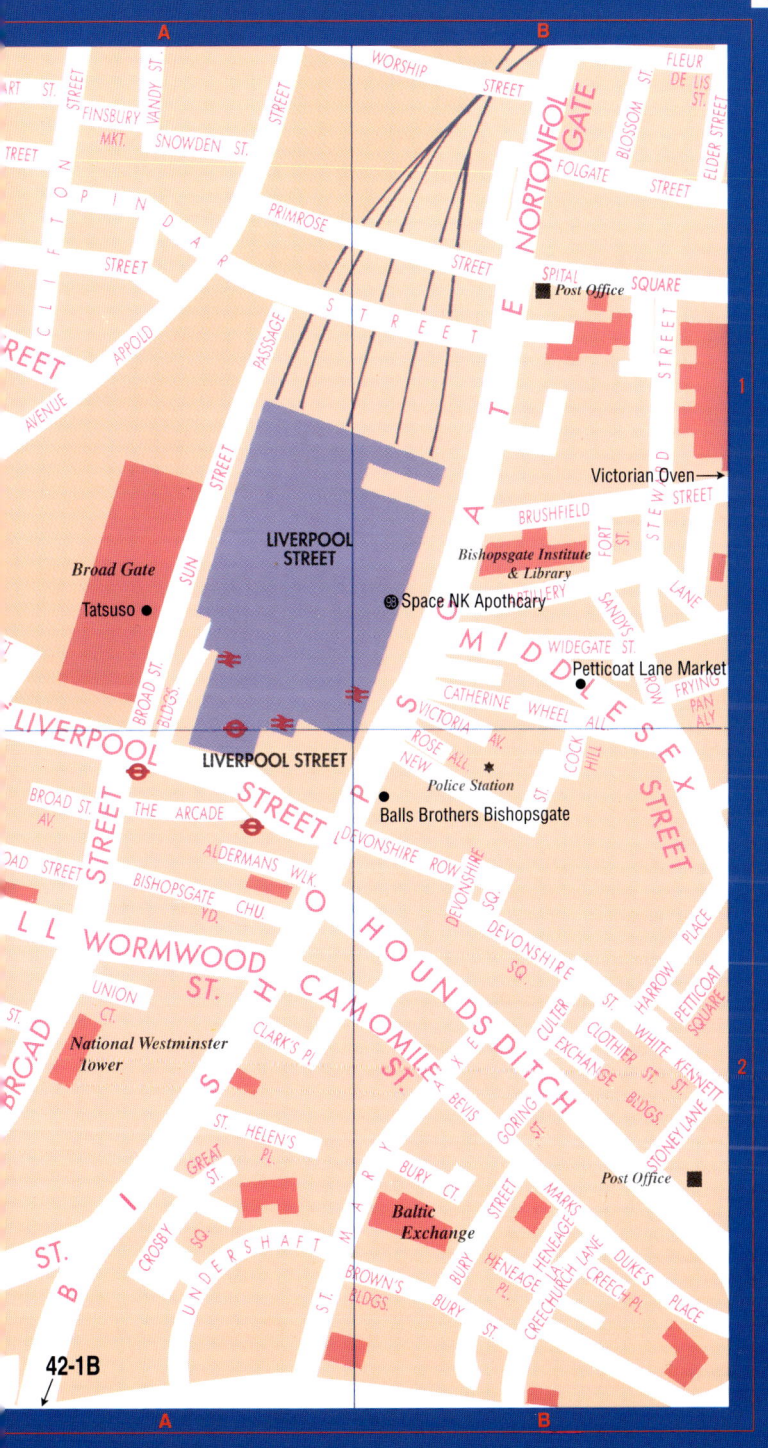

A | B

Broad Gate
Tatsuso

LIVERPOOL STREET

Post Office
Victorian Oven →
Bishopsgate Institute & Library
Space NK Apothecary
Petticoat Lane Market

LIVERPOOL STREET
Police Station
Balls Brothers Bishopsgate

National Westminster Tower

Post Office

Baltic Exchange

42-1B

Streets and labels
CLIFTON ST, FINSBURY MKT, VANDY ST, SNOWDEN ST, APPOLD ST, PRIMROSE ST, WORSHIP STREET, NORTON FOLGATE, BLOSSOM ST, FLEUR DE LIS ST, ELDER STREET, FOLGATE STREET, SPITAL SQUARE, BROAD ST AV, SUN STREET PASSAGE, BROAD ST BLDGS, THE ARCADE, ALDERMANS WLK, BISHOPSGATE CHU. YD., BRUSHFIELD, FORT ST, STEWARD STREET, SANDYS ROW, WIDEGATE ST, CATHERINE WHEEL AL, FRYING PAN ALY, VICTORIA AV, ROSE ALL, NEW ST, COCK HILL, MIDDLESEX STREET, HOUNDSDITCH, DEVONSHIRE ROW, DEVONSHIRE SQ, CUTLER ST, EXCHANGE BLDGS, HARROW PLACE, CLOTHIER ST, WHITE KENNETT ST, PETTICOAT SQUARE, WORMWOOD ST, UNION CT, CLARK'S PL, ST. HELEN'S PL, GREAT ST, CROSBY SQ, UNDERSHAFT, ST. MARY AXE, CAMOMILE ST, BEVIS MARKS, BURY CT, GORING ST, STONEY LANE, BROWN'S BLDGS, BURY ST, HENEAGE LANE, HENEAGE PL, CREECHURCH LANE, CREECH PL, DUKE'S PLACE, BROAD STREET, BISHOPSGATE

A | B

42 CANNON ST., BANK, LONDON BRIDGE, TOWER HILL

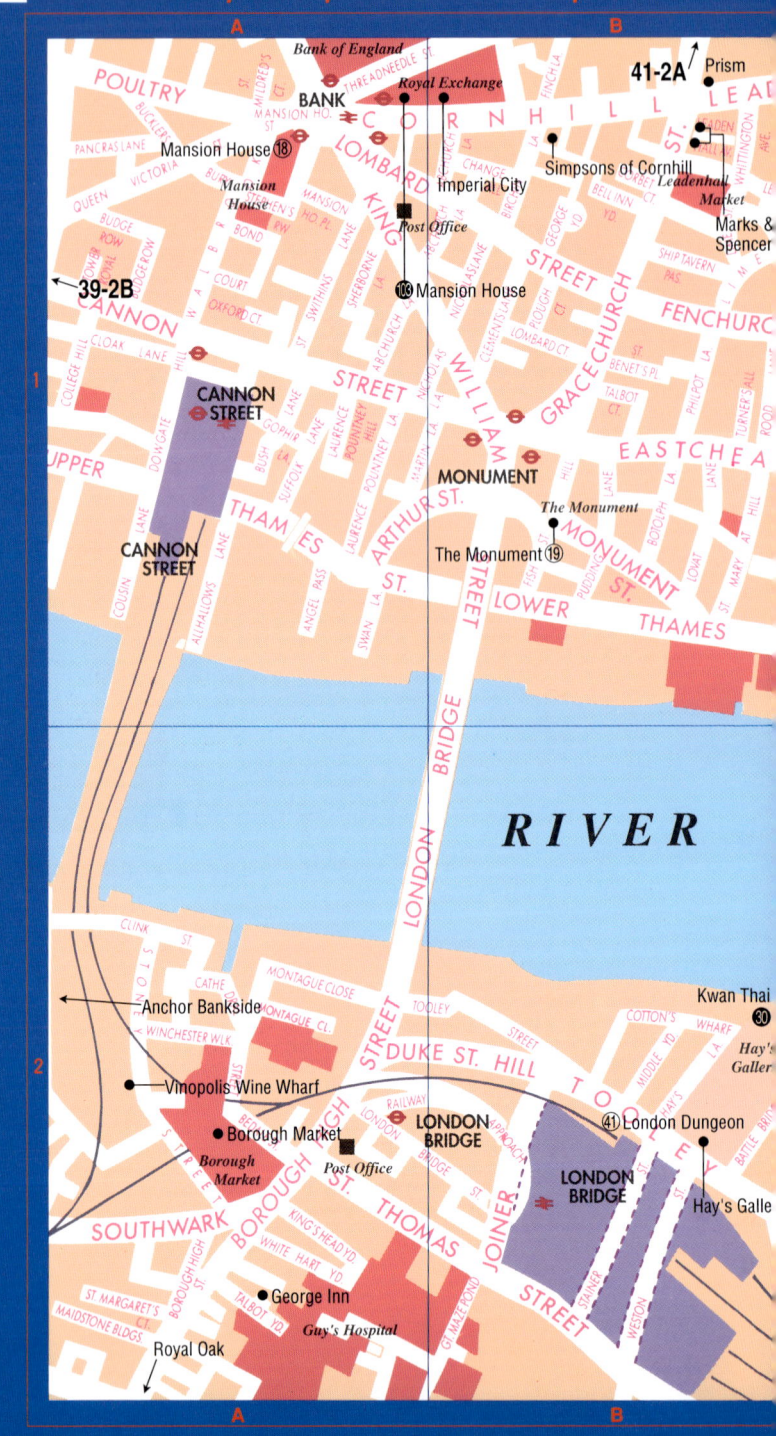

43

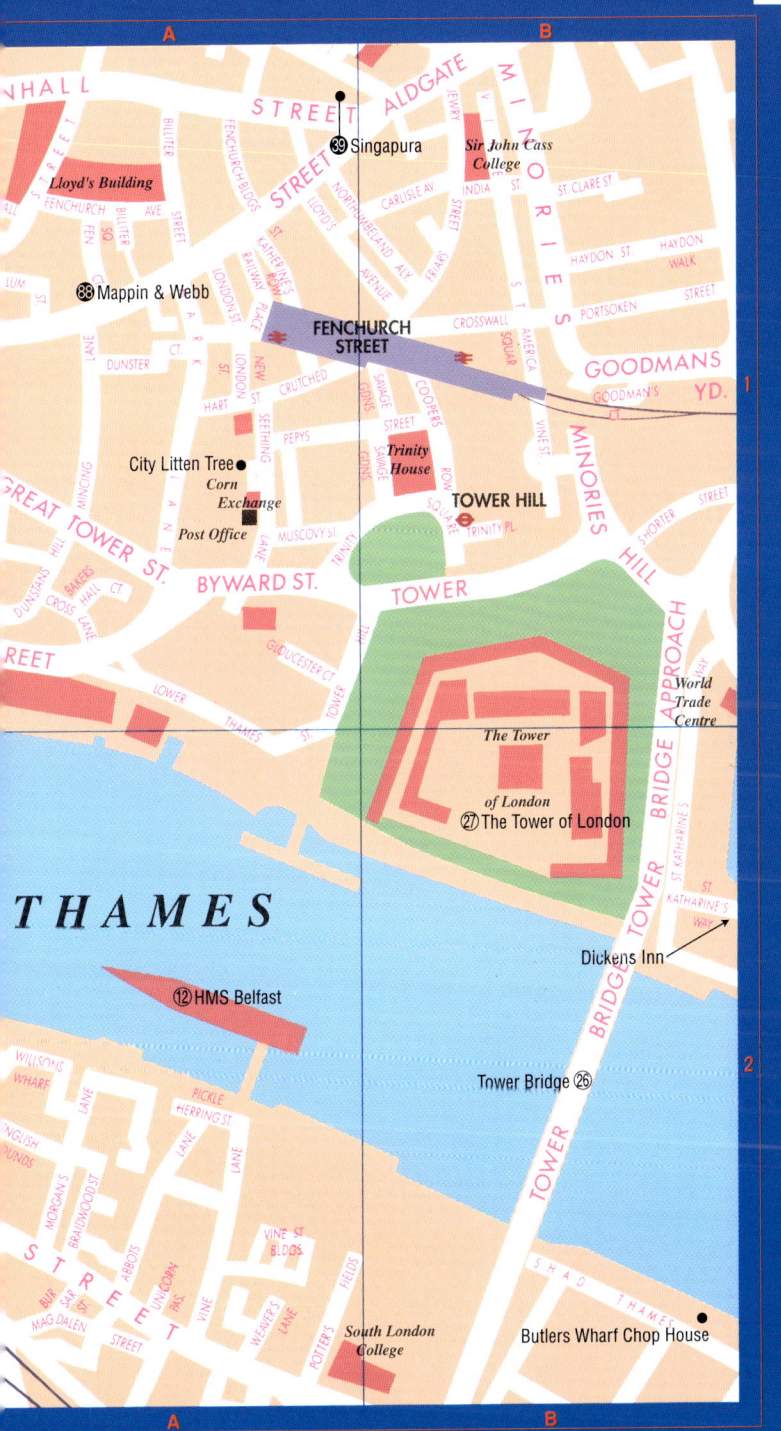

A | B

STREET ALDGATE
㊷ Singapura
Sir John Cass College

Lloyd's Building

㊶ Mappin & Webb

FENCHURCH STREET

GOODMANS YD.

City Litten Tree
Corn Exchange
Post Office

Trinity House

TOWER HILL

GREAT TOWER ST.

BYWARD ST.

TOWER

HILL

World Trade Centre

The Tower of London
㉗ The Tower of London

THAMES

⑫ HMS Belfast

Dickens Inn

Tower Bridge ㉖

South London College

Butlers Wharf Chop House

44 HIGH ST. KENSINGTON, NOTTING HILL GATE

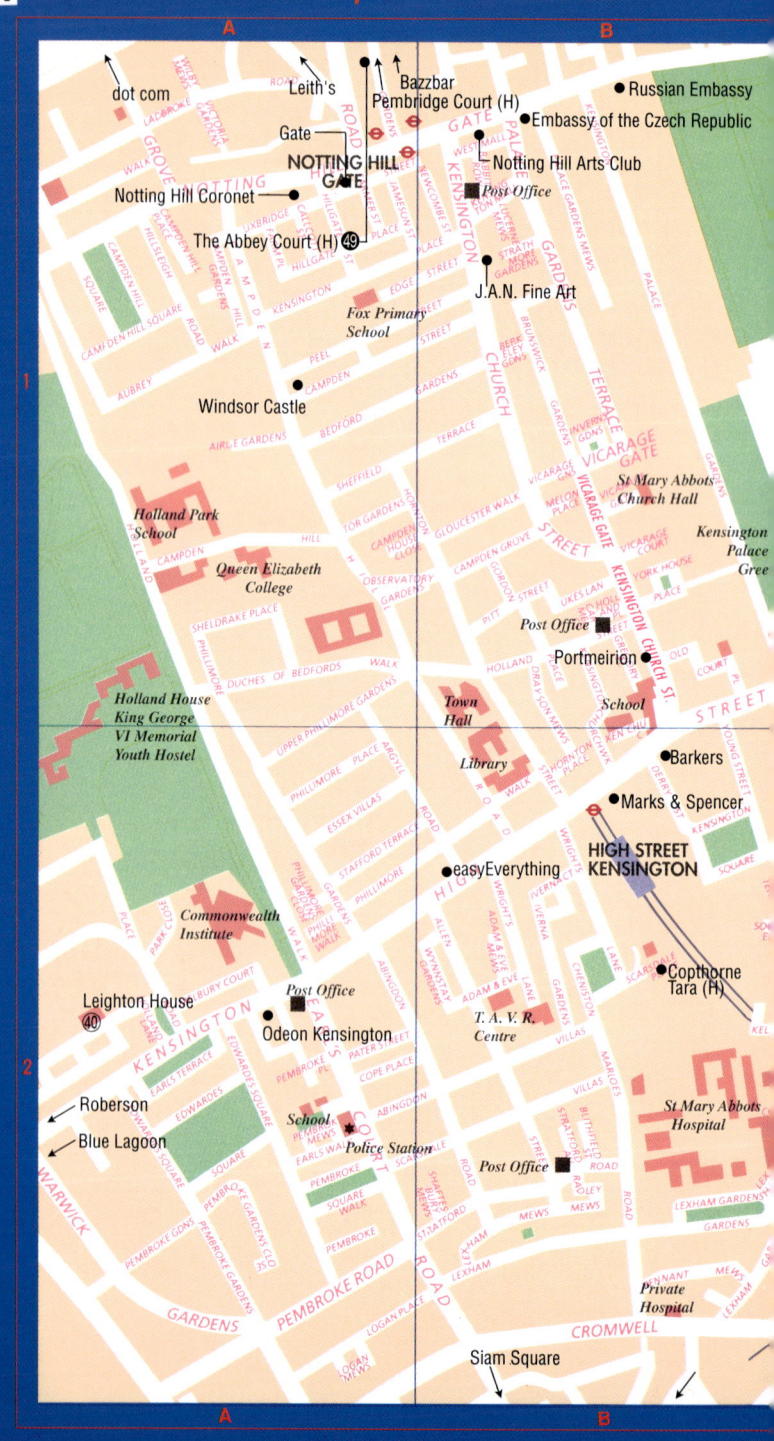

45

Kensington Gardens area map

- Internet Exchange
- UCI Whiteleys
- Speke's Monument
- Peter Pan
- **KENSINGTON GARDENS**
- Round Pond
- (14) Kensington Palace
- The Orangery
- Kensington Palace
- Serpentine Gallery (55)
- Serpentine Gallery
- (64) Royal Garden (H)
- Connoisseur Club
- The Palace Gate
- Queen's Gate
- Albert Memorial
- Alexandra Gate
- Royal College of Arts
- Royal Netherlands Embassy
- Royal Albert Hall
- Royal Geographical Society
- Imperial College
- The Gore (H)
- Royal College of Music
- Fish at 190
- Jacob's
- Post Office
- Imperial College of Science & Technology
- The Royal Thai Embassy
- Royal College of Art
- Science Museum (54)
- Science Museum
- National History Museum
- The Natural History Museum (49)
- 46-2A →
- The Delhi Brasserie (24)
- (58) The Gainsborough (H)
- French Consulate General
- (59) The Gallery (H)
- Ciné Lumière
- GLOUCESTER ROAD
- Bombay Brasserie
- Millennium Gloucester (21)
- Pelham (H)

46 KNIGHTSBRIDGE, BROMPTON RD., SOUTH KENSINGTO

DANE ST.

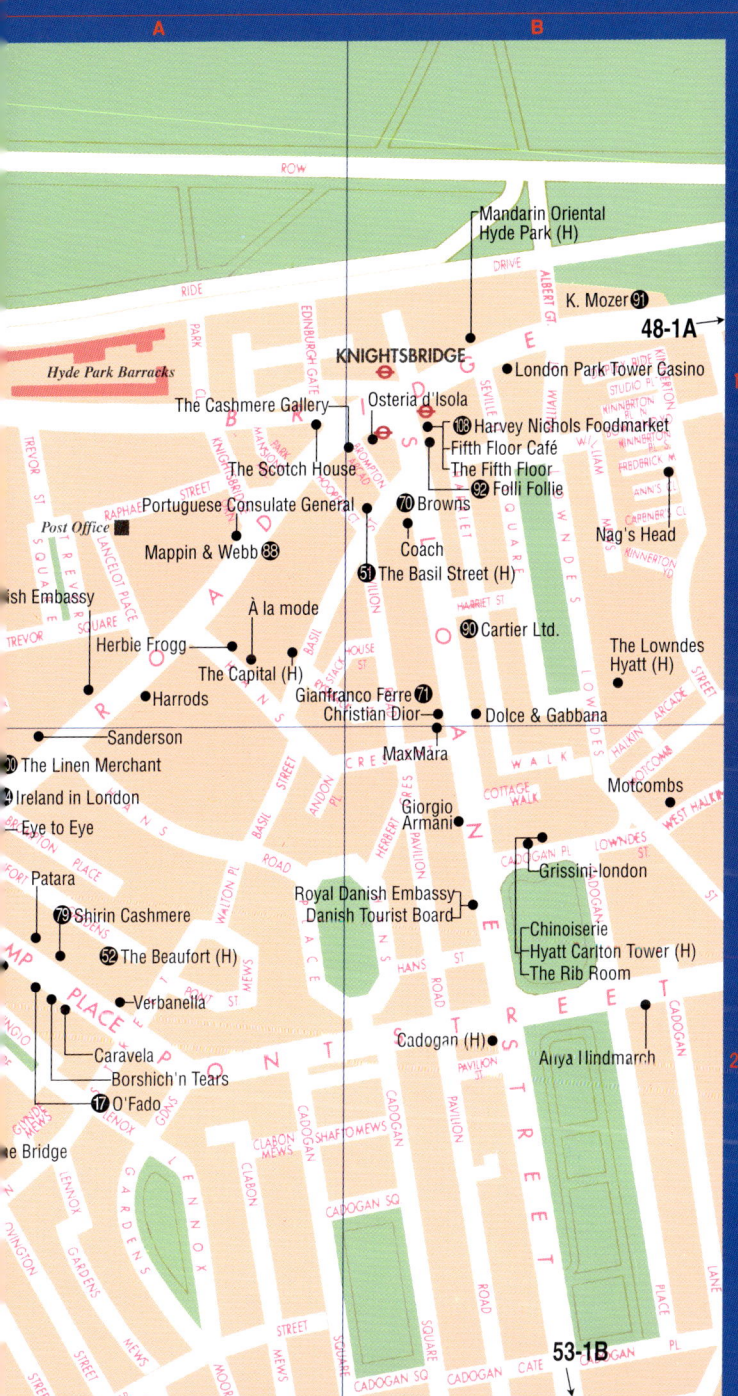

47

48-1A →

53-1B ↓

Map labels

- KNIGHTSBRIDGE
- Hyde Park Barracks
- Mandarin Oriental Hyde Park (H)
- K. Mozer 91
- London Park Tower Casino
- The Cashmere Gallery
- Osteria d'Isola
- Harvey Nichols Foodmarket 108
- Fifth Floor Café
- The Fifth Floor
- The Scotch House
- Folli Follie 82
- Portuguese Consulate General
- Browns 70
- Post Office
- Mappin & Webb 88
- Coach
- Nag's Head
- The Basil Street (H) 51
- À la mode
- Cartier Ltd. 90
- Herbie Frogg
- The Lowndes Hyatt (H)
- The Capital (H)
- Gianfranco Ferre 71
- Harrods
- Christian Dior
- Dolce & Gabbana
- Sanderson
- MaxMara
- The Linen Merchant
- Ireland in London
- Giorgio Armani
- Eye to Eye
- Motcombs
- Patara
- Royal Danish Embassy
- Shirin Cashmere 79
- Danish Tourist Board
- Grissini-london
- The Beaufort (H) 52
- Chinoiserie
- Hyatt Carlton Tower (H)
- Verbanella
- The Rib Room
- Caravela
- Borshich'n Tears
- Cadogan (H)
- Anya Hindmarch
- O'Fado 17
- ish Embassy
- Bridge

48 VICTORIA, HYDE PARK CORNER, BELGRAVIA

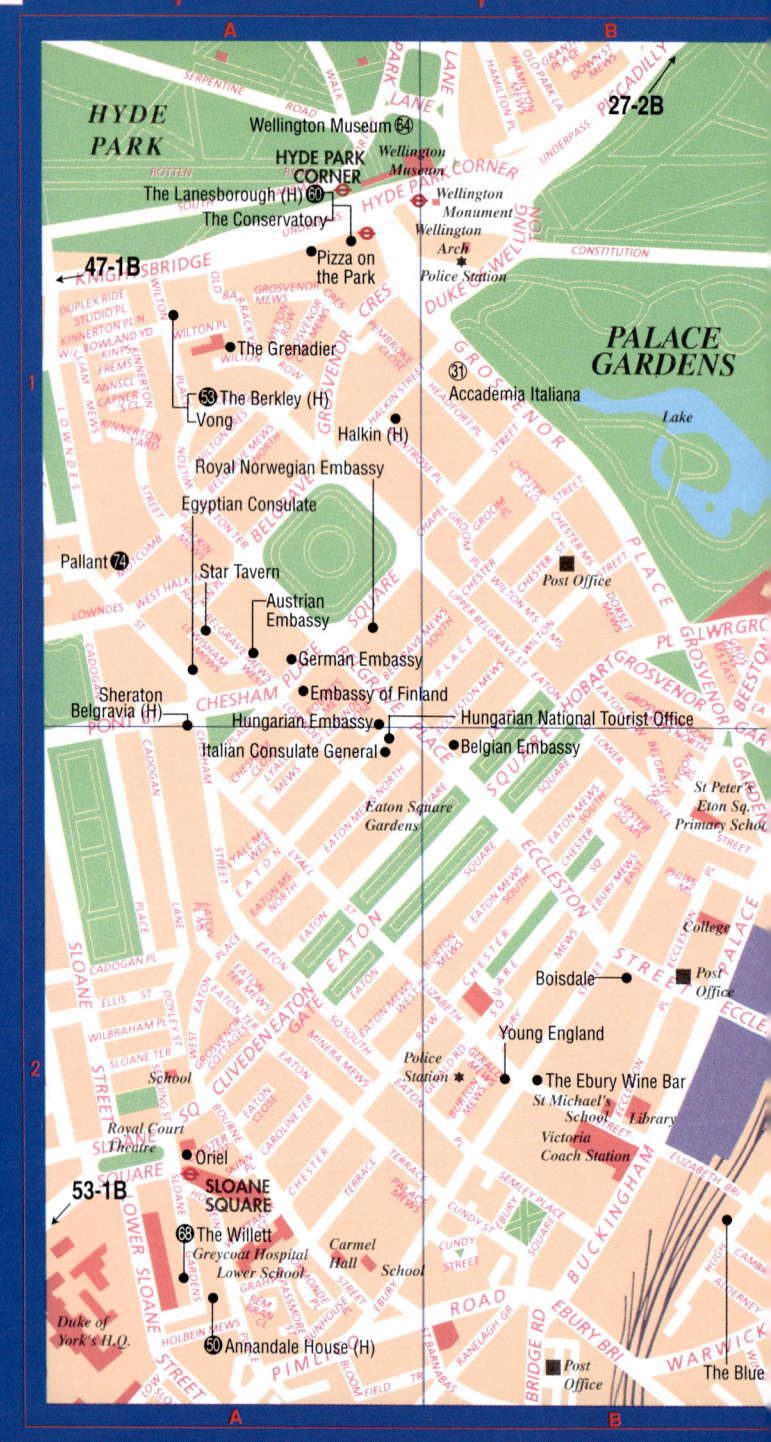

49

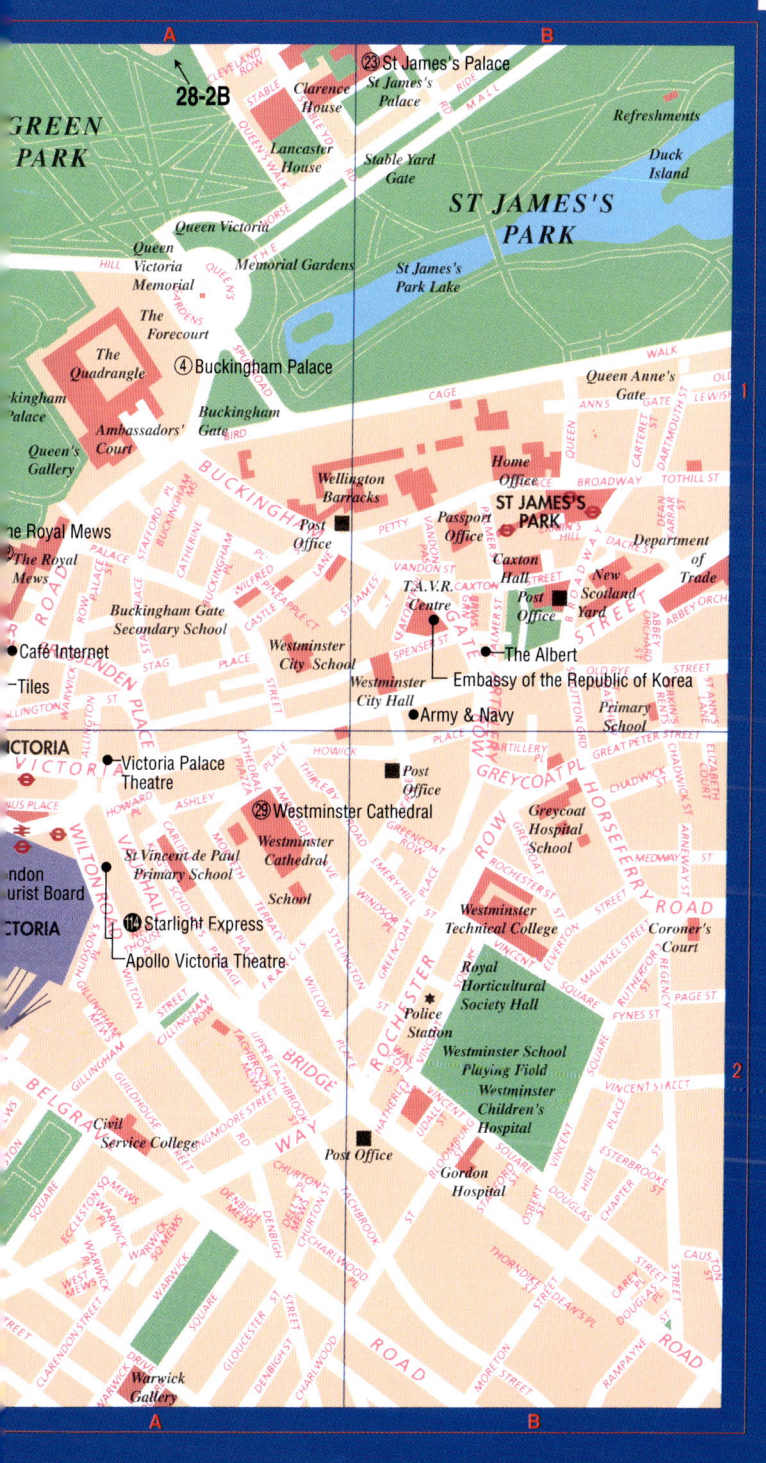

A / B

28-2B

GREEN PARK

Cleveland Row
Queen's Walk
Clarence House
Lancaster House

㉓ St James's Palace
St James's Palace
Stable Yard Gate

ST JAMES'S PARK

Refreshments
Duck Island

Queen Victoria Memorial Gardens
Queen Victoria Memorial
The Forecourt
The Quadrangle
St James's Park Lake

Buckingham Palace
④ Buckingham Palace
Ambassadors' Court
Buckingham Gate
Queen's Gallery

Queen Anne's Gate
Old Queen St
Carteret St
Dartmouth St
Tothill St
Lewisham St

The Royal Mews
The Royal Mews

Wellington Barracks
Post Office

Home Office
ST JAMES'S PARK
Broadway
Department of Trade

Passport Office
Caxton Hall
T.A.V.R. Centre
Post Office
New Scotland Yard

Café Internet
Tiles

Buckingham Gate Secondary School
Westminster City School
Westminster City Hall
● The Albert
Embassy of the Republic of Korea

Primary School

● Army & Navy

VICTORIA
● Victoria Palace Theatre

■ Post Office

㉙ Westminster Cathedral
Westminster Cathedral School

Greycoat Hospital School

London Tourist Board
VICTORIA

St Vincent de Paul Primary School

⑭ Starlight Express
Apollo Victoria Theatre

Westminster Technical College

Coroner's Court

★ Police Station

Royal Horticultural Society Hall
Westminster School Playing Field
Westminster Children's Hospital

Civil Service College

Post Office

Gordon Hospital

Warwick Gallery

A / B

50 WESTMINSTER, TRAFALGAR SQ., CHARING CROSS, W

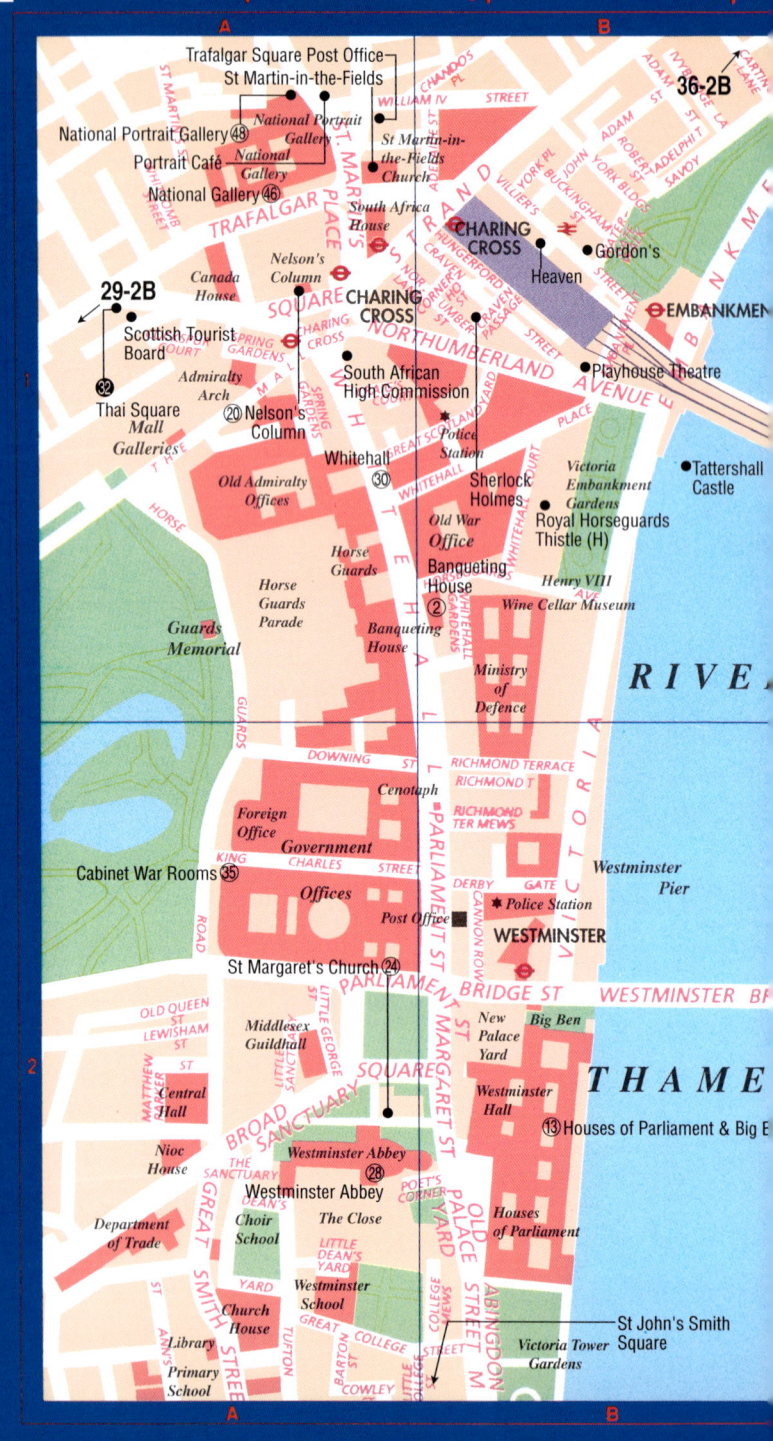

51

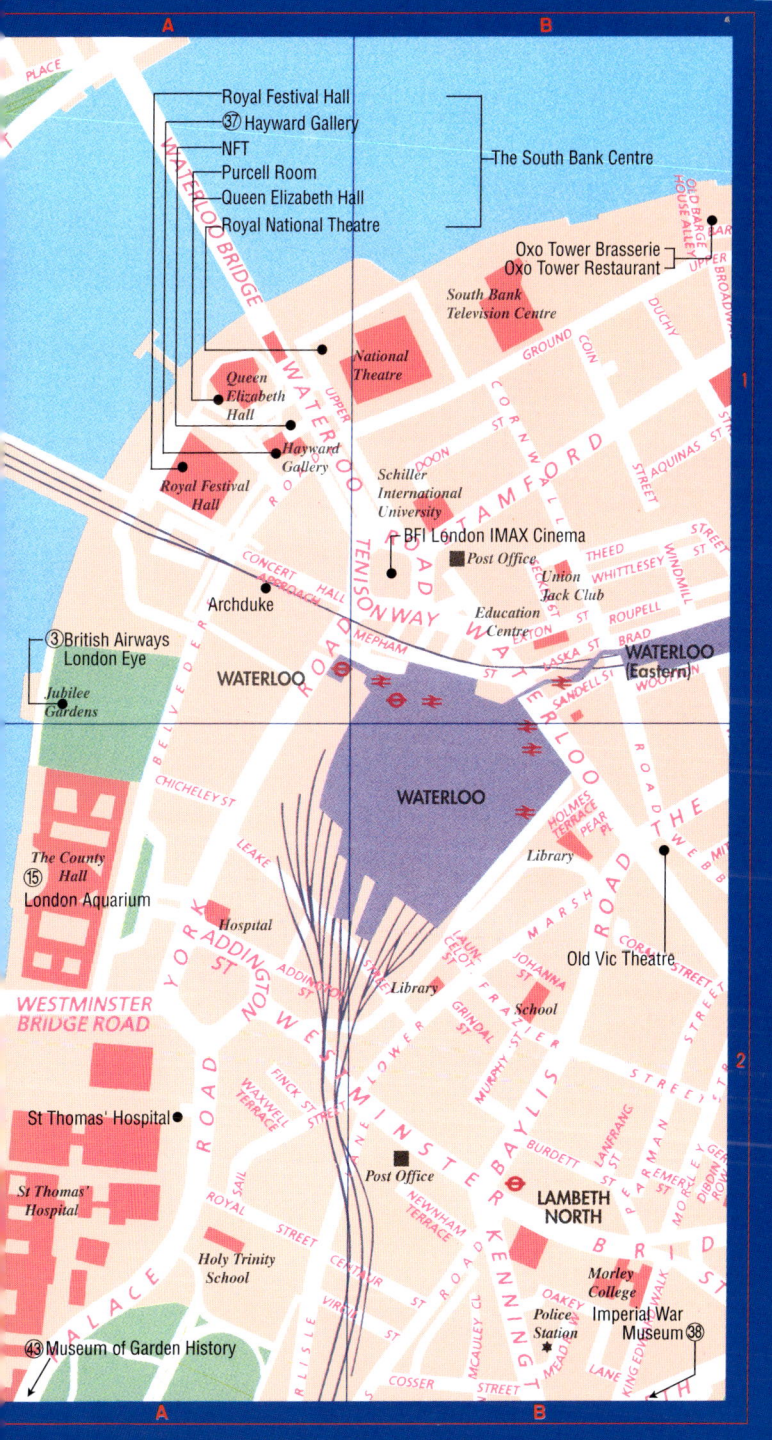

The South Bank Centre
- Royal Festival Hall
- ㊲ Hayward Gallery
- NFT
- Purcell Room
- Queen Elizabeth Hall
- Royal National Theatre

Oxo Tower Brasserie
Oxo Tower Restaurant

South Bank Television Centre

National Theatre

Queen Elizabeth Hall

Hayward Gallery

Royal Festival Hall

Schiller International University

BFI London IMAX Cinema
Post Office

Union Jack Club

Archduke

Education Centre

WATERLOO (Eastern)

③ British Airways London Eye

Jubilee Gardens

WATERLOO

WATERLOO

The County Hall
⑮ London Aquarium

Library

Hospital

Library

Old Vic Theatre

School

St Thomas' Hospital

St Thomas' Hospital

Post Office

LAMBETH NORTH

Holy Trinity School

Morley College

Police Station

Imperial War Museum ㊳

㊸ Museum of Garden History

WESTMINSTER BRIDGE ROAD

52 CHELSEA, SLOANE SQ., KING'S RD.

A

- Daquise
- SOUTH KENSINGTON
- Post Office
- Café Lazeez
- Brompton Hospital
- Royal Marsden Hospital
- Brompton Hospital
- Cemy
- Zaika
- UGC Fulham Road
- Bridgewater
- Chelsea College of Science & Technology
- UGC Chelsea
- Dôme
- Bluebird
- Space NK Apothecary
- Post Office
- Burial Ground

B

46-2B

- Cox & Power
- The Collection
- Tokio
- Itsu
- Poissonnerie de L'Avenue ❼
- Bibendum
- The Conran Shop
- Galerie Gaultier
- Zen Chelsea
- The Crescent
- Tandori of Chelsea
- Chelsea Green
- St Luke's Church
- Chelsea Hospital for Women
- St Luke's Hospital
- The Builders Arms
- Neal's Yard Remedies ❾⓻
- Post Offi
- Chelsea School of Art
- Sports Centre
- Old Town Hall
- ⑤ Carlyle's House
- Carlyle's House

53

A **B**

47-2B

Partick Cox •

Hackett • **48-2A**

The Cliveden Town House 56

SLOANE

Peter Jones

• The Spanish Consulate **SLOANE SQUARE**

Post Office

The Sloane (H) 66 • El Blasson

— Jane Asher's Tea Room

Duke of York's H.Q.

• Reiss

• Marks & Spencer

sea Cinema

Burton's Court

— Antiquarius

Chelsea Royal Hospital

National Army Museum

㊻ National Army Museum

Post Office

Royal Hospital

• Gordon Ramsay

Botanic Gardens

EMBANKMENT

A **B**

Bentley's
Seafood Restaurant & Oyster Bar

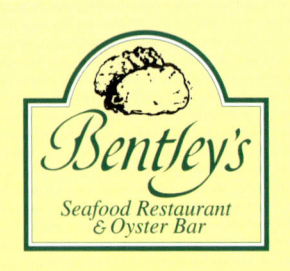

Bentley's has been synonymous with seafood since 1916. Only the freshest produce from sea and river finds its way into the kitchens, and onto your table. This is a place where the traditional and the modern sit happily together, where you'll enjoy up-to-the-minute cooking in the discreet comfort of gloriously old-fashioned booths. You might start with the plumpest of oysters or spaghetti of lobster and continue with classic grilled Dover sole or roast turbot with Ravigote sauce and asparagus. From fish and chips to caviar Bentley's believes in quality.

1916年の創業以来、「ベントリーズ」はシーフードの代名詞。極めつけの新鮮な魚介類だけがテーブルを彩ります。懐古調の心地よい座席とモダンが調和した店内。丸々と太ったアイルランド産の牡蠣やロブスターのスパゲッティを前菜に、特製ヨーグルトソースを添えた舌平目のグリルや大平目など、できたての味をご堪能ください。フィッシュ＆チップスからキャビアまで、食のクオリティが光ります。

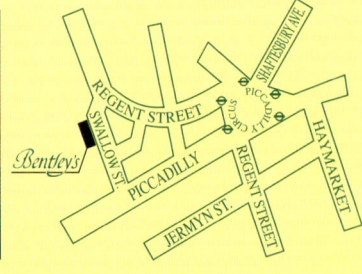

11-15 Swallow Street, London W1R 7HD *Tube: Piccadilly Circus*
Tel: 020-7734-4756/7439-6903 Fax: 020-7287-2972
Amex, Visa, Mastercard, Diners, JCB

◆ ◆ ◆ ◆ ◆

lunch, dinner: 7 days a week
menu: lunch £14.75-£19.50, dinner £14.75-£19.50, a la carte £35.00

Eating London &
Satisfying all the Senses

The right environments for eating alone
or with companions, and foods that delight
in aesthetics, taste, aroma and perhaps more…

EAT-TRENDY

Eat Trendy
Fashion, passion & dining

Defy convention, follow fashion ~ follow no one, defy by convention ~ but basically it's the punters who set the scene of a restaurant or bar. So whilst *sublime* might be the rightful claim of all this *engineered* interior design, adventurous cuisine and wild World wines, it's down to you to add the…*sparkle*.

Fruity French Sophistication

Cellar Gascon offers a bar menu that's a delicatessen's dream. It's a modest affair of sharp cheeses, melt-in-the-mouth meats and *'oh order me some more of those... olives!'* This gastronomy meets brasserie is served by France's own *Men in Black*, in a steel, leather and bare brick bar. Amongst their highly recommendable wine list are *Madiran, Tursan, Cotes de Gascogne* and *Saussignac*, and their gin and tonic also hits the mark. Neither over nor under designed, they've created the right balance, with a very comfortable ambience and an air of the romantic.

Biting Edge

If your appetite is for Thai food, then *'O's Thai Cafe'* or the more recent **'O's Bar'** are perfect and both are very reasonably priced and good value for money. ***O's Bar*** has tons of noodle options, seafood steamed in banana leaves, green curry sauce, lemon grass, and lime leaves… tantalising ingredients a plenty. The restaurant area has a basic table-

Cellar Gascon

O's Bar

Gresslin's

Cellar Gascon
59 West Smithfield EC1
⊖Barbican
☎020-7796-0600
⊙12.00-0.00
⊗Sun
£18
Map:39-1A

O's Bar
115 Park Rd. N8
⊖Finsbury Park
☎020-8340-7845
⊙12.00-0.00(Sun 23.00)
⊗No
£15
Map:24-1B

Gresslin's
13 Heath St. NW3
⊖Hampstead
☎020-7794-8386
⊙12.00-14.30(Ex. Mon), 19.00-22.30
⊗Sun
£20
Map:24-1A

EAT-TRENDY 57

and-bench interior rather like a noodle bar. This leads out of the main bar which has a cool slate floor and funky bar stools *designed by Stefano Giovannoni*, for those into *names* - but what matters more is that they *are* comfy and sitting on one of these is rather like putting yourself on a pedestal.

Zen Chic

This has to describe the strength of design at **Gresslin's**, red leather dining chairs opposite black leather banquette seating, offset by clean white table cloths, with an eccentric wall of bicycle wheels to add the necessary humour. It has to be said, that stepping inside a really well designed restaurant could make any-one feel special, and who would deny themselves that? As for the menu, that is modern European with Oriental influences, and combining fish with lychee is a big hit.

Satsuma is a modern minimalist Japanese restaurant. It has a rather bare interior but a very upbeat atmosphere, attracting customers of every nationality. Their colourful bento is a good choice, especially if you want to try out lots of different Japanese food without committing yourself to one dish. Their tempura and sushi are also popular, and are partnered well by plum wine or beer.

Satsuma

The Bridge

Oxo Tower Brasserie

River Cool

Views of the Thames are more often tones of grey than shades of blue, but the landscape of ***The Bridge*** restaurant and bar has great lighting, and is bathed in varying atmospheric blues. If the *al fresco* dining option doesn't live up to expectation, *The Bridge* has a striking interior with its blue suede chair covers, royal blue bar, beech wood tables, and quite a sophisti-cated mood. Many of their wines and champagnes are served by the glass, and the menu has a large dim sum selection, with main courses such as Mongolian lamb or duck, and desserts including lemon and elderflower tart….um!

London's city skyline is certainly impressive at night, and the ***Oxo Tower Brasserie*** is both a super viewing tower and a rather swanky place to dine.

Satsuma	**The Bridge**	**Oxo Tower Brasserie**
56 Wardour St. W1	1 Paul's Walk EC4	Oxo Tower Wharf, Barge House St. SE1
⊖Piccadilly Circus	⊖Blackfriars	⊖Waterloo
☎020-7437-8338	☎020-7236-0000	☎020-7803-3888
◎12.00-23.00(Sat 23.30, Sun 22.30)	◎10.30-16.30(Ex. Sat), 18.00-23.30	◎11.00-23.00(Sun 12.00-22.30)
⊗No	⊗Sun	⊗No
£20	£25	£35
Map:29-1A	Map:39-2B	Map:51-1B

58 EAT-POSH

Eat Posh
Bon Appetit

Gordon Ramsay

Caviar House

The New End

Too Beautiful for You

Sensitively designed modern interior with carpet underfoot and glorious glass screens that hide... nothing, and certainly not your blushes, as you enter into an exciting affair with gourmet cooking at **Gordon Ramsay**'s. A glamorous setting for marvellous dishes, lobster, beef, pigeon...*heaven*.... Book well in advance!

The *Caviar House*, the epitome of indulgence and luxuriance. French blue glass plates lie helpless under the flirtatious charms of the house's symphonies of caviar. The connoisseur staff will conduct you well through their current menu, while the champagne and wine listing will simply have you in raptures. At least once in a lifetime, if not once in a while, spoil yourself.

The Earnest Chef

Wasn't it Dr. Samuel Johnson who said that a man rarely thinks about anything more earnestly than his dinner ? Perhaps it is enough if such intense conviction is left in the hands of the chef, and few chefs would really want their dishes tasted in a mood of 'earnest consumption.' Fortunately London has a bold list of such dedicated chefs and **The New End** is home to at least one of these, leaving the customer at ease to think with nothing more than the palate. The menu is contemporary European and the ingredients are feisty choices

---

Gordon Ramsay's
68-69 Royal Hospital Rd. SW3
⊖Sloane Square
☎020-7352-4441
⊙12.00-14.00, 18.45-23.00
⊗Sat, Sun
⊙70
Map:53-2A

Caviar House
161 Piccadilly W1
⊖Green Park
☎020-7409-0445
⊙10.00-23.00
⊗Sun
⊙65
Map:30-2B

The New End
102 Heath St. NW3
⊖Hampstead
☎020-7431-4423
⊙12.00-14.30(Ex. Tue),
18.00-23.00
⊗Mon
⊙40
Map:24-1A

EAT-POSH 59

such as pigeon, veal, oyster, aged balsamic, chorizo and black-eyed beans. When it comes to the dessert menu that too has some dominating features, not least the white truffle ice cream - *scrumptious*, or the roast apricots. The wines are selected from both New and Old Worlds, and the setting likewise combines old and new with an aged brick wall opposite the bright white one bedecked with ebullient contemporary art.

The **Prism** is as architecturally fun as some of its dessert designs. The classical 1920's features of the restaurant make it a really classy city dining space. Its high ceiling and colossal columns put you in mind of a posh railway waiting room, filled with elegant diners in place of passengers. There is no Orient Express awaiting but a wonderful team of sommeliers and waiters to direct you through the menu. The Modern British dishes are all wonderful, and in particular the Whitby cod, peppered haddock, and Cumberland sausage main courses. Then to follow - the lime parfait with roasted liquorice is very clever and delicious, and their pineapple dessert with basil sorbet... complete perfection... *doesn't everyone have two desserts?!...*

Prism

Fifth Floor

Oxo Tower Restaurant

World View

Clement weather, it seems, can't be guaranteed at any time of year in London, so clear views of the city or river can only ever be a lucky addition to any dining experience. That means that none of the *'restaurants with a view,'* can rest on their laurels, as no London diners are ever so distracted from what they're eating, by the skyline... quite right too. Thankfully, the **Fifth Floor** at Harvey Nichols has a delicately coloured interior to relax in, expecting the table fare to do all the work it should. The service is polished and attentive, and their sommelier - worldly wise and humorous. Their apricots with mint sorbet are a truly inspired combination.

Down on the South Bank, the **Oxo Tower Restaurant** serves Keta caviar and lightly seared tuna that often upstages the view. Feast the appetite...and enjoy.

Prism	**The Fifth Floor**	**Oxo Tower Restaurant**
147 Leadenhall St. EC3	Harvey Nichols SW1	Oxo Tower Wharf, Barge House St. SE1
⊖Bank	⊖Knightsbridge	⊖Waterloo
☎020-7256-3888	☎020-7235-5250	☎020-7803-3888
⊙11.30-15.00, 18.00-22.00	⊙11.00-23.00(Sun 12.00-18.00)	⊙11.00-23.00(Sun 12.00-22.30)
⊗Sat, Sun	⊗No	⊗No
£43	£40	£45
Map:42-1B	Map:47-1B	Map:51-1B

EAT-FOR LESS

Eat For Less
Lite bites & satisfaction

The Coffee Gallery

Le Tea Cosy

Buon Appetito

Rhyme & Reasonable

Very close to the British Museum you will find **The Coffee Gallery**, and just as the name suggests it is a place for coffee and a place for art. The cafe itself is painted in brilliant Van Gogh colours, and its walls are decked with contemporary art that's often for sale. They open early enough for breakfast and have the morning newspapers ready for you. There are also great coffees, hot chocolate, cakes and lunches at realistic prices. It has the kind of warm friendly service that puts you at ease if you're having coffee or lunch alone.

Pale, sunny yellow walls in Primrose hill, that's the interior and indeed the mood at **Le Tea Cosy**. Hanging flower baskets as you enter this modest little place. It serves fresh salads, a huge sandwich list, impressive homemade cakes and all manner of freshly squeezed juices. This hospitable teashop also offers breakfast, and afternoon tea to almost rival the Ritz, at about one third of the price.

Modest but Mighty

There's a great Sicilian eatery in Holborn that puts the cheerful in *'cheap and.....'* You can have ciabatta or focaccia with all kinds of delicious fillings, savour that basil, and their risotto takes some beating. By complete contrast they also serve up a full English breakfast, and why not. They have a selection of top Italian ice creams, and the coffees are LARGE. Polite service that's not intrusive, clean, cheap and cheerful by the right measure, **Buon Appetito**.

The Coffee Gallery
23 Museum St. WC1
⊖ Tottenham Court Road
☎ 020-7436-0455
◎ 8.30 (Sat 10.00, Sun 12.30) - 17.30
⊗ No
© 5
Map:36-1A

Le Tea Cosy
51A Regents Park Rd. NW1
⊖ Chalk Farm
☎ 020-7483-3378
◎ 8.00-19.00
⊗ No
© 6
Map:24-1B

Buon Appetito
27 Sicilian Av. WC1
⊖ Holborn
☎ 020-7242-7993
◎ 6.30-16.30
⊗ No
© 6
Map:36-1B

EAT-NO FUSS

Eat No Fuss

Keep it simple.
Eating without too much sauce.

There are signs all over London and on food packaging saying *"Food to go"*. When speed takes precedence over all culinary considerations you have to ask what happened to *"Food to eat ?"* But take heart, indeed literally so if your fancy is meat. There are several great restaurants ready to stir the appetite with quality meats, in time served highly recommended recipes, dished up with only a modicum of fuss. Sound good ? Then you might want to try **St. John** and what they have excelled in and entitled 'nose to tail' eating. They pride themselves on using as much of the animal as possible and wasting little. The menus are always varied, *"passer du coq a l'ane"* you might say, or if not a menu running from cockerels to donkeys, it does at least jump from eel to veal. Wooden tables, stone floor and their own bakery in operation, what a setting, with smells of freshly baked breads and draught beers to tickle the taste buds, and polite if brusque service.

Just Feed Me

You might also want to step back in time to the 1869 **Quality Chop House**, boasting progressive working class fare, no-nonsense foods and impeccable standards. Victorian benches and tables, top grub including liver and bacon to die for. Less traditional, but a clean and unfussy environment for eating good Modern-European food, try out **La Ventura**.

St. John

Quality Chop House

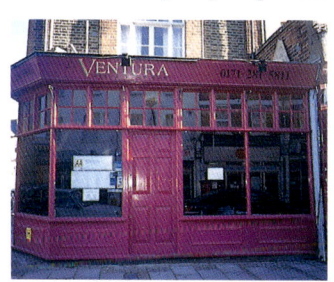

La Ventura

St. John
26 St John St. EC1
⊖Farringdon
☎020-7251-0848
◎11.00(Sat 18.00)-23.00
⊗Sun
©35
Map:38-1B

Quality Chop House
94 Farringdon Rd. EC1
⊖Farringdon
☎020-7837-5093
◎12.00-15.00(Sun 16.00, Ex. Sat), 18.30(Sun 19.00)-11.30
⊗No
©32
Map:25-1A

La Ventura
28 Crouch Hill N4
⊖Finsbury Park
☎020-7281-5811
◎10.30-1.00
⊗No
©25
Map:24-1B

62 EAT-AUTHENTIC

Eat Authentic
Peruse at leisure & enjoy in measure.

Rules

Simpsons of Cornhill

Veronica's

Opened in 1798, *Rules* is the oldest restaurant in London and its panelled walls simply ooze historical and political gossip. This is where the Prince of Wales entertained the adored, late nineteenth century actress, Lillie Langtry. The prince would enter by the tradesmen's entrance and dine with his Jersey Lily behind screens in the King Edward V11 room. Throughout history, Rules has been a popular haunt for thespians and writers including Charles Dickens, Evelyn Waugh, Charlie Chaplin, Clark Gable and Laurence Olivier.

Politics & Whiskey

In more recent years *Rules* has been frequented by many political figures, and the Charles Dickens room displays a collection of whiskey signed by Margaret Thatcher's entire 1990 Cabinet. Outside this glass case you'll also find a solitary whisky bottle, apparently signed by Tony Blair, make of this what you will. Rules' private dining rooms cater for up to 24 people, but for anyone in *Prince & Langtry mood*, you are welcome to book an entire room for two… at some cost. The menu is divine English country cooking, pheasant and partridge making appearances and applauded by terrine of strawberries in champagne jelly, lucky Lillie! *Simpsons of Cornhill's* bill of fare is full of English classics. Steamed puddings and fruit crumbles follow shepherds pie or roast leg of lamb. Old wooden, high backed benches and tables reminiscent of school days from another era. The service is warm, even motherly, and you rub shoulders with port and wine drinking city gents.

Rules
35 Maiden La. WC2
⊖Covent Garden
☎020-7836-5314
◎12.00-0.00
⊗No
ⓒ45
Map:36-2B

Simpsons of Cornhill
38 1/2 Cornhill EC3V
⊖Bank
☎020-7626-9985
◎11.30-15.00
⊗Sat, Sun
ⓒ30
Map:42-1B

Veronica's
3 Hereford Rd. W2
⊖Bayswater/Queensway
☎020-7229-5079
◎12.00-14.30(Ex. Sat),
18.00-11.30
⊗Sun
ⓒ32
Map:24-1A

EAT-AUTHEMTIC

Historic Britain, Literary Britain

At *Veronica's* the menus are taken from many periods in British history, Roman, Georgian, Edwardian, and are so authentically produced that the restaurant often caters for banquets at Royal Palaces. But along with catering for big affairs, you can enjoy really super lunches and dinners from a thought provoking and appetising menu. If there was an award to be gained for the longest dish title, then *Lord John Russell's Frozen Pudding with Butterscotch Sauce*, would surely be in the running. Rest assured that this marriage of 1860's new found passion for ice cream with the later discovery of butterscotch sauce, lives up to its lengthy introduction. It's worth making enquiries in advance if you're interested in Veronica's Literary Luncheons and Dinners. Speakers have included Hilary Spurling on Matisse and David Starkey on Elizabeth I & Henry VIII.

Club Gascon

Alounak

The Bon Vivants

Club Gascon is a celebration of cooking from the south-west of France, specialising in dishes from Toulouse, Bordeaux and Biarritz. The waiter takes on the role of guide as you journey through the courses with well-chosen wines to celebrate the flavours. What this restaurant can't do with *foie gras* is nobody's business, they even replace the rice in sushi with it, and although that means it's strictly speaking *not* sushi, it is still divine. The chef, when asked if he was surprised, that to many, he and his team of seven are

Al-Casbah

thought to out cook the English, gave a wry and satisfied smile. The *foie gras, magrets and confits* have been favourably reviewed from New York to Japan. The marble and mirrors interior has a Parisian sophistication and that expected *je ne sais quoi*.

Olympia is the place to find London's best Iranian cooking and the *Alounak* serves its lamb in true Persian fashion. The air is filled with the scent of okra and oven-baked breads and by the music of the Middle East.

Moroccan Moods

Can be found and accompanied by really great North African food at *Al-Casbah*, where a satisfied stomach can, on occasion, be met by a rolling one, as they even have a belly dancer!

Club Gascon
57 West Smithfield EC1
⊖Barbican
☎020-7796-0600
◎12.00-14.00(Ex. Fri), 19.00-23.00(Sat. 22.30)
⊗Sun
©32
Map:39-1A

Alounak
10 Russell Gdns. W14
⊖Olympia
☎020-7603-7645
◎12.00-0.00
⊗No
©20
Map:24-2A

Al-Casbah
42 Hampstead High St. NW3
⊖Hampstead
☎020-7431-6356
◎10.00-0.00(Sun 23.00)
⊗No
©30
Map:24-1A

The Gateway to India

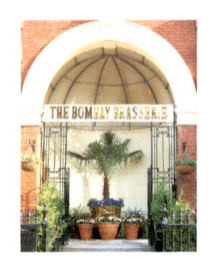

Every day The Bombay Brasserie serves an excellent 8 dish buffet, plus soup, 2 starters, 5 salads, naans, 3 desserts and coffee, all for just £16.95 per person. At dinner our new a la carte menu offers the finest cuisine India can offer.

London and Bombay are this close.

The Bombay Brasserie

Courtfield Road   London SW7
opp. Gloucester Rd tube
Reservations: 020 7370 4040 or 020 7373 0971
Open: 12.30pm - 3pm and 7.30pm - Midnight 7 days a week

EAT-AMBIENCE 65

Eat Ambience
Feed the senses
Forget the soul

Just Because You Can – Indulge
George Bernard Shaw once wrote that there was no love more sincere than that of food, and who would disagree…? If you eat out at **Mesculn** it will certainly reinforce any love relationship you've formed with food, and any culinary courting you may have already done. The fish dishes vary according to what's best at the market on the day, and are always a gastronomic success. The *mis en place* here is quite finely tuned, all the food is prepared with devotion, and the service is both courteous and unobtrusive, a quietly confident Modern European restaurant. Truly worth a step out of the city.

No Pain, Just Gain
There are an incredible number of Modern Italian restaurants emerging all over London, many boast impressive menus and wine lists, but **Artigiano** sets the standard in terms of interior and service. Natural light coming through the glass roof gives it a very refreshing atmosphere, and the floor and ceiling lights provide the subtle light show that complement the restaurant's *Giacometti-esque* sculpture. The restaurant's clean lines in presentation and service is also carried through its enticing menu.

Deliberate Delight
If you're looking for an *'Out of India'* as opposed to an *'Out of Africa,'* experience, the **Bombay Brasserie** is reminiscent of the *'last days of the Raj'* with its cocktail bar and lush, green conservatory. Their lamb dishes come highly recommended, especially when flattered by the house cocktail, comprised of champagne and sumptuous mango.

Mesclun

Artigiano

Bombay Brasserie

Mesclun	**Artigiano**	**Bombay Brasserie**
24 Stoke Newington Church St. N16	12 Belsize Terrace NW3	Courtfield Rd. SW7
⚐Stoke Newington	⚐Belsize Park	⚐Gloucester Road
☎020-7249-5029	☎020-7794-4288	☎020-7370-4040
◎18.00-23.00	◎12.00-15.00, 19.00-0.00	◎12.30-15.00, 19.00-0.00
⊗Sun	⊗No	⊗No
◉25	◉35	◉40
Map:25-1A	Map:24-1A	Map:45-2A

EAT - PIZZA

Eat Pizza
Pizza Passion
Do it the Italian Way

Pizza Paradiso

La Porchetta

Hoxton Furnace

Pizza Paradise
Pizza, pizza, pizza, but where can you get authentic Italian pizza ? Well there are a few to choose from, but those run independently by Italian families have to be the best. At *Pizza Paradiso*, the owner hails from Milan but the pizza's are made in true Sicilian fashion, thin crust, one size fits all as they are not made for sharing, and rightly so, they're too good. There are plenty of different pizzas to choose from and vegetarians are catered for just as well as meat lovers.

Italian Fashion
From Milan down to Sicily and then back up to Naples and London's family run *La Porchetta*. Here you can even see the bases freshly prepared. As you enter, the pizza dough is flying high as the guys spin it into those gargantuan discs in readiness for generous toppings. For those on the look out for a more sophisticated environment you might check out the self proclaimed 'superior pizzeria,' the *Hoxton Furnace*. Smart pine tables and chairs with the minimalism hitting the size of the pizzas, but that doesn't have to be a problem as the menu is reasonable and the various pasta dishes are obvious and delicious fillers…and then of course there's the dessert menu… this plays a bit of a blinder with specials such as their homemade tiramisu. And whilst you're in the area, pop into the local happening bar the *"Shoreditch Electricity Showrooms,"* for a buzz and a beer.

Pizza Paradiso
31 Catherine St. WC2
⊖ Covent Garden
☎ 020-7836-3609
◎ 12.00-0.00
✕ No
£ 17
Map:36-2B

La Porchetta
147 Stroud Green Rd. N4
⊖ Finsbury Park
☎ 020-7281-2892
◎ 18.00(Sat, Sun 12.00)-0.00
✕ No
£ 15
Map:25-1A

Hoxton Furnace
1 Rufus St. N1
⊖ Old Street
☎ 020-7613-0598
◎ 12.00-15.00(Ex. Sat), 18.00(Sat 19.00)-23.00
✕ Sun
£ 15
Map:25-1A

EAT - FISH

Eat Fish
Like it raw, like it cooked
Scream for more

Rhythm of the Tide
All thanks to Marie-Antoine Careme in the 1800's for establishing certain gastronomic rules and maxims; one of these being that sauces should enhance and not hide flavours. Smithfield's *Stream Bubble and Shell* restaurant serves a seafood menu with subtle sauces that even the great haute cuisine chef, Careme himself, might have admired. Their grilled squid and polenta are titillation to the tongue, and the shellfish crab platter…with oysters so fresh you can almost hear them sing; lobster, prawns, winkles and whelks – the total taste sensation. They serve a selection of daily fresh fruits of the sea that simply dance to the rhythm of sea and sensuality. A trendy but friendly atmosphere, minimalist wood and steel decor, a full bar, and a menu to make you blush with pleasure.

Clamorous Clams
Clams, langoustine, scallops and an impressive list of swimmers at *Fish at 190*. A rather more intimate atmosphere where you can relax and reflect alone or with company over the well-balanced fish menu and sea of world wines. At *Rasa Samudra* strawberry pink walls and dark raspberry chairs form the evocative and spicy interior. The fish dishes are prepared in Keralan fashion with all the exciting and enlivening flavours of the region. Green and red chillies, garlic, onion and coconut provide the taste of southern India; not as hot as other Indian cooking just a beautiful complement to the food of the sea.

Stream Bubble and Shell

Fish at 190

Rasa Samudra

Stream Bubble and Shell
50-52 Long La. EC1
⊖Barbican
☎020-7796-0070
◎12.00(Sat 18.00)-0.00
⊗Sun
£30
Map:39-1A

Fish at 190
190 Queen's Gate, SW7
⊖Gloucester Road
☎020-7581-5666
◎7.00(Sat, Sun 7.30)-23.15
⊗No
£30
Map:45-2B

Rasa Samudra
5 Charlotte St. W1
⊖Goodge Street
☎020-7637-0222
◎12.00-14.45(Ex. Sun), 18.00-22.45
⊗No
£33
Map:35-1A

Royal China

**Cuisine worthy of an emperor
from London's most sophisticated Chinese restaurants.**

Experience real Dim Sum
from the chef's selection of the week,
or enjoy lobster noodles with ginger and scallions
from our exquisite seafood menu.

· Cocktail bar · Private room

Royal China (Queensway): 13 Queensway London W2 4QJ   TEL: 020-7221-2535
12.00-23.00 (Fri, Sat 12.00-23.30, Sun 11.00-22.00)

Royal China (Baker St.): 40 Baker St. London W1M 1DA   TEL: 020-7487-4688
12.00-23.00 (Fri, Sat 12.00-23.30, Sun 11.00-22.00)

Royal China (St John's Wood): 68 Queens Grove NW8 6WR   TEL: 020-7586-4280
12.00-23.00 (Fri, Sat 12.00-23.30, Sun 12.00-22.30)

EAT-DIM SUM

Eat Dim Sum
Savour the flavours
Devour the dream

Steamed Sensations

These Chinese dishes of small steamed, fried or grilled dumplings can be devilishly delicious or none-too-delicate dissters. Fortunately London really plays host to some dim sum winners. Originally a Cantonese custom, dim sum can be eaten as a snack or as dishes in themselves. Although the London restaurants can't yet boast the 2,000 varieties developed by the Cantonese, they offer up enough to stimulate the taste for more, and if you choose carefully that can be *without the MSG (monosodium glutamate)*. They are designed to satisfy with taste, fragrance and some with their presentation. Gold and black lacquer forms the untamed decor at the **Royal China,** and it makes for a dramatic introduction to its highly acclaimed, gold bound menu, and an amazing dim sum production. Here they are especially proud of their *cheung fun*, pork being a favourite but the choice includes mushrooms, prawns, beef and plenty more. All the atmospheric busy bustle that makes for the *wake-up-and-eat-up* of a good Chinese restaurant.

Imperial City is deliberately less authentically Chinese. The somewhat Westernised but popular menu, is MSG-free and blends surprisingly well with the choice of either Chinese beers like Tsing Tao, Harbin or Tiger, or European wines.

Daring Dumplings

The **Royal Dragon** are Cantonese dim sum specialists, with 'sums' of turnip paste, pork & crab, that can be added to sweet lotus or cream custard buns to equal – *sheer pleasure*.

Royal China

Imperial City

Royal Dragon

Royal China	**Imperial City**	**Royal Dragon**
13 Queensway W2	Royal Exchange EC3	30 Gerrard St. W1
⊖Queensway	⊖Bank	⊖Leicester Square/ Piccadilly Circus
☎020-7221-2535	☎020-7626-3437	☎020-7734-1388
◎12.00-23.00(Fri, Sat 23.30, Sun 11.00-22.00)	◎11.30-21.00	◎12.00(Sun 11.00)-3.00
⊗No	⊗Sat, Sun	⊗No
ⓒ30	ⓒ32	ⓒ22
Map:24-2A	Map:42-1B	Map:29-1B

EAT-VEG.

Eat Veg.
Don't tell the meat eaters

Manna

The Gate

Rasa

Who was it that coined the phrase *"Beef is the soul of cooking"* ? What blasphemy to the vegetarian chef; thankfully vegetarian cooking has long seen the back of those who would simply replace the meat element with a few unambitious veg. London's vegetarian restaurants now boast that they are often the preferred choice of hitherto stalwart meat eaters. The new generation of vegetarian eateries cater for those seeking reliable, non GM, organic foods, and many of these restaurants can facilitate vegans, gluten-free diets and other dietary considerations such as allergies.

Victorious Veg.
As a rule, chefs argue that vegetarian food is the most labour intensive, as they constantly strive to create new and more adventurous recipes that provide a culinary feast. Fortunately the element of competition pervading, keeps these chefs on their toes and what they're cooking up is really worth checking out.

Culinary Calm
Manna's pale green ceiling is a roof of calm above its exciting gourmet vegetarian list; worth a mention are the apple and potato gratin and their buckwheat blinis. The pace is very laid back here and it's an excellent choice for those with particular dietary requirements as the staff are pleased to try and accommodate these as much as possible.

Manna
4 Erskine Rd. NW3
⊖Chalk Farm
☎020-7722-8028
◎12.30-14.30(Sat Sun only), 18.00-23.00
⊗No ⓒ25
Map:24-1B

The Gate
51 Queen Caroline St. W6
⊖Hammersmith
☎020-8748-6932
◎12.00-15.00(Ex. Sat), 18.00-22.45
⊗Sun ⓒ27
Map:22-2B

Rasa
55 Stoke Newington Church St. N16
⇌Stoke Newington
☎020-7249-0344
◎12.00-15.00(Sat, Sun only), 18.00-23.00(Fri, Sat 0.00)
⊗No ⓒ25
Map:25-1B

EAT-VEG.

The Gate to Heaven
The Gate restaurant, set near a church, has a high ceiling and lots of natural light, and it is something of an altar to vegetarian cuisine. The food is imaginative in composition and truly appetising, with ingredients such as salsa, chilli and horseradish used by modest degree to flatter and not inflame the palate. At **Rasa**, the vegetarian food of southern India's Kerala is served, and this is an exuberant feast of aroma, colour, and flavour that dances through the senses. Think of mandarin, coconut, ginger and chillies and the fresh scent of coriander, mustard, and fennel seed and you'll begin to have something of a nose for this stimulating and festive food.

Cosy in the Capital
Unpretentious surroundings can be difficult to find in the capital, but it is possible at **Food For Thought**. Their various bakes, quiches and scones provide plenty of thoughts on food, as you relax in the basement's cosy nooks on cushions at floor level or on wooden stools at a table; not a lot of space, healthy dining and a convivial air. *Fiction* gained its name rather romantically, since the restaurant was previously a bookshop, and the owner thought it fitting, as vegetarian cuisine is often itself, an act of fiction. It has to be said that their menu really does have a few best-sellers, and even some poetic specials such as its miso, black bean and sesame *haiku*. There is seating outside in a part-covered garden with climbing wisteria and Japanese anemone; it's a pretty and relaxing environment. They play an eclectic selection of music inside which massages the old stone walls and wooden floors ..., or is that just the organic wine talking...? Certainly worth a special visit.

Original Bliss
The Place Below is situated in the Norman crypt of Wren's beautiful Bow Bell's church. The restaurant has a proud and innovative menu with adventurous performances from ingredients like onion marmalade, green pea guacamole and garlic and almond dressing. The dishes here are brimming with originality, composed by a chef with passion and taste.

Food For Thought

Fiction

The Place Below

Food for Thought
31 Neal St. WC2
⊖Covent Garden
☎020-7836-9072
◎9.30-20.30(Sun 12.00-17.00)
⊗No
ⓒ15
Map:36-1A

Fiction
60 Crouch End Hill N8
⊖Finsbury Park
☎020-8340-3403
◎12.30-16.30(Sun only), 18.30-23.00
⊗Mon, Tue
ⓒ20
Map:24-1B

The Place Below
St Mary-le-Bow, Cheapside, EC2
⊖Bank/St Paul's
☎020-7329-0789
◎11.30-14.30
⊗Sat, Sun
ⓒ18
Map:39-2B

Authentic Indian Food

CHUTNEY MARY

535 KINGS ROAD
CHELSEA LONDON SW10
RESERVATIONS: 020 7351 3113

Best Indian Restaurant in the UK Good Curry Guide Award
- A unique gourmet trail of the many regions of India
- Winner of more major awards than any other Indian Restaurant
- Sunday Jazz Lunch £15 for 3 courses

Veeraswamy

VICTORY HOUSE
99 REGENT STREET LONDON W1
ENTRANCE ON SWALLOW ST -
MEZZANINE FLOOR
RESERVATIONS: 020 7734 1401

Best Indian Restaurant Time Out Award
- Britain's oldest Indian restaurant in a vibrant modern style
- Unusual food from Indian homes, palaces and wayside stalls
- Lunch & pre & post theatre dinner £11 - 2 courses prix fixe menu

For Special Offers, Information and Recipes -
visit our website, www.realindianfood.com

Eating Global London & the Luxury of Choice

Officially the most cosmopolitan city in the world, London offers up a feast of culinary celebration.

74 EAT-BRITAIN

❶ Bentley's 31-2A

11/15 Swallow St. W1
☎020-7734-4756/7439-6903
Ⓕ020-7287-2972
⊖Piccadilly Circus
12.00-23.30 ⊗Sun
[VISA] [M/C] [AMEX] [D]

A respected fish restaurant, established in 1916, synonymous with the finest seafood, oysters and selected champagnes. A traditional setting in which to enjoy a meal.

❷ The Crescent 32-2A

The Montcalm/Hotel Nikko London, Great Cumberland Pl. W1
☎020-7402-4288 Ⓕ020-7724-9180
Ⓔmontcalm@montcalm.co.uk
⊖Marble Arch
12.30-14.30(Ex. Sat, Sun), 18.30-22.30
⊗No
[VISA] [M/C] [AMEX] [D] [JCB]

The Montcalm/Hotel Nikko provides a sophisticated setting with modern art interior, just a few minutes' walk from Oxford Street. Modern British cuisine to be enjoyed at reasonable prices.

❸ Seashell 24-1A

49/51 Lisson Grove NW1
☎020-7224-9000 Ⓕ020-7724-9071
⊖Marylebone / Baker Street
12.00-14.30, 17.00-22.30 ⊗Sun
[VISA] [M/C] [AMEX] [D] [JCB]

The Seashell restaurant serves traditional fish and chips in a relaxing, friendly and informal atmosphere. The decor is the customary black and white marble with wooden panelling and hand painted walls.

❹ Simpson's-in-the-Strand 36-2B

100 Strand WC2
☎020-7836-9112 Ⓕ020-7836-1381
Ⓔsimpsons@savoy-group.co.uk
⊖Charing Cross
7.15-10.15, 12.00-14.15, 17.30-22.45
⊗No
[VISA] [M/C] [AMEX] [D] [JCB]

Simpson's-in-the-Strand has an impeccable reputation for serving excellent roasts from silver trolleys and other English dishes. Simply Simpson's on the first floor provides a relaxed and informal alternative.

EAT-BRITAIN | 75

Alfred   36-1A
245 Shaftesbury Av. WC2 ⊖ Tottenham Court Road ☎020-7240-2566 ⒻO20-7497-0672 ◎12.00-15.30(Ex. Sat), 18.00-23.30 ⊗Sun

Bentley's   ➡See p74   31-2A
11/15 Swallow St. W1 ⊖ Piccadilly Circus ☎020-7734-4756 Ⓕ020-7287-2972 ◎12.00-23.30 ⊗Sun

Butlers Wharf Chop House   43-2B
Butlers Wharf Bldg. 36E Shad Thames SE1 ⊖Tower Hill/London Bridge ☎020-7403-3414 Ⓕ020-7403-3414 ◎12.00-15.00(Ex Sat), 18.00-22.45(Ex Sun) ⊗No

The Crescent   ➡See p74   32-2A
The Montcalm/Hotel Nikko London, Great Cumberland Pl. W1 ⊖Marble Arch ☎020-7402-4288 Ⓕ020-7724-9180 ◎12.30-14.30(Ex. Sat, Sun), 18.30-22.30 ⊗No

Green's   31-2A
36 Duke St. SW1 ⊖Piccadilly Circus ☎020-7930-4566 ◎11.30-15.00, 17.30-23.30 ⊗Sun(May-Sep)

Greenhouse   27-2B
27A Hay's Mews W1 ⊖ Green Park ☎020-7499-3331 Ⓕ020-7499-5368 ◎12.00-14.30(Sun 12.30-15.00, Ex. Sat), 18.30-23.00(Sun 22.00) ⊗No

Leith's   44-1A
92 Kensington Park Rd. W11 ⊖Notting Hill Gate ☎020-7229-4481 Ⓕ020-7221-1246 ◎12.15-14.15(Tue-Fri Only), 19.00-23.30 ⊗Sun

The Rib Room   47-2B
Hyatt Carlton Tower, Cadgan Pl. SW1 ⊖Knightsbridge ☎020-7235-1234 Ⓕ020-7235-9129 ◎12.30-14.45, 19.00-23.15(Sun 22.15) ⊗No

Rules   36-2B
35 Maiden La. WC2 ⊖Covent Garden/Charing Cross ☎020-7836-5314 Ⓕ020-7497-1081 ◎12.00-23.30(Sun 22.30) ⊗No

St John   38-1B
26 St John St. EC1 ⊖Farringdon ☎020-7251-0848 Ⓕ020-7251-4090 ◎11.00(Sat 18.00)-23.00 ⊗Sun

The Savoy Grill   36-2B
The Savoy Hotel, Strand WC2 ⊖Covent Garden/Charing Cross ☎020-7836-4343 Ⓕ020-7240-6040 ◎12.30-14.30(Ex. Sat), 18.00-23.15 ⊗Sun

Seashell   ➡See p74   24-1A
49/51 Lisson Grove NW1 ⊖Marylebone / Baker Street ☎020-7224-9000 ◎12.00-14.30, 17.00-22.30 ⊗Sun

Simpson's-in-the-Strand   ➡See p74   36-2B
100 Strand WC2 ⊖Charing Cross ☎020-7836-9112 Ⓕ020-7836-1381 ◎7.15-10.15, 12.00-14.15, 17.30-22.45 ⊗No

EAT-FRANCE

❺ The Lobster Pot　　　　　　　　25-2A

3 Kennington Lane SE11
☎ 020-7582-5556
⊖ Kennington
12.00-14.30, 19.00-22.45 ⊗ Mon,Sun
VISA M/C AMEX D JCB

This family-run seafood restaurant specialises in genuine "Plateau De Fruits De Mer" and of course their fresh lobster is always a triumph served grilled or poached. And where better to try fishermen's fare than in this most nautical of onshore interiors.

❻ Nico Central　　　　　　　　34-2A

35 Great Portland St. W1
☎ 020-7436-8846 📠 020-7436-3455
📧 nicocentral@trpplc.com 🌐 www.trpplc.com
⊖ Oxford Circus
12.30-14.30, 18.00-22.30 (Ex. Sat)
⊗ Sun　　　　　　　　　VISA M/C AMEX D

Inspired modern French cuisine of the highest quality. Food is prepared using the freshest ingredients with great attention to detail. The impression is of simplicity, yet the flavours are rich and satisfying. Ideal for business or social entertaining.

❼ Poissonnerie de L'Avenue　　52-1B

82 Sloane Av. SW3
☎ 020-7589-2457/5774 📠 020-7581-3360
📧 info@poissonnerie.co.uk
🌐 www.poissonnerie.co.uk
⊖ South Kensington
12.00-15.00, 19.00-23.30 ⊗ Sun
VISA M/C AMEX D JCB

Poissonnerie de L'Avenue has a delightful fish menu with everything from shellfish to homemade fish cakes, supplemented by delicious fresh pasta & meat dishes. Dining room available for private parties.

❽ Terrace　　　　　　　　　　31-2B

Le Meridien Piccadilly, 21 Piccadilly W1
☎ 020-7465-1642 📠 020-7465-1616
⊖ Piccadilly Circus
7.00-10.30(Sun 7.30-11.00), 12.00-14.30,
18.00-23.00(Sun 22.30) ⊗ No
VISA M/C AMEX D

Overlooking Piccadilly, on the second floor of Le Meridien Piccadilly Hotel. Recently refurbished, this is the first joint venture for renowned Parisian chef Michel Rostang who has two Michelin stars.

EAT-FRANCE

Aubergine   24-2A
11 Park Walk, SW10 ⊖South Kensington ☎020-7352-3449 Ⓕ020-7351-1770 ◎12.00-14.30(Ex. Sat), 19.00-22.45 ⊗Sun

Chez Gerard   36-2B
The Opera Terrace, The Piazza WC2 ⊖Covent Garden ☎020-7379-0666 Ⓕ020-7497-9060 ◎12.00-15.00, 17.30-23.30(Sun 22.30) ⊗No

Criterion   31-2B
224 Piccadilly W1 ⊖Piccadilly Circus ☎020-7930-0488 Ⓕ020-7930-8380 ◎12.00-14.30(Ex. Sun), 18.00-23.30(Sun 22.30) ⊗No

Le Gavroche   26-1B
43 Upper Brook St. W1 ⊖Marble Arch ☎020-7408-0881 Ⓕ020-7409-0939 ◎12.00-14.00, 19.00-23.00 ⊗Sat, Sun

Gordon Ramsay   53-2A
68-69 Royal Hospital Rd. SW3 ⊖Sloane Square ☎020-7352-4441 ◎12.00-14.00, 18.45-23.00 ⊗Sat, Sun

The Lobster Pot → See p76   25-2A
3 Kennington Lane SE11 ⊖Kennington ☎020-7582-5556 ◎12.00-14.30, 19.00-22.45 ⊗Mon,Sun

Maison Noveli   25-1A
29 Clerkenwell Green EC1 ⊖Farringdon ☎020-7251-6606 Ⓕ020-7490-1083 ◎12.00-15.00(Ex. Sat), 18.00-23.00 ⊗Sun

The Mirabelle   28-2A
56 Curzon St. W1 ⊖Green Park ☎020-7499-4636 Ⓕ020-7499-5449 ◎12.00-14.30, 19.00-23.30(Sun 22.30) ⊗No

Mon Plaisir   36-1A
21 Monmouth St. WC2 ⊖Covent Garden ☎020-7240-3757 Ⓕ020-7240-4774 ◎12.00-14.15(Ex. Sat), 18.00-23.15 ⊗Sun

Nico Central → See p76   34-2A
35 Great Portland St. W1 ⊖Oxford Circus ☎020-7436-8846 Ⓕ020-7436-3455 ◎12.30-14.30, 18.00-22.30(Ex. Sat) ⊗Sun

The Oak Room   31-2B
Le Meridien Piccadilly, 21 Piccadilly W1 ⊖Piccadilly Circus ☎020-7437-0202 Ⓕ020-7437-3574 ◎12.00-14.30(Ex. Sat), 19.00-23.15 ⊗Sun

Poissonnerie de L'Avenue → See p76   52-1B
82 Sloane Av. SW3 ⊖South Kensington ☎020-7589-2457 Ⓕ020-7581-3360 ◎12.00-15.00, 19.00-23.30 ⊗Sun

Terrace → See p76   31-2B
Le Meridien Piccadilly, 21 Piccadilly W1V ⊖Piccadilly Circus ☎020-7465-1642 Ⓕ020-7465-1616 ◎7.00-10.30(Sun 7.30-11.00), 12.00-14.30, 18.00-23.00(Sun 22.30) ⊗No

78 EAT-ITALY

⑨ Da Paolo 35-1A

3 Charlotte Pl. W1
☎020-7580-0021 ℱ020-7580-9055
ⓗwww.DaPaoloRestaurant.co.uk
⊖Goodge Street
12.00-15.00(Ex.Sat, Sun),17.30-23.30
⊗No

A village restaurant in the heart of London. Traditional Italian cooking served in a warm, family atmosphere. Private dining, business lunches and dinners are also catered for, using only the finest ingredients.

⑩ Elena's L'Etoile 35-1A

30 Charlotte St.W1
☎020-7636-7189 ℱ020-7637-0122
ⓔletoile@trpplc.com ⓗwww.trpplc.com
⊖Goodge Street
12.00-14.30(Ex. Sat), 18.00-22.30 ⊗Sun

Popular and successful restaurant with award winning chef Kevin Hopgood highly acclaimed menus offering a wide choice of French/Italian dishes. The combination of superb food and buzzing ambience is simply addictive.

⑪ Franco's 30-2B

63 Jermyn St. SW1
☎020-7493-3645 ℱ020-7499-2211
⊖Green Park
12.00-15.00, 18.00-23.00 ⊗Sun

The only classical Italian restaurant in Jermyn St. kept under the watchful eye of owners Luigi and Carlo. Expert in specialities from the north of Italy as well as international cuisine. Private room with bar for parties.

⑫ Pescatori 30-2B

11 Dover St. W1
☎020-7493-2652 ℱ020-7499-3180
ⓗwww.pescatori.co.uk
⊖Green Park
12.00-15.00(Ex. Sat), 18.00-23.00 ⊗Sun

Superb fish & seafood restaurants situated in London's West End, stylish contemporary & Mediterranian, offering the freshest fish & seafood available. The 'Lobster Spaghetti' is highly recommended. Branch on Charlotte St. 35-1A

EAT-ITALY 79

Alloro 30-2A
19-20 Dover St. W1X ⊖Green Park ☎020-7495-4768 ⓕ020-7629-5348 ◎12.00-14.30(Ex. Sat), 19.00-22.30 ⊗Sun

Artigiano 24-1A
12A Belsize Terrace NW3 ⊖Belsize Park ☎020-7794-4288 ◎12.00-15.00(Ex. Mon), 18.15-23.00(Sat 23.30, Sun 22.00) ⊗Mon

Assaggi 24-2A
39 Chepstow Pl. W2 ⊖Notting Hill Gate ☎020-7792-5501 ◎12.30-14.30, 19.30-23.00 ⊗Sun

Da Paolo ➝See p78 35-1A
3 Charlotte Pl. W1 ⊖Goodge Street ☎020-7580-0021 ⓕ020-7580-9055 ◎12.00-15.00(Ex.Sat, Sun),17.30-23.30 ⊗No

Elena's L'Etoile ➝See p78 35-1A
30 Charlotte St. W1 ⊖Goodge Street ☎020-7636-7189 ⓕ020-7637-0122 ◎12.00-14.30(Ex. Sat), 18.00-22.30 ⊗Sun

Emporio Armani Caffè 46-2B
191 Brompton Rd. SW3 ⊖Knightsbridge ☎020-7823-8818 ⓕ020-7823-8854 ◎10.00-18.00 ⊗Sun

Franco's ➝See p78 30-2B
63 Jermyn St. SW1 ⊖Green Park ☎020-7493-3645 ⓕ020-7499-2211 ◎12.00-15.00, 18.00-23.00 ⊗Sun

Grissini-london 47-2B
Hyatt Carlton Tower, Cadgan Pl. SW1 ⊖Knightsbridge ☎020-7858-7171 ⓕ020-7235-9129 ◎7.00(Sun 8.00)-11.00, 12.30-14.45(Ex. Sat, Sun), 18.30-22.45(Ex. Sun) ⊗No

The Neal Street 36-2A
26 Neal St. WC2 ⊖Covent Garden ☎020-7836-8368 ⓕ020-7240-3964 ◎12.30-14.30, 18.00-23.00 ⊗Sun

Pescatori ➝See p78 30 2B
11 Dover St. W1 ⊖Groon Park ☎020 7493 2652 ⓕ020-7499-3100 ◎12.00-15.00(Ex Sat), 18.00-23.00 ⊗Sun

Sartoria 30-1B
20 Savile Row W1 ⊖Oxford Circus/Piccadilly Circus ☎020-7534-7000 ⓕ020-7534-7070 ◎12.00-15.00, 18.30-23.00(Sun 22.00) ⊗No

Spiga 35-2A
84-86 Wardour St. W1 ⊖Oxford Circus/Tottenham Court Road ☎020-7734-3444 ◎12.00-15.00, 18.00-0.00(Mon, Tue , Sun 23.00) ⊗No

Verbanella 47-2A
30 Beauchamp Pl. SW3 ⊖Knightsbridge ☎020-7584-1107 ◎12.00-15.00, 18.00-23.15 ⊗No

⑬ Costa Dorada 35-2B

47/55 Hanway St. W1
☎020-7631-5117 ⓕ020-7636-7139
ⓔCosta@Dorada.fsbusiness.co.uk
⊖Tottenham Court Road
19.00-3.00 ⊗Sun   visa M/C AMEX ID JCB

A distinctive, warm southern Spanish atmosphere is enjoyed by diners in this lively restaurant, with live music and flamenco dancers to entertain after 8.30pm. Paella is the most popular dish on the menu.

⑭ La Mancha 31-2B

32 Putney High St. SW15
☎020-8780-1022 ⓕ020-8780-2202
⊖Putney Bridge/East Putney
12.00-23.00(Fri, Sat 23.30, Sun22.30)
⊗No
visa M/C AMEX ID JCB

A typical Spanish atmosphere - with live music seven nights a week. They serve paella made from a traditional Spanish recipe. Spanish wines, beers, cocktails and sangria are available in the new conservatory and bar.

⑮ El Pirata of Mayfair 27-2B

5/6 Down St. W1
☎020-7491-3810 ⓕ020-7491-0853
⊖Green Park
12.00-23.30 ⊗Sun   visa M/C AMEX ID JCB

One of London's leading Spanish tapas bars and restaurants. Stylish decor with a superb range of tapas dishes and main courses, all at extremely reasonable prices. It has a dedicated following, especially Japanese and American customers.

⑯ Salvador's El Bodegon 24-2A

9 Park Walk SW10
☎020-7352-1330 ⓕ020-7352-1330
ⓔsalvador@bodegon.demon.co.uk
⊖South Kensington
12.00-15.00, 18.00-0.00 ⊗No   visa M/C AMEX ID

Established in 1965, the restaurant is family owned and run, with the menu developed by the same chef since 1976. Your own dining room can be arranged creating a relaxing atmosphere to enjoy paellas, zarzuela, excellent gaspacho and much more.

EAT-SPAIN 81

Baradero 25-2A
Turberry Quay off Papper St. E14 ⊖Crossharbour ☎020-7537-1666 ◎11.00(Sat 18.00)-23.00 ⊗Sun

El Blasón 53-1B
8-9 Blacklands Terrace SW3 ⊖Sloane Square ☎020-7823-7383 ◎12.00-15.00, 18.00-23.00 ⊗Sun

Café Loco 22-1B
266 Muswell hill Broadway N10 ⊖Highgate ☎020-8444-3370 ◎10.00-2.00 (Sun 1.00) ⊗No

Costa Dorada →See p80 35-2B
47/55 Hanway St. W1 ⊖Tottenham Court Road ☎020-7631-5117 Ⓕ020-7636-7139 ◎19.00-3.00 ⊗Sun

Don Pepe 24-1A
99 Frampton St. NW8 ⊖Edgware Road ☎020-7262-3834 Ⓕ020-7724-8305 ◎12.00-15.00, 18.00-1.00 ⊗Sun

The Finca 24-1B
96-98 Pentonville Rd. N1 ⊖Angel ☎020-7837-5387 ◎12.00-0.00(Fri, Sat 2.00) ⊗No

Gaudí 25-1A
63 Clerkenwell Rd. EC1 ⊖Farringdon ☎020-7608-3220 ◎12.00-14.30, 19.00-22.30 ⊗Sat, Sun

Goya 24-2B
34 Lupus St. SW1 ⊖Pimlico ☎020-7976-5309 Ⓕ020-7976-6940 ◎12.00-23.30 ⊗No

La Mancha →See p80 24-2A
32 Putney High St. SW15 ⊖Putney Bridge/East Putney ☎020-8780-1022 Ⓕ020-8780-2202 ◎19.00-23.00(Fri, Sat 23.30, Sun 22.30) ⊗No

El Molino 24-1B
379 Holloway Rd. N7 ⊖Holloway Road ☎020-7700-4312 ◎11.00-22.30 (Fri, Sat 23.00) ⊗Sun

El Pirata of Mayfair →See p80 27-2B
5/6 Down St. W1 ⊖Green Park ☎020-7491-3891 Ⓕ020-7491-0853 ◎12.00-23.30 ⊗Sun

Los Remos 24-1A
38A Southwick St. W2 ⊖Paddington/Edgware Road ☎020-7723-5056 Ⓕ020-7723-5055 ◎12.00-15.00, 18.00-0.00(Mon, Tue, Sun 23.00) ⊗No

Salvador's El Bodegon →See p80 24-2A
9 Park Walk SW10 ⊖South Kensington ☎020-7352-1330 Ⓕ020-7352-1330 ◎12.00-15.00, 18.00-0.00 ⊗No

82 EAT-EUROPE

Portuguese

⑰ O'Fado — 47-2A

49/50 Beauchamp Pl. SW3
☎020-7589-3002 Ⓕ020-8961-5584
⊖Knightsbridge
12.00-15.00, 18.30-1.00 ⊗No
VISA M/C AMEX JCB

A wide range of meat and fish dishes prepared in Portuguese style; whole dressed crab and cod cooked with potatoes, olive oil and garlic. Live Fado music creates a sunny Mediterranean atmosphere.

Swiss

⑱ St Moritz — 35-2A

161 Wardour St. W1
☎020-7734-3324 Ⓕ020-7734-8995
⊖Oxford Circus / Piccadilly Circus
12.00-15.00 (Ex Sat),18.00-23.30
⊗Sun
VISA M/C AMEX D

Authentic Swiss restaurant, well established and specialising in Swiss meats, bratwurst and fondues; vegetarians also catered for. Swiss wines, liqueur coffees and a wonderful selection of Swiss cheeses complement the menu.

Austrian

⑲ Tiroler Hut — 24-1A

27 Westbourne Grove W2
☎020-7727-3981 Ⓕ020-7727-3981
⊖Queensway / Bayswater / Royal Oak
18.30-0.30 ⊗No
VISA M/C AMEX

The Tiroler Hut established in 1967 offers traditional live music including cow bell shows, Austrian hospitality and authentic cuisine.

Hungarian

⑳ The Gay Hussar — 35-2B

2 Greek St. W1
☎020-7437-0973 Ⓕ020-7437-4631
Ⓔgayhussar@trpplc.com Ⓦwww.trpplc.com
⊖Tottenham Court Road
12.30-14.30, 18.00-22.30 ⊗Sun
VISA M/C AMEX D

In the hub of Soho and acclaimed as one of Europe's top Hungarian restaurants, a favourite haunt of artists, writers and politicians alike. Clubby ambience and a distinctive menu with many Transylvanian dishes.

EAT·EUROPE 83

Caravela — 47-2A — PORTUGUESE
39 Beauchamp Pl. SW3 ⊖ Knightsbridge ☎ 020-7581-2366 Ⓕ 020-8770-0340 ◎ 12.00-15.00, 19.00-0.30(Sun 23.30) ⊗ No

O' Fado → See p82 — 47-2A — PORTUGUESE
49/50 Beauchamp Pl. SW3 ⊖ Knightsbridge ☎ 020-7589-3002 Ⓕ 020-8961-5584 ◎ 12.00-15.00, 18.30-1.00 ⊗ No

St. Moritz → See p82 — 35-2A — SWISS
161 Wardour St. W1 ⊖ Oxford Circus / Piccadilly Circus ☎ 020-7734-3324 Ⓕ 020-7734-8995 ◎ 12.00-15.00 (Ex Sat), 18.00-23.30 ⊗ Sun

Tiroler Hut → See p82 — 24-1A — AUSTRIAN
27 Westbourne Grove W2 ⊖ Queensway / Bayswater / Royal Oak ☎ 020-7727-3981 Ⓕ 020-7727-3981 ◎ 18.30-0.30 ⊗ No

Jägerhütte — 24-2A — GERMAN
36 Queensway W2 ⊖ Bayswater/Queensway ☎ 020-7229-7941 ◎ 12.00-0.00 ⊗ No

Lemonia — 24-1B — GREEK
89 Regent's Park Rd. NW1 ⊖ Chalk Farm ☎ 020-7586-7454 Ⓕ 020-7483-2630 ◎ 12.00-15.00(Ex. Sat), 18.00-23.30(Ex.Sun) ⊗ No

Ozer — 34-1A
5 Langham Pl. Regent St. W1 ⊖ Oxford Circus ☎ 020-7323-0505 Ⓕ 020-7323-0111 ◎ 12.00-23.00 ⊗ No

Jacob's — 45-2A — ARMENIAN
20 Gloucester Rd. SW7 ⊖ Gloucester Road ☎ 020-7581-9292 ◎ 9.00-22.00(Sun 17.00) ⊗ No

Czech & Slovak House — 24-1A — CZECH
74 West End La. NW6 ⊖ West Hampstead ☎ 020-7372-5251 ◎ 18.00-22.00(Sat, Sun 11.00-15.00) ⊗ Mon

The Gay Hussar → See p82 — 35-2B — HUNGARIAN
2 Greek St. W1 ⊖ Tottenham Court Road ☎ 020-7437-0973 Ⓕ 020-7437-4631 ◎ 12.30-14.30, 18.00-22.30 ⊗ Sun

Daquise — 52-1A — POLISH
20 Thurloe St. SW7 ⊖ South Kensington ☎ 020-7589-6117 ◎ 11.30-23.00 ⊗ No

Borshtch'n Tears — 47-2A — RUSSIAN
46 Beauchamp Place SW3 ⊖ Knightsbridge ☎ 020-7584-9911 ◎ 18.00-1.00 ⊗ Mon

Nikita's — 24-2A
65 Ifield Rd. SW10 ⊖ Earl's Court ☎ 020-7352-6326 Ⓕ 020-7352-6969 ◎ 19.30-23.30 ⊗ Sun

84 EAT-INDIA

㉑ Bombay Brasserie 45-2A

Courtfield Cl., Courtfield Rd. SW7
☎020-7370-4040 Ⓕ020-7835-1669
⊖Gloucester Road
12.30-15.00, 19.00-0.00 ⊗No
VISA M/C D JCB

An elegant colonial-style conservatory provides a pleasing dining area. The menu emphasises the various distinctive regional dishes found throughout India, such as chicken tikka achari and ragara pattice.

㉒ Bombay Palace 24-1A

50 Connaught St. W2
☎020-7723-8855 Ⓕ020-7706-8072
Ⓔwww.bombay-palace.co.uk
⊖Marble Arch
12.00-14.45, 18.00-23.30 ⊗No
VISA M/C AMEX D JCB

London branch of distinguished international group, specializing in North Indian foods. Award winner for all-round excellence and noted as 'the very best Indian cuisine in this country'. Elegant and fully air-conditioned.

㉓ Chutney Mary 24-2A

535 King's Rd. SW10
☎020-7351-3113 Ⓕ020-7351-7694
Ⓗwww.realindianfood.com
⊖Fulham Broadway
12.00-15.00, 19.00-23.30 ⊗No
VISA M/C AMEX D

Fashionable, evocative and unique with unusual Indian dishes from as many as six different regions, prepared by special regional chefs. Twice voted top Indian restaurant in UK by the Good Curry Guide.

㉔ The Delhi Brasserie 35-2B

44 Frith St. W1
☎020-7437-8261 Ⓕ020-7437-3789
⊖Leicester Square/Tottenham Court Road
12.00-0.00 ⊗No
●134 Cromwell Rd. SW7: 45-2A
☎020-7370-7617 Ⓕ020-7244-8639
⊖Gloucester Road
12.00-23.30 ⊗No
VISA M/C AMEX D

Dishes from various regions, cooked to perfection and served with style.

EAT-INDIA 85

Bombay Brasserie →See p84   45-2A
Courtfield Cl. Courtfield Rd. SW7 ↔Gloucester Road ☎020-7370-4040 Ⓕ020-7835-1669 ◎12.30-15.00, 19.00-0.00 ⊗No

Bombay Palace →See p84   24-1A
50 Connaught St. W2 ↔Marble Arch ☎020-7723-8855 Ⓕ020-7706-8072 ◎12.00-14.45, 18.00-23.30 ⊗No

Café Lazeez   52-1A
93/95 Old Brompton Rd. SW7 ↔South Kensington ☎020-7581-9993 Ⓕ020-7581-8200 ◎11.00-0.30(Sun 22.30) ⊗No

Chor Bizarre   30-2B
16 Albemarle St. W1 ↔Green Park ☎020-7629-9802 Ⓕ020-7493-7756 ◎12.00-15.00, 18.00-23.30(Sun 22.30) ⊗No

Chutney Mary →See p84   24-2A
535 King's Rd. SW10 ↔Fulham Broadway ☎020-7351-3113 Ⓕ020-7351-7694 ◎12.00-15.00, 19.00-23.30 ⊗No

The Delhi Brasserie →See p84   35-2B
44 Frith St. W1 ↔Leicester Square/Tottenham Court Road ☎020-7437-8261 Ⓕ020-7437-3789 ◎12.00-0.00 ⊗No

Gaylord   34-1A
79/81 Mortimer St. W1 ↔Oxford Circus ☎020-7580-3615 Ⓕ020-7636-0860 ◎12.00-15.00, 18.00-23.45 ⊗No

Geeta   24-1A
57-59 Willesden La. NW6 ↔Kilburn ☎020-7624-1713 ◎12.00-14.30, 28.00-22.30(Fri, Sat 23.30) ⊗No

Khan's →See p86   24-1A
13/15 Westbourne Grove W2 ↔Royal Oak / Bayswater / Queensway ☎020-7727-5420 Ⓕ020-7229-1835 ◎12.00-0.00(Mon-Thur Ex. 15.00-18.00) ⊗No

Malabar Junction   35-1B
107 Great Russel St. WC2 ↔Tottenham Court Road ☎020-7580-5230 Ⓕ020-7436-9942 ◎12.00-15.00, 18.00-23.30 ⊗No

La Porte des Indes   32-2B
32 Bryanston St. W1 ↔Marble Arch ☎020-7224-0055 Ⓕ020-7224-1144 ◎12.00-14.30(Ex. Sat), 19.00-0.00 ⊗No

Rasa   25-1A
55 Stoke Newington Church St. N16 ⇄Stoke Newington ☎020-7249-0344 Ⓕ020-7249-8748 ◎12.00-14.30(Sat, Sun only), 18.00-23.00(Fri, Sat 0.00) ⊗No

Rasa Samudra   35-1A
5 Charlotte St. W1 ↔Goodge Street ☎020-7637-0222 Ⓕ020-7637-0224 ◎12.00-14.45(Ex. Sun), 18.00-22.45 ⊗No

86 EAT-INDIA, MIDDLE EAST, AFRICA

㉕ Khan's
24-1A

13/15 Westbourne Grove W2
☎020-7727-5420 ℱ020-7229-1835
ⓔinfo@khansrestaurant.com
ⓗwww.khansrestaurant.com
⊖Bayswater/Queensway/Royal Oak
12.00-0.00 (Mon-Thur Ex.15.00-18.00)
⊗No

It is no exaggeration to describe Khan's as the closest you will get to India in central London. Renowned for its high standard of food/service, 100% Halal, fully air conditioned, with a great atmosphere.

㉖ Veeraswamy
31-2A

Mezzanine Fl., Victory House, 99 Regent St. W1
☎020-7734-1401 ℱ020-7439-8434
ⓗwww.realindianfood.com
⊖Piccadilly Circus
12.00-14.30(Sun 15.00), 17.30-23.15 (Sun 18.00-22.00) ⊗No

Britain's oldest Indian restaurant, refashioned into a vibrant, contemporary space with real Indian food from Indian homes in the heart of the West End. Winner of prestigious Time Out Best Indian Restaurant Award.

㉗ Ayoush
33-2A

58 James St. W1
☎020-7935-9839 ℱ020-7935-1708
ⓔayoush@eps.prestel.co.uk
ⓗwww.ayoush.com
⊖Bond Street 12.00-23.30 ⊗No

Ayoush serves exotic North African foods including stuffed pastries and special lamb, chicken or vegetable couscous. Ayoush is a tapestry of images, warm, sensual, mysterious and exciting. It has a magical atmosphere and yet its mood is informal.

㉘ Souk
36-2A

27 Litchfield St. WC2
☎020-7240-1796 ℱ020-7240-8833
ⓔbook@soukrestaurant.co.uk
ⓗwww.soukwc2.com
⊖Leicester Square
12.00-23.30 ⊗No

Souk restaurant offers an authentic North African mood and menu. It is full of enchanting ornamentation and has a very friendly and lively atmosphere in this basement setting. They also offer vegetarian dishes.

EAT-INDIA, MIDDLE EAST, AFRICA 87

Tandori of Chelsea — 52-1B
153 Fulham Rd. SW3 ↔ South Kensington ☎020-7589-7617 ◎12.00-14.30(Ex. Sun), 6.30-0.00(Sun 23.00) ⊗No

Top Curry Centre — 24-2B
3 Lupus St. SW1 ↔ Pimlico ☎020-7821-7572 ◎112.00-15.00, 18.00-0.00 ⊗No

Veeraswamy → See p86 — 31-2A
99 Regent St. W1 ↔ Piccadilly Circus ☎020-7734-1401 ⒻO20-7439-8434 ◎12.00-14.30(Sun 15.00), 17.30-23.15 (Sun 18.00-22.00) ⊗No

Zaika — 52-2A
257-259 Fulham Rd. SW3 ↔ South Kensington ☎020-7351-7823 Ⓕ020-7376-4971 ◎12.00-14.30(Ex. Sat), 18.30-22.30 ⊗Sun

▸ INDIAN

Alounak — 24-2A
10 Russell Gdns. W14 ↔ Olympia ☎020-7603-7645 ◎12.00-0.00 ⊗No

Patogh — 24-1A
8 Crawford Pl. W1 ↔ Edgware Road ☎020-7262-4015 ◎12.00-23.30 ⊗No

▸ IRANIAN

Al Fawer — 32-1B
50 Baker St. W1 ↔ Baker Street ☎020-7224-4777 Ⓕ020-7224-1616 ◎12.00-0.00 ⊗Sun

Al Sultan — 27-2B
51-52 Hertford St. W1 ↔ Green Park ☎020-7408-1155 ◎12.00-0.00 ⊗No

Ali Baba — 32-1A
32 Ivor Pl. NW1 ↔ Baker Street ☎020-7723-7474 ◎12.00-0.00 ⊗No

▸ LEBANESE

Ayoush → See p86 — 33-2A
58 James St. W1 ↔ Bond Street ☎020-7935-9839 Ⓕ020-7935-1708 ◎12.00-23.30 ⊗Sun

Souk → See p86 — 36-2A
27 Litchfield St. WC2 ↔ Leicester Square ☎020-7240-1796 Ⓕ020-7240-8833 ◎12.00-23.30 ⊗No

▸ EGYPTIAN
▸ NORTH AFRICAN

Lalibela — 24-1B
137 Fortress Rd. N5 ↔ Tufnell Park ☎020-7284-0600 ◎18.00-0.00(Fri, Sat, Sun 23.00) ⊗No

Calabash — 36-2B
The Africa Centre, 38 King St. WC2 ↔ Covent Garden ☎020-7836-1976 ◎17.30-23.00 ⊗Sun

▸ ETHIOPIAN
▸ WEST AFRICAN

EAT-THAILAND

㉙ Blue Elephant　　　　　　　　　24-2A

4/6 Fulham Broadway SW6
☎020-7385-6595 Ⓕ020-7386-7665
⊖Fulham Broadway
12.00-14.30(Sun 16.00), 19.00(Sat 18.30)-0.00(Sun 22.30) ⊗No
VISA M/C D

A unique venue specialising in Royal Thai cuisine, for which all the ingredients are flown in directly from Thailand. Diners eat in a lush, tropical setting, surrounded by exotic greenery and served by waiters in national costume.

㉚ Kwan Thai　　　　　　　　　42-2B

Unit 1, The Riverfront, Hay's Galleria SE1
☎020-7403-7373 Ⓕ020-7357-9850
Ⓔkwanthai@btinternet.com
Ⓗwww.kwanthairestaurant.co.uk
⊖London Bridge/Monument
11.30-15.00(Ex. Sat), 18.00-22.00 ⊗Sun
VISA M/C AMEX D JCB

Situated between London Bridge and Tower Bridge, with outdoor tables by the Thames, in summer. Interior is spacious. Popular dishes include Tom Yam Goong and Green Curry.

㉛ Thai Pavilion　　　　　　　　　29-1A

42 Rupert St. W1
☎020-7287-6333 Ⓕ020-7587-0484
Ⓔenquiries@thaipavilion.com
Ⓗwww.thaipavilion.com
⊖Piccadilly Circus/Leicester Square
12.00-14.30(Sun 12.30-16.30), 18.00-23.15 (Sun 22.30) ⊗No
VISA M/C AMEX D JCB

Embroideries and a waterfall provide an Oriental setting in which to enjoy tasty classical cuisine, with ingredients fresh from Thailand. Reservations and exclusive offers at the website.

㉜ Thai Square　　　　　　　　　50-1A

21/24 Cockspur St. SW1
☎020-7839-4000 Ⓕ020-7839-0839
⊖Piccadilly Circus/Charing Cross
12.00-15.00, 17.00-23.30(Sun 23.00) ⊗No
VISA M/C AMEX

Sumptuous decor by top Bangkok designers creates an intimate feel to this new restaurant, which actually has a capacity of 500. Green curry, steamed squid with lemon grass, and papaya salad use ingredients flown in from Thailand.

EAT-THAILAND 89

Blue Elephant ➡ See p88   24-2A
4/6 Fulham Broadway SW6 ⊖Fulham Broadway ☎020-7385-6595 Ⓕ020-7386-7665 ◎12.00-14.30(Sun 16.00), 19.00 (Sat 18.30)-0.00(Sun 22.30) ⊗No

The Blue Jade   48-2B
44 High St. SW1 ⊖Victoria ☎020-7828-0321 ◎12.00-14.30(Ex. Sat), 18.00-23.00 ⊗Sun

Blue Lagoon   44-2A
284 High Street Kensington W8 ⊖High Street Kensington ☎020-7603-1231 ◎12.00-23.30 ⊗No

Chiang Mai   35-2B
48 Frith St. W1 ⊖Leicester Square/ Tottenham Court Road ☎020-7437-7444 ◎12.00-15.00(Ex. Sun), 18.00-23.00(Sun 22.30) ⊗No

Kwan Thai ➡ See p88   42-2B
Unit 1, The Riverfront, Hay's Galleria SE1 ⊖London Bridge/Tower Hill ☎020-7403-7373 Ⓕ020-7357-9850 ◎11.30-15.00 (Ex.Sat), 18.00-22.00 ⊗Sun

Manorom   36-2B
35 Southampton St. WC2 ⊖Covent Garden ☎020-7240-1030 ◎12.00-14.30, 18.00-23.00 ⊗Sun

Patara   47-2A
9 Beauchamp Pl. SW3 ⊖Knightsbridge ☎020-7581-8820 Ⓕ020-7581-2155 ◎12.00-14.30, 18.30-22.30 ⊗No

Pin-Petch   24-2A
4-12 Barkston Gdns. SW5 ⊖Earl's Court ☎020-7370-1371 Ⓕ020-7370-1372 ◎18.00-23.00 ⊗No

PU's Brasserie   37-1A
10 Gate St. WC2 ⊖Holborn ☎020-7404-2126 Ⓕ020-7404-2132 ◎12.00-15.00, 17.30-22.30(Mon, Tue 17.00-22.00) ⊗Sun

Siam Square   44-2B
310C Earl's Court Sq. SW5 ⊖Earl's Court ☎020-7370 2224 ◎17.00-23.30 ⊗No

Thai Pavilion ➡ See p88   29-1A
42 Rupert St. W1 ⊖Piccadilly Circus/Leicester Square ☎020-7287-6333 Ⓕ020-7587-0484 ◎12.00-14.30 (Sun 12.30-16.30), 18.00-23.15 (Sun 22.30) ⊗No

Thai Pot   36-2A
1 Bedfordbury WC2 ⊖Covent Garden ☎020-7379-4580 Ⓕ020-7379-9885 ◎12.00-15.00, 17.30-23.15 ⊗Sun

Thai Square ➡ See p88   50-1A
21/24 Cockspur St. SW1 ⊖Piccadilly Circus/Charing Cross ☎020-7839-4000 Ⓕ020-7839-0839 ◎12.00-15.00, 17.00-23.30(Sun 23.00) ⊗No

EAT-CHINA

㉝ China City Restaurant 29-1B

25A Lisle St. WC2
☎020-7734-3388 Ⓕ020-7734-3833
Ⓔ Leicester Square
12.00-23.45 ⊗No
VISA M/C AMEX JCB

Authentic Chinese cuisine, including Cantonese dim sum, crispy duck with pancakes and lobster. Offering 52 wines and over 150 dishes, the huge restaurant can seat 500 people. Private rooms ideal for business parties.

㉞ China Rendezvous 33-2A

62 Marylebone Lane W1
☎020-7486-2004
Ⓔk.constant@virgin.net
Ⓔ Bond Street
12.00-15.00(Ex. Sat), 18.00-23.00 ⊗Sun
VISA AMEX

London's widest selection of dishes from all provinces of China, such as the Mongolian Grill, north China charcoal steamboat, Taiwan-style stone pot. Diners are welcomed by friendly staff.

㉟ Fung Shing 29-1B

15 Lisle St. WC2
☎020-7437-1539 Ⓕ020-7734-0284
Ⓗwww.fungshing.com
Ⓔ Leicester Square
12.00-23.30 ⊗No
VISA M/C AMEX D

One of the best up-market Chinese restaurants in town. Luxurious yellow and blue decor with two private rooms. Exciting dishes include pork-stuffed aubergine with black bean sauce and lobster with fresh noodles.

㊱ Harbour City 29-1B

46 Gerrard St. W1
☎020-7439-7859/7120
Ⓕ020-7734-7745
Ⓔ Leicester Square/Piccadilly Circus
12.00-23.30(Sun 11.00-22.30) ⊗No
VISA M/C AMEX D JCB

Spacious dining area popular with local Chinese diners, situated in the heart of Chinatown. Authentic dishes and dim sum served by friendly and helpful staff.

EAT-CHINA 91

China City Restaurant ➜ See p90   29-1B
25A Lisle St. WC2 ⊖ Leicester Square ☎020-7734-3388 Ⓕ020-7734-3833 ◎12.00-23.45 ⊗No

China Rendezvous ➜ See p90   33-2A
62 Marylebone Lane W1 ⊖Bond Street ☎020-7486-2004 ◎12.00-15.00(Ex. Sat), 18.00-23.00 ⊗Sun

Chung's   29-1B
22 Wordour St. W1 ⊖Leicester Square/Piccadilly Circus ☎020-7287-3886 Ⓕ020-7287-0630 ◎12.00-23.30 ⊗No

Fung Shing ➜ See p90   29-1B
15 Lisle St. WC2 ⊖Leicester Square ☎020-7437-1539 Ⓕ020-7734-0284 ◎12.00-23.30 ⊗No

Furama   29-1B
5 Macclesfield St. W1 ⊖ Piccadilly Circus/Leisecter Square ☎020-7734-1382 Ⓕ020-7287-0363 ◎12.00-0.00 ⊗No

Golden Dragon   29-1B
28/29 Gerrard St. W1 ⊖Leicester Square ☎020-7734-2763 Ⓕ020-7734-1073 ◎12.00-23.15 ⊗No

Harbour City ➜See p90   29-1B
46 Gerrard St. W1 ⊖Leicester Square/Piccadilly Cirucus ☎020-7439-7859 Ⓕ020-7734-7745 ◎12.00-23.30 ⊗No

The Immortals   29-1B
58/60 Shaftesbury Av. W1 ⊖Leicester Square/Piccadilly Circus ☎020-7437-3119 Ⓕ020-7437-3118 ◎12.00-23.30(Sun 11.30-22.30) ⊗No

Kai Mayfair   27-1A
65 South Audley St. W1 ⊖Bond Street ☎020-7493-8988 Ⓕ020-7493-1456 ◎12.00-14.30(Sat, Sun 15.00), 18.30-23.30(Sun 22.30) ⊗No

New Fook Lam Moon   29-1B
10 Gerrard St. W1 ⊖Leicester Square ☎020-7734-7615 Ⓕ020-7439-0563 ◎12.00-23.30(Sun 22.30) ⊗No

New Mayflower   29-1B
68/70 Shaftesbury Av. W1 ⊖ Piccadilly Circus/Leicester Square ☎020-7734-9207 ◎17.00-4.00 ⊗No

New World   29-1B
1 Gerrard Pl. W1 ⊖Leicester Square ☎020-7734-0677 ◎11.00-0.00 ⊗No

Orient ➜See p92   30-2B
1st Fl., 160 Piccadilly W1 ⊖Green Park ☎020-7499-6888 Ⓕ020-7659-9300 ◎12.00-14.30 (Ex.Sat), 18.00-23.30 ⊗Sun

92 EAT-CHINA, ASIA

Chinese

㊲ Orient　　　　　　　　　　　　　　　　30-2B

1st Fl. 160 Piccadilly W1
☎020-7499-6888 Ⓕ020-7659-9300
Ⓗwww.chinahouse.co.uk
⊖Green Park
12.00-14.30 (Ex.Sat), 18.00-23.30　⊗Sun
VISA M/C AMEX

This restaurant offers a sophisticated menu of modern Chinese dishes in relaxed contemporary surroundings, overlooking Piccadilly.

㊳ Royal China　　　　　　　　　　　　　24-2A

13 Queensway W2
☎020-7221-2535 Ⓕ020-7792-5752
⊖Queensway
12.00-23.00(Fri, Sat 23.30, Sun 11.00-22.00) ⊗No
VISA M/C AMEX JCB
● 40/42 Baker St. W1 :　　　　　　　　32-2B
☎020-7487-4688　⊖Baker Street
● 68 Queens Grove NW8 :　　　　　　24-1A
☎020-7586-4280　⊖St John's Wood

Luxurious Cantonese restaurant. Dim sum is served till 5pm daily.

Singaporean

㊴ Singapura　　　　　　　　　　　　　　38-2B

1/2 Limeburner Lane EC4
☎020-7329-1133 Ⓕ020-7236-2325
⊖St Paul's/Blackfriars
12.00-15.00, 17.30-22.30
⊗Sat, Sun
VISA M/C AMEX ID

Two of Singapore's great culinary traditions, Chinese and Malay, fuse in Nonya cuisine. Also served at the sister restaurant at Broadgate Circle.

Asian

㊵ Oriental City Food Court　　　　　　22-1B

399 Edgware Rd. NW9
☎020-8200-0009 Ⓕ020-8200-0848
⊖Colindale
10.00- 22.00 ⊗No
VISA M/C AMEX JCB

Self service style restaurant situated in London's largest Oriental shopping centre. They offer a fantastic array of Japanese, Chinese, Korean, Thai, and Indonesian dishes at affordable prices. The environment is suitable for family lunches & dinners.

EAT-CHINA, ASIA 93

CHINESE

Oriental Garden — 24-1A
23A Malvern Rd. NW8 ↔ Maida Vale ☎ 020-7625-8888 ◎ 12.00-15.00(Sun 13.00-23.30), 18.00-11.30 ⊗ No

Royal China ➜ See p92 — 24-2A
13 Queensway W2 ↔ Queensway ☎ 020-7221-2535 Ⓕ 020-7792-5752 ◎ 12.00-23.00(Fri, Sat 23.30, Sun 11.00-22.00) ⊗ No

Young Cheng — 29-1B
22 Lisle Street WC2A ↔ Leicester Square ☎ 020-7287-3045 ◎ 12.00-23.30 ⊗ No

Zen Chelsea — 52-1B
Chelsea Cloisters, 85 Sloane Av. SW3 ↔ South Kensington ☎ 020-7589-1781 Ⓕ 020-7584-0596 ◎ 12.00(Sun 11.30)-23.30(Fri, Sat 0.00, Sun 22.30) ⊗ No

COREAN

Arirang — 34-2B
31-32 Poland St. W1 ↔ Oxford Circus ☎ 020-7437-6633 ◎ 12.00-15.00, 18.00-23.00 ⊗ Sun

Kaya — 30-2B
42 Albemarle St. W1 ↔ Green Park ☎ 020-7499-0622 ◎ 12.00-15.00(Ex. Sun), 18.00-10.45 ⊗ No

VIETNAMESE

Mekong River — 24-2A
48 Queensway W2 ↔ Queensway/Bayswater ☎ 020-7229-9111 ◎ 12.00-23.30 ⊗ No

SIGAPOREAN

Singapura ➜ See p92 — 38-2B
1/2 Limeburner Lane EC4 ↔ St Paul's/Blackfriars ☎ 020-7329-1133 Ⓕ 020-7236-2325 ◎ 12.00-15.00, 17.30-22.30 ⊗ Sat, Sun

INDONESIAN

Satay Bar — 25-2A
450 Coldharbour La. SW9 ↔ Brixton ☎ 020-7326-5001 Ⓕ 020-7737-2042 ◎ 12.00-23.00(Fri 2.00, Sat 13.00-2.00, Sun 13.00-22.30) ⊗ No

MALAYSIAN

Satay House — 24-1A
13 Sale Pl. W2 ↔ Paddington ☎ 020-7723-6763 ◎ 12.00-15.00, 18.00-23.00 ⊗ Mon

MONGOLIAN

The Mongolian Barbecue — 36-2B
12 Maiden La. WC2 ↔ Covent Garden ☎ 020-7379-7722 ◎ 12.00-15.00(Ex. Sun), 18.00-23.00 ⊗ No

TIBETAN

The Tibetan — 29-1B
17 Irving St. WC2 ↔ Leicester Square/Charing Cross ☎ 020-7839-2090 ◎ 12.00-14.45(Ex Wed), 17.00-22.45 ⊗ Sun

ASIAN

Oriental City Food Court ➜ See p92 — 22-1B
399 Edgware Rd. NW9 ↔ Colindale ☎ 020-8200-0009 Ⓕ 020-8200-0848 ◎ 10.00-22.00 ⊗ No

EAT-JAPAN

㊶ Matsuri St James's 28-2B

15 Bury St. SW1
☎020-7839-1101 Ⓕ020-7930-7010
Ⓔmatsuri@japanglobe.net
Ⓗwww.matsuri-restaurant.com
⊖Green Park 12.00-14.30, 18.00-22.30
⊗Sun   VISA M/C AMEX D JCB

One of the most fashionable Japanese restaurants in London, serving sushi and teppan-yaki of exceptional quality. Wide choice includes fresh seafood and finest quality beef. A unique dining experience.

㊷ Mitsukoshi Restaurant 29-2A

14/20 Regent St. SW1
☎020-7930-0317 Ⓕ020-7839-1167
Ⓔlonrest@mitsukoshi.co.jp
⊖Piccadilly Circus 12.00-14.00, 18.00-21.30
⊗Sun   VISA M/C AMEX D JCB

Very popular especially for its sushi bar, lunch sets and evening a la carte. Sukiyaki, Shabushabu and special seasonal dishes are also recommended. Ideal for both formal and informal occasions. Japanese and Western style private rooms availble. Mitsukoshi's usual high standard of service.

㊸ Noto Restaurant 40-2A

2/3 Bassishaw Highwalk, London Wall EC2
☎020-7256-9433 Ⓕ020-7588-5656
⊖Moorgate/Bank
12.00-14.30, 18.00-22.15 ⊗Sat, Sun
VISA M/C JCB
● Ramen House Noto: 39-2B
7 Bread St. EC4 ☎020-7329-8056

Popular City restaurant, recently refurbished, with proper sushi and tempura bars. Also specializes in udon noodles and set meals.

㊹ Suntory 28-2B

72/73 St James's St. SW1
☎020-7409-0201 Ⓕ020-7499-0208
⊖Green Park
12.00-14.00(Ex. Sun), 18.00-22.00(Sun 21.00) ⊗No
VISA M/C AMEX D JCB

Very popular among Japanese and locals alike for its traditional Japanese atmosphere. The teppan-yaki tables, with food served straight from the hot plate, are also a big draw. Branches in major cities across the world.

EAT-JAPAN 95

Ikeda   27-1B
30 Brook St. W1 ⊖ Bond Street ☎020-7629-2730 ⓕ020-7499-7145 ◎12.30-14.30(Ex. Sat), 18.30-22.30(Sat 18.00-22.00) ⊗Sun

Kiku   27-2B
17 Half Moon St. W1 ⊖ Green Park ☎020-7499-4208 ◎12.00-14.30, 18.00-22.15 ⊗Sun

Matsuri St James's → See p94   28-2B
15 Bury St. SW1 ⊖ Green Park ☎020-7839-1101 ⓕ020-7930-7010 ◎12.00-14.30, 18.00-22.30 ⊗Sun

Mitsukoshi Restaurant → See p94   29-2A
14/20 Regent St. SW1 ⊖ Piccadilly Circus ☎020-7930-0317 ⓕ020-7839-1167 ◎12.00-14.00, 18.00-21.30 ⊗Sun

Nobu   27-2A
19 Old Park La. W1 ⊖ Hyde Park Corner ☎020-7447-4747 ⓕ020-7447-4749 ◎12.00-14.15(Ex. Sat), 18.00-22.30 ⊗Sun

Noto Restaurant → See p94   40-2A
2/3 Bassishaw Highwalk, London Wall EC2 ⊖ Moorgate / Bank ☎020-7256-9433 ⓕ020-7588-5656 ◎12.00-14.30, 18.00-22.15 ⊗Sat, Sun

Ramen House Noto   39-2B
7 Bread St. EC4 ⊖ St Paul's/Mansion House ☎020-7329-8056 ◎11.30-20.45 ⊗Sat.Sun

Ryo Noodle Bar   31-1A
84 Brewer St. W1 ⊖ Piccadilly Circus ☎020-7287-1318 ⓕ020-7287-1319 ◎12.00(Sun 11.30)-0.00(Thur-Sat 1.00) ⊗No

Saga   33-2B
43 South Molton St. W1 ⊖ Bond Street ☎020-7408-2236 ⓕ020-7629-7507 ◎12.30-14.30(Ex. Sun), 18.30-22.00(Sun 18.00-21.30) ⊗No

Satsuma   29-1B
56 Wardour St. W1 ⊖ Piccadilly Circus ☎020-7437-8338 ⓕ020-7437-3389 ◎12.00-23.00(Sat 23.30, Sun 22.30) ⊗No

Suntory → See p94   28-2B
72/73 St James's St. SW1 ⊖ Green Park ☎020-7409-0201 ⓕ020-7499-0208 ◎12.00-14.00(Ex. Sun), 18.00-22.00(Sun 21.00) ⊗No

Tatsuso   41-1A
32 Broadgate Circle EC2 ⊖ Liverpool Street ☎020-7638-5863 ⓕ020-7638-5864 ◎11.30-14.30, 18.00-21.45 ⊗Sat, Sun

Yo! Sushi   34-2B
52 Poland St. W1 ⊖ Oxford Circus ☎020-7287-0443 ⓕ020-7287-2324 ◎12.00-24.00 ⊗No

96 EAT-INTERNATIONAL

Seafood

㊺ Caviar House 30-2B

161 Piccadilly W1
☎020-7409-0445 Ⓕ020-7493-1667
↺Green Park
10.00-23.00 ⊗Sun
VISA M/C AMEX D JCB

Caviar, seafood, and daily specialities. Cafe Nikolaj restaurant offers contemporary dishes in a relaxing setting, and is the perfect location for business and social occasions. The adjacent shop offers a wide range of products including caviar, balik & foie gras.

Modern European

㊻ Langan's Brasserie 28-2A

Stratton St. W1
☎020-7491-8822
↺Green Park
12.15(Sat 19.00)-23.45 ⊗Sun
VISA M/C AMEX D JCB

Good, unpretentious favourite dishes have kept the reputation of this legendary brasserie as high as ever. The lower dining room is lined with paintings and books, while a mural adorns the walls of the Venetian Room.

㊼ Mezzo 35-2A

100 Wardour St. W1
☎020-7314-4000 Ⓕ020-7314-4040
↺Piccadilly Circus/Tottenham Court Road
12.00(Sun 12.30)-14.30, 18.00-23.45
(Fri, Sat 0.45, Sun 22.45) ⊗No
VISA M/C AMEX D

A spacious but bustling Conran restaurant in Soho, lavishly decorated with mirrors. Cuisine is modern British, and there is live music on most nights. Upstairs, the Mezzonine serves faster meals at lower prices.

㊽ Orrery 33-1A

55/57 Marylebone High St. W1
☎020-7616-8000 Ⓕ020-7616-8080
↺Baker Street
12.00-15.00, 19.00-23.00
⊗No
VISA M/C AMEX D JCB

Situated above a Conran store, this Conran restaurant offers beautiful views of a neighbouring church from all tables. Reservations essential for lunch and dinner.

EAT-INTERNATIONAL 97

Caviar House → See p96 — 30-2B
161 Piccadilly W1 ⊖ Green Park ☎020-7409-0445 Ⓕ020-7493-1667 ◎10.00-23.00 ⊗Sun

SEAFOOD

Livebait — 37-2A
21 Wellington St. WC2 ⊖ Covent Garden ☎020-7836-7161 ◎12.00-15.00, 17.30-23.30 ⊗Sun

The Collection — 52-1B
264 Brompton Rd. SW3 ⊖ South Kensington ☎020-7225-1212 Ⓕ020-7225-1050 ◎12.00-15.00(Sat, Sun 16.00), 18.30-23.15(Sun 22.30) ⊗No

FUSION

Globe — 24-1A
100 Avenue Rd. NW3 ⊖ Swiss Cottage ☎020-7722-7200 ◎12.00(Sun 11.30)-15.00, 18.00-23.00(Sun 22.00) ⊗No

Bibendum — 52-1B
Michelin House, 81 Fulham Rd. SW3 ⊖ South Kensington ☎020-7581-5817 ◎12.00-14.30(Sat,Sun 12.30-15.00), 19.30-23.00(Sat, Sun 22.30) ⊗No

MODERN EUROPEAN

Che — 28-2B
23 St James's St. SW1A ⊖ Green Park/Piccadilly Circus ☎020-7747-9380 Ⓕ020-7747-9389 ◎12.00-15.00(Ex. Sat), 18.00-23.00 ⊗Sun

Circus — 31-1A
1 Upper James St.W1 ⊖ Piccadilly Circus ☎020-7534-4000 Ⓕ020-7534-4010 ◎12.00(Sat in Winter 18.00)-0.00 ⊗Sun

Langan's Brasserie → See p96 — 28-2A
Stratton St. W1 ⊖ Green Park ☎020-7491-8822 ◎12.15(Sat 19.00)-23.45 ⊗Sun

Mezzo → See p96 — 35-2A
100 Wardour St. W1 ⊖ Piccadilly Circus/Tottenham Court Road ☎020-7314-4000 Ⓕ020-7314-4040 ◎12.00(Sun 12.30)-15.00, 18.00-11.30(Fru, Sat 0.30, Sun 22.30) ⊗No

Orrery → See p96 — 33-1A
55/57 Marylebone High St. W1 ⊖ Baker Street ☎020-7616-8000 Ⓕ020-7616-8080 ◎12.00-15.00, 19.00-23.00 ⊗No

Cassia — 28-1A
12 Berkeley Square W1 ⊖ Green Park ☎020-7629-8886 Ⓕ020-7491-8883 ◎12.00-15.00, 18.00-23.30 ⊗Sun

MODERN ORIENTAL

Itsu — 52-1B
118 Draycott Av. W10 ⊖ South Kensington ☎020-7584-5522 Ⓕ020-7581-8716 ◎12.00-23.00(Sun 22.00) ⊗No

Vong — 48-1A
The Berkeley Hotel, Wilton Pl. SW1 ⊖ Knightsbridge ☎020-7235-1010 Ⓕ020-7235-1011 ◎12.00(Sat, Sun 11.30)-14.30(Sun 14.00), 18.00-23.30(Sun 22.00) ⊗No

Treat yourself to affordable luxury.

Each of The Savoy Group's famous hotels has its own special reputation for service and luxury, born out of its own particular heritage. Rooms are spacious and comfortable with large bathrooms and equipped with unobtrusive state-of-the-art communications and entertainment systems. Choose from *The Berkeley*, a sanctuary of gracious living in Knightsbridge, *Claridge's* and *The Connaught* in Mayfair or *The Savoy* beside the River Thames in the heart of London's theatre district. Whilst for country lovers, *The Lygon Arms* in the Cotswold hills, just 2 hours from London, offers one and two night Luxury Breaks in some of England's prettiest countryside.

Our prices may pleasantly surprise you. Special rates are available at quieter times of the year, whilst our *Luxury Breaks* represent savings of up to 40%!

The Savoy Group
England's most distinguished and individual hotels

For reservations and further information telephone 44 (0) 20 7872 8080, email info@savoy-group.co.uk or visit www.savoygroup.com for full details and online bookings.

Eat & Sleep in London's Best Hotels

Comfortable, convivial and elegant places to stay.

(49) The Abbey Court 44-1A

20 Pembridge Gdns. W2
☎020-7221-7518 Ⓕ020-7792-0858
Ⓔinfo@abbeycourthotel.co.uk
Ⓗwww.abbeycourthotel.co.uk
⊖Notting Hill Gate VISA M/C AMEX D JCB

A 4 star townhouse hotel with 22 individually designed bedrooms in a quiet residential location, just 100 metres from Notting Hill Gate station. All rooms with en-suite jacuzzi bath and shower, and satelite TV. Ideal for business or leisure visitors.

(50) Annandale House Hotel 48-2A

39 Sloane Gdns. SW1
☎020-7730-6291 Ⓕ020-7730-2727
Ⓔmail@annandale-hotel.co.uk
Ⓗwww.annandale-hotel.co.uk
⊖Sloane Square VISA M/C AMEX D JCB

Elegant, yet informal Victorian town house with private gardens. All rooms are en suite. Situated in a safe and quiet area, near Sloane Square station. A short distance from Knightsbridge & all the designer boutiques. Single ; £60-70, double/twin; £90-110 (incl.tax).

(51) The Basil Street Hotel 47-1B

Basil St. SW3
☎020-7581-3311 Ⓕ020-7581-3693
Ⓔinfo@thebasil.com Ⓗwww.thebasil.com
⊖Knightsbridge
VISA M/C AMEX JCB

A privately owned hotel in the heart of fashionable Knightsbridge. It is close to the city's theatreland, finest art galleries and museums, and the hotel is in itself a treasure trove of fine paintings and antiques.

(52) The Beaufort 47-2A

33 Beaufort Gdns. SW3
☎020-7584-5252 Ⓕ020-7589-2834
Ⓔthebeaufort@nol.co.uk
Ⓗwww.thebeaufort.co.uk
⊖Knightsbridge
VISA M/C AMEX D JCB

Situated 100 yards from Harrods in a peaceful tree-lined Knightsbridge square, this 28 bedroom hotel is privately owned by Sir Michael and Lady Wilmot, and have won the agents' highest rating for good service in London, twice.

HOTELS 101

22 Jermyn Street — 31-2B
22 Jermyn St. SW1 ⊖ Piccadilly Circus ☎ 020-7734-2353 Ⓕ 020-7734-0750 £ S:205-, W:290-

47 Park Street — 26-1B
47 Park St. W1 ⊖ Marble Arch ☎ 020-7491-7282 Ⓕ 020-7491-7281 £ W:285-

The Abbey Court →See p100 — 44-1A
20 Pembridge Gdns. W2 ⊖ Notting Hill Gate ☎ 020-7221-7518 Ⓕ 020-7792-0858 £ S:99-, W:145-

Annandale House Hotel →See p100 — 48-2A
39 Sloane Gdns. SW1 ⊖ Sloane Square ☎ 020-7730-6291 Ⓕ 020-7730-2727 £ S:50-, W:74-

Athenaeum — 27-2B
116 Piccadilly W1 ⊖ Green Park ☎ 020-7499-3464 Ⓕ 020-7493-1866 £ S:250-, W:270-

The Basil Street Hotel →See p100 — 47-1B
8 Basil St. SW3 ⊖ Knightsbridge ☎ 020-7581-3311 Ⓕ 020-7581-3693 £ S:128-, W:190-

The Beaufort →See p102 — 47-2A
33 Beaufort Gdns. SW3 ⊖ Knightsbridge ☎ 020-7584-5252 Ⓕ 020-7589-2834 £ S:155-, W:180-

The Berkeley →See p102 — 48-1A
Wilton Pl. SW1 ⊖ Knightsbridge ☎ 020-7235-6000 Ⓕ 020-7235-4330 £ S:225-, W:275-

Berkshire — 33-2B
350 Oxford St. W1 ⊖ Bond Street ☎ 020-7629-7474 Ⓕ 020-7629-8156 £ S:145-, W:145-

The Berners — 35-2A
10 Berners St. W1 ⊖ Oxford Circus/Tottenham Court Road ☎ 020-7666-2000 Ⓕ 020-7666-2001 £ S:175-, W:225-

Blakes — 24-2A
33 Roland Gdns SW7 ⊖ South Kensington ☎ 020-7370-6701 Ⓕ 020-7373-0442 £ S:182-, W:258-

Blooms — 36-1A
7 Montague St WC1 ⊖ Russel Square/Holborn ☎ 020-7323-1717 Ⓕ 020-7636-6498 £ S:100-, W:150-

Brown's — 30-2A
Albemarle St. W1 ⊖ Green Park ☎ 020-7493-6020 Ⓕ 020-7493-9381 £ S:258-, W:262-

*S: Single Room   W: Double Room   Prices are exclusive of VAT

102 HOTELS

⑤③ The Berkeley — 48-1A

Wilton Pl. SW1
☎020-7235-6000 (F)020-7235-4330
(E)info@the-berkeley.co.uk
(H)www.savoygroup.com
⊖Hyde Park Corner / Victoria VISA M/C AMEX D JCB

This elegant 5 star hotel is based in the heart of residential Knightsbridge, close to Harrods & Harvey Nichols. It has two exceptional restaurants: the French-Thai, Vong and the French, La Tante Claire. The Berkeley also boasts a Christian Dior Spa on the roof.

⑤④ Chelsea Green — 52-1B

35 Ixworth Pl. SW3
☎020-7225-7500 (F)020-7225-7555
(E)CGHOTEL@dircon.co.uk
(H)www.Welcome2London.com
⊖South Kensington VISA M/C AMEX

The Chelsea Green Hotel is a relaxing and elegant townhouse situated in the heart of Chelsea & close to fashionable shopping areas, museums & sightseeing. It is also a perfect corporate venue with full banquet & conference facilities.

⑤⑤ Churchill Inter-Continental — 32-2B

30 Portman Sq. W1
☎020-7486-5800 (F)020-7486-1255
(E)churchill@interconti.com
(H)www.interconti.com
⊖Marble Arch / Bond Street
VISA M/C AMEX D JCB

An elegant 5 star hotel near Oxford Street. It has an impressive 440 rooms, 6 meeting rooms, a business centre, 2 Club Inter-Continental floors, beauty salon/barber, theatre desk and a large number of garage spaces.

⑤⑥ The Cliveden Town House — 53-1B

26 Cadogan Gdns. SW3
☎020-7730-6466 (F)020-7730-0236
(E)reservations@clivedentownhouse.co.uk
(H)www.clivedentowhouse.co.uk
⊖Sloane Square / Victoria VISA M/C AMEX D JCB

The perfect balance of luxury, service and privacy at this tranquil location. Splendidly decorated Edwardian style rooms with 24hr. service and state-of-the-art technology. A gym, fashionable shops & West End theatres all within easy reach.

HOTELS

Cadogan — 47-2B
75 Sloane St. SW1 ⊖ Knightsbridge/Sloane Square ☎ 020-7235-7141 Ⓕ 020-7245-0994 Ⓒ S:175-, W:190-

The Capital — 47-1A
22 Basil St. SW3 ⊖ Hyde Park Corner/Knigtsbridge ☎ 020-7589-5171 Ⓕ 020-7225-0011 Ⓒ S:217-, W:287-

Cavendish — 31-2A
81 Jermyn St. SW1 ⊖ Piccadilly Circus/Green Park ☎ 020-7930-2111 Ⓕ 020-7839-2125 Ⓒ S:71-, W:137-

Chelsea Green →See p102 — 52-1B
35 Ixworth Pl. SW3 ⊖ South Kensington ☎ 020-7225-7500 Ⓕ 020-7225-7555 Ⓒ S:135-, W:180-

Churchill Inter-Continental →See p102 — 32-2B
30 Portman Sq. W1 ⊖ Marble Arch ☎ 020-7486-5800 Ⓕ 020-7486-1255 Ⓒ S:250-, W:270-

Claridge's — 27-1B
Brook St. W1 ⊖ Bond Street ☎ 020-7629-8860 Ⓕ 020-7499-2210 Ⓒ S:295-, W:370-

The Cliveden Town House →See p102 — 53-1B
26 Cadogan Gardens SW3 ⊖ Sloane Square / Victoria ☎ 020-7730-6466 Ⓕ 020-7730-0236 Ⓒ S:247-, W:256-

The Connaught — 27-1A
16 Carlos Pl. W1 ⊖ Bond Street ☎ 020-7499-7070 Ⓕ 020-7495-3262 Ⓒ S:265-, W:335-

Conrad International — 24-2A
Chelsea Harbour SW10 ⊖ Earl's Court ☎ 020-7823-3000 Ⓕ 020-7351-6525 Ⓒ S:193-, W:215-

Copthorne Tara — 44-2B
Wright's Lane W8 ⊖ High Street Kensington ☎ 020-7872-2000 Ⓕ 020-7937-7100 Ⓒ S:190-, W:230-

The Cranley →See p104 — 24-2A
10/12 Bina Gdns. SW5 ⊖ Gloucester Road / Victoria ☎ 020-7373-0123 Ⓕ 020-7373-9497 Ⓒ S:145-, W:160-

The Dorchester — 27-2A
53 Park Lane W1 ⊖ Hyde Park Corner ☎ 020-7629-8888 Ⓕ 020-7495-7342 Ⓒ S:332-, W:388-

Dorset Square — 32-1A
39 Dorset Sq. NW1 ⊖ Marylebone/Baker Street ☎ 020-7723-7874 Ⓕ 020-7724-3328 Ⓒ S:98-, W:130-

(57) The Cranley 24-2A

10/12 Bina Gdns. SW5
☎020-7373-0123 Ⓕ020-7373-9497
Ⓔinfo@thecranley.com
Ⓗwww.thecranley.com
⊖Gloucester Road VISA M/C AMEX D JCB

The Cranley situated in South Kensington, sets out to bring together the best of established tradition and modern technology: air conditioning; voice mail, ISDN lines; Internet access, television. Some rooms with 4 poster beds, or dramatic canopied beds.

(58) The Gainsborough 45-2B

7/11 Queensberry Pl. SW7
☎020-7957-0000 Ⓕ020-7957-0001
Ⓔgainsborough@eeh.co.uk
Ⓗwww.eeh.co.uk
⊖South Kensington
VISA M/C AMEX D JCB

Imagine an English Country Home but set in an exclusive London borough, and you have the Gainsborough. Stay here to enjoy fashionable South Kensington for its shopping, restaurants and pubs. Visit the website for a virtual tour.

(59) The Gallery 45-2B

8/10 Queensberry Pl. SW7
☎020-7915-0000 Ⓕ020-7915-4400
Ⓔgallery@eeh.co.uk Ⓗwww.eeh.co.uk
⊖South Kensington
VISA M/C AMEX D JCB

An imposing Victorian residence is tailormade for business or leisure travellers, the atmosphere is one of quiet refinement. It displays original framed art in every room & is close to museums and fashionable city life. Visit the website for a virtual tour.

(60) The Lanesborough 48-1A

Hyde Park Corner SW1
☎020-7259-5599 Ⓕ020-7259-5606
Ⓔreservations@lanesborough.co.uk
Ⓗwww.lanesborough.com
⊖Hyde Park Corner
VISA M/C AMEX D JCB

An incredibly luxurious hotel, which captures the warmth of hospitality of an early 19th century residence. It boasts 24-hour butler service, business and fitness centres, extensive on-screen film library, CD & DVD players in all rooms & baby sitting service.

HOTELS 105

Dukes   28-2B
35 St James's Pl. SW1 ⊖Green Park ☎020-7491-4840 ⒻO20-7493-1264
ⒸS:190-, W:210-

Flemings Mayfair   27-2B
7/12 Half Moon St. W1 ⊖Green Park ☎020-7499-2964 Ⓕ020-7629-4063
ⒸS:125-, W:145-

Four Seasons   27-2A
Hamilton Pl. W1 ⊖Hyde Park Corner ☎020-7499-0888 Ⓕ020-7493-1895
ⒸS:317-, W:370-

The Gainsborough →See p104   45-2B
7/11 Queensberry Pl. SW7 ⊖South Kensington ☎020-7957-0000 Ⓕ020-7957-0001 ⒸS:67-, W:120-

The Gallery →See p104   45-2B
8/10 Queensberry Pl. SW7 ⊖South Kensington ☎020-7915-0000 Ⓕ020-7915-4400 ⒸW:120-

The Gore   45-2B
189 Queen's Gate SW7 ⊖Gloucester Road ☎020-7584-6601 Ⓕ020-7589-8127
ⒸS:84-, W:106-

Grosvenor Court   24-2A
Devonshire Terrace W2 ⊖Lancaster Gate ☎020-7262-2204 Ⓕ020-7402-9351
ⒸS:99-, W:120-

Grosvenor House   26-1B
86/90 Park Lane W1 ⊖Marble Arch ☎020-7499-6363 Ⓕ020-7493-3341
ⒸS:267-, W:322-

The Halkin   48-1A
5 Halkin St. SW1 ⊖Hyde Park Corner ☎020-7333-1000 Ⓕ020-7333-1100
ⒸS:190-, W:190-

The Howard   37-2B
12 Temple Pl. WC2 ⊖Temple ☎020-7836-3555 Ⓕ020-7379-1547 ⒸW:255-

Hyatt Carlton Tower   47-2B
2 Cadogan Pl. SW1 ⊖Knightsbridge ☎020-7235-1234 Ⓕ020-7235-9129
ⒸS:200-, W:220-

Inter-Continental   27-2A
1 Hamilton Pl. W1 ⊖Hyde Park Corner ☎020-7409-3131 Ⓕ020-7493-3476
ⒸS:295-, W:295-

Kensington Court   24-2A
33-35 Nevern Pl. SW5 ⊖Earl's Court ☎020-7370-5151 Ⓕ020-7370-3499
ⒸS:65-, W:85-

(61) The Leonard 32-2B

15 Seymour St. W1
☎020-7935-2010 Ⓕ020-7935-6700
Ⓔthe.leonard@dial.pipex.com
Ⓗwww.theleonard.com
⊖Marble Arch
VISA M/C AMEX D JCB

Johansens' London Hotel of The Year 1997. The Leonard has 31 rooms including 20 suites. Each room has a marble bathroom, bar, satellite TV, with the emphasis on luxury. Room service is available 24 hours.

(62) The Montcalm Hotel Nikko London 32-2A

Great Cumberland Pl. W1
☎020-7402-4288 Ⓕ020-7724-9180
Ⓔmontcalm@montcalm.co.uk
Ⓗwww.nikkohotels.com
⊖Marble Arch
VISA M/C AMEX D JCB

A beautiful crescent-shaped Georgian building, owned and run by the Japan Airline Group since 1985. They offer modern British & authentic Japanese breakfasts and both are very popular.

(63) The Ritz, London 28-2A

150 Piccadilly W1
☎020-7493-8181 Ⓕ020-7493-2687
Ⓗwww.theritzlondon.com
⊖Green Park
VISA M/C AMEX D JCB

Ideally located on Piccadilly, over-looking Green Park and close to Bond St., the Ritz has completed a £28, 000,000 renovation, restoring the hotel to its former Louis XV1 magnifi-cence. The service is as always, impec-cable.

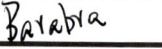

(64) Royal Garden Barabra 45-1A

2/24 Kensington High St. W8
☎020-7937-8000 Ⓕ020-7361-1909
Ⓔguest@royalgdn.co.uk
Ⓗwww.royalgardenhotel.co.uk
⊖High Street Kensington
VISA M/C AMEX JCB

Situated next to Hyde Park and Kensington Palace, this hotel has some lovely views, especially from the top floor restaurant. It also boasts another restaurant, a bar, a fitness centre and a conference room.

HOTELS 107

Landmark London   32-1A
222 Marylebone Rd. NW1 ⊖ Marylebone ☎020-7631-8030 Ⓕ020-7631-8080 ⓒS:336-, W:355-

The Lanesborough →See p104   48-1A
Hyde Park Corner SW1 ⊖Hyde Park Corner ☎020-7259-5599 Ⓕ020-7259-5606 ⓒS:255-, W:340-

Langham Hilton   34-1A
1 Portland Pl. W1 ⊖Oxford Circus ☎020-7636-1000 Ⓕ020-7323-2340 ⓒW:378-

The Leonard →See p106   32-2B
15 Seymour St. W1 ⊖Marble Arch ☎020-7935-2010 Ⓕ020-7935-6700 ⓒS:180-, W:200-

The Lowndes Hyatt   47-1B
21 Lowndes St. SW1 ⊖Knightsbridge ☎020-7823-1234 Ⓕ020-7235-1154 ⓒS:205-, W:215-

Mandarin Oriental Hyde Park   47-1B
66 Knightsbridge SW1 ⊖Knightsbridge ☎020-7253-2000 Ⓕ020-7235-4552 ⓒS:295-, W:295-

Le Meridien Piccadilly   31-2B
21 Piccadilly W1 ⊖Piccadilly Circus ☎020-7465-1608 Ⓕ020-7465-1601 ⓒS:342-, W:395-

Millennium Gloucester   45-2A
4/18 Harrington Gdns. SW7 ⊖Gloucester Road ☎020-7373-6030 Ⓕ020-7373-0409 ⓒS:230-, W:230-

The Montcalm Hotel Nikko London →See p106   32-2A
34 Great Cumberland Pl. W1 ⊖Marble Arch ☎020-7402-4288 Ⓕ020-7724-9180 ⓒS:220-, W:240-

Park Lane   27-2B
Piccadilly W1 ⊖Green Park ☎020-7499-6321 Ⓕ020-7499-1965 ⓒS:156-, W:156-

The Pelham   45-2B
15 Cromwell Pl. SW7 ⊖South Kensington ☎020-7589-8288 Ⓕ020-7584-8444 ⓒS:145-, W:175-

Pembridge Court   44-1A
34 Pembridge Gdns. W2 ⊖Notting Hill Gate ☎020-7229-9977 Ⓕ020-7724-4982 ⓒS:120-, W:150-

Radisson Mountbatten   36-2A
20 Monmouth St. WC2 ⊖Covent Garden ☎020-7836-4300 Ⓕ020-7240-3540 ⓒS:171-, W:184-

HOTELS

⑥⑤ The Savoy
36-2B

Strand WC2
☎ 020-7836-4343 ℱ 020-7240-6040
Ⓔ info@the-savoy.co.uk
Ⓗ www.savoygroup.com
⊖ Charing Cross / Embankment
VISA M/C AMEX D JCB

The incomparable Savoy continues to provide excellent levels of comfort & luxury. Its 3 restaurants offer a choice of dining venues from its Brasserie to its romantic River Restaurant, to the renowned Savoy Grill. Its American Bar serves the best martini in town.

⑥⑥ The Sloane
53-1A

29 Draycott Pl. SW3
☎ 020-7581-5757 ℱ 020-7584-1348
Ⓔ Sloanehotel@BTINTERNET.COM
⊖ Sloane Square
VISA M/C AMEX D JCB

The Sloane is a small luxury town-house hotel with 12 air-conditioned rooms with en-suite marble bathrooms. Each room is decorated with hand-picked antiques from auctions in France & the UK, and every single item is available for purchase.

⑥⑦ Stanton House Hotel
22-2A

The Avenue, Stanton Fitzwarren, Swindon, Wiltshire SN6
☎ 01793-861777 ℱ 01793-861857
⇌ Swindon
VISA M/C AMEX D JCB

Stanton House Hotel is a beautiful Cotswold stone house in the most peaceful setting. The rooms boast en suite facilities, telephones and satelite TV. The Stanton also caters for conferences for British/Japanese business & can provide interpreting services.

⑥⑧ The Willett
48-2A

32 Sloane Gdns. SW1
☎ 020-7824-8415 ℱ 020-7730-4830
Ⓔ willett@eeh.co.uk
Ⓗ www.eeh.co.uk
⊖ Sloane Square
VISA M/C AMEX D JCB

Your home from home in London's charming Sloane Gardens. A quiet retreat of terracotta terraces, seemingly far from the world of work, but close enough to the best that Chelsea has to offer. En-suite facilities. Visit the website for a virtual tour.

HOTELS 109

Rembrandt 46-2B
11 Thurloe Pl. SW7 ⊖South Kensington ☎020-7589-8100 Ⓕ020-7225-3363 ⓒS:175-, W:195-

The Ritz ➡See p106 28-2A
150 Piccadilly W1 ⊖Green Park ☎020-7493-8181 Ⓕ020-7493-2687 ⓒS:285-, W:325-

Royal Garden ➡See p106 45-1A
2/24 Kensington High St. W8 ⊖High Street Kensington ☎020-7937-8000 Ⓕ020-7361-1909 ⓒS:150-, W:170-

Royal Horseguards Thistle 50-1B
2 Whitehall Court SW1 ⊖Embankment ☎020-7839-3400 Ⓕ020-7925-2263 ⓒS:155-, W:155-

Royal Lancaster 24-2A
Lancaster Terrace, London W2 ⊖Lancaster Gate ☎020-7262-6737 Ⓕ020-7724-3191 ⓒS:293-, W:313-

St George's 34-1A
Langham Pl. W1 ⊖Oxford Circus ☎020-7580-0111 Ⓕ020-7436-7997 ⓒS:170-, W:192-

The Savoy ➡See p108 36-2B
Strand WC2 ⊖Charing Cross/Embankment ☎020-7836-4343 Ⓕ020-7240-6040 ⓒS:280-, W:330-

Sheraton Belgravia 48-1A
20 Chesham Pl. SW1 ⊖Knightsbridge ☎020-7201-1922 Ⓕ020-7259-6243 ⓒS:204-, W:217-

The Sloane ➡See p108 53-1A
29 Draycott Pl. SW3 ⊖Sloane Square ☎020-7581-5757 Ⓕ020-7584-1348 ⓒW:140-

Stanton House Hotel ➡See p108 22-2A
The Avenue, Stanton Fitzwarren, Swindon, Wiltshire SN6 ⇌Swindon ☎01793-861777 Ⓕ01793-861857 ⓒS:59-, T:93-

Strand Palace 36-2B
372 Strand WC2 ⊖Charing Cross ☎020-7836-8080 Ⓕ020-7836-2077 ⓒS:145-, W:145-

Westbury 30-1A
Conduit St, W1 ⊖Oxford Circus ☎020-7629-7755 Ⓕ020-7495-1163 ⓒS:45-, W:65-

The Willett ➡See p108 48-2A
32 Sloane Gdns. SW1 ⊖Sloane Square ☎020-7824-8415 Ⓕ020-7730-4830 ⓒW:90-

Chor Bizarre
India's Restaurant

Capturing the spirit of the 'chor bazaar' or 'thieves market' within it's kaleidoscopic interiors, **Chor Bizarre- India's Restaurant**, is dedicated to serving authentic Indian cuisine in a unique atmosphere. The resplendent furnishings and decor have been collected from various bazaars of India and have been creatively arranged so as to inspire the diner to venture beyond his immediate and uniquely decorated surrounds and explore the wealth of objects d'art displayed in each corner of the restaurant.

The chefs brought in from Chor Bizarre, New Delhi, are amongst a handful to have access to the secrets of the **'Wazwan'** - the legendary Kashmiri community feast of 36 courses from which selections are available. Chor Bizarre has also matched every dish on the menu with three wines in order of preference, painstakingly put together by the internationally acclaimed wine presenter **Charles Metcalfe**. Menu in Japanese available on request.

"One of The Best 50 Restaurants in London and amongst The Best 10 for fun and atmosphere"
The Independent

"Romantic Setting, Pukka Cooking"
Time Out

"It's a fabulous and magical setting"
The Economist

"There is a playfulness about Chor Bizarre...hard to resist when combined with competent cooking and an Aladdin's cave decor..."
Fay Maschler, Evening Standard

"Authentic Indian Food with a 'Bazaar' setting"
Charles Campion, Restaurant Writer

"A romantic hangout"
The Tatler Ashe Park Restaurant Guide

ROYAL PRE-THEATRE DINNER
£11 **Two courses**
£18 **Maharaja Thai** inclusive of 33cl Cobra lager and free car drop to any West End theatre

PRIVATE PARTY ROOM & CATERING
An elegant Private Dining Room, seating 30 peaple, available for both parties and full day conferences with all conference aids. We undertake catering for conferences, birthday parties, wedding receptions, and get togethers with varied cuisine options at your venue.
We offer this service for a minimum of 15 people and are equipped to take care of your complete needs including decor or theme setups.

OPEN SEVEN DAYS A WEEK
For reservations please call
Tel: 020-7629-9802/8542 Fax: 020-7493-7756
E-mail: chorbizarrelondon@oldworldhospitality.com
16 Albemarle Street, Mayfair, London W1X 3HA
1 minute walk from Old Bond Street via Stafford Street. Underground: Green Park

Eat & Shop in London's Shopping Paradise

Fashion, cosmetics, jewellery, antiques, glass, china & silverware; toys, stationary and of course…food !

112 FASHION

㊽ Aquascutum   31-1A

100 Regent St. W1
☎020-7675-8200 📠020-7675-9250
🌐www.aquascutum.co.uk ⊖Piccadilly Circus
10.00-18.30(Thur 19.00, Sun 12.00-17.00)
⊗No

Aquascutum celebrates their 150th anniversary this year. An in-store exhibition will highlight the company's heritage dating back to 1851. Promotional activity will occur throughout the year and the collections will concentrate on tradition and innovation.

㊹ Browns   33-2B

23/27 South Molton St. W1
☎020-7514-0000 ⊖Bond Street
● 6C Sloane St. SW1:   47-1B
⊖Knightsbridge
● Browns Labels for Less: 33-2B
50 South Molton St. W1
● Browns Focus: 33-2B
38/39 South Molton St. W1
⊖Bond Street
10.00-18.00(Thur 19.00) ⊗Sun

㊸ Gianfranco Ferre   47-1B

29 Sloane St. SW1
☎020-7838-9576 📠020-7838-9576
⊖Knightsbridge
10.00-19.00 ⊗Sun

Home of the ladies' collection from this talented designer. Decorative designs, with generous prints and embroidery.

㊺ Laura Ashley   34-2A

256/258 Regent St. W1
☎020-7437-9760 📠020-7437-0640
⊖Oxford Circus
10.00(Sat 9.30, Sun 12.00)-19.00(Mon, Tue 18.30, Thur20.00,Sun18.00) ⊗No

The essential English country style. The timeless floral prints and simple designs are loved by young and old alike. Laura Ashley also produces a range of interior design materials.

FASHION 113

À la mode 47-1A
36 Hans Crescent SW1 ↔Knightsbridge ☎020-7584-2133 ⒻE020-7584-2801 ◎10.00-18.00 ⊗Sun

Agnès B 36-2A
35/36 Floral St. WC2 ↔Covent Garden ☎020-7379-1992 Ⓕ020-7379-3318 ◎10.30(Sun 12.00)-18.30(Thur 19.00, Sun 17.00) ⊗No

Aquascutum →See p112 31-1A
100 Regent St. W1 ↔Piccadilly Circus ☎020-7675-8200 Ⓕ020-7675-9250 ◎10.00-18.30(Thur 19.00, Sun 12.00-17.00) ⊗No

Browns →See p112 33-2B
23/27 South Molton St. W1 ↔Bond Street ☎020-7514-0000 ◎10.00 - 18.00(Thur 19.00) ⊗Sun

Christian Dior 47-1B
31 Sloane St. SW1 ↔Knightsbridge ☎020-7235-1357 Ⓕ020-7225-1781 ◎10.00-18.00 ⊗Sun

Comme des Garçons 27-1B
59 Brook St. W1 ↔Bond Street ☎020-7493-1258 Ⓕ020-7408-1281 ◎10.00-18.00(Thur 19.00) ⊗Sun

Dolice & Gabbana 47-1B
175 Sloane St. SW1 ↔Knightsbridge ☎020-7235-0335 Ⓕ020-7235-0816 ◎10.00(Sat 10.30)-18.00(Wed 19.00) ⊗Sun

Donna Karan 30-1A
19 New Bond St. W1 ↔Bond Street/Green Park ☎020-7495-3100 Ⓕ020-7495-3500 ◎10.00-18.00(Thur 19.00) ⊗Sun

Galerie Gaultier 52-1B
171/175 Draycott Av. SW3 ↔South Kensington ☎020-7584-4648 Ⓕ020-7581-9092 ◎10.30-18.30(Sat 18.00) ⊗Sun

Gianfranco Ferre →See p112 47-1B
29 Sloane St. SW1 ↔Knightsbridge ☎020-7838-9576 Ⓕ020-7838-9576 ◎10.00-19.00 ⊗Sun

Gianni Versace 30-2B
34/36 Old Bond St. W1 ↔Green Park ☎020-7499-1862 Ⓕ020-7499-1719 ◎10.00-18.00 ⊗Sun

Giorgio Armani 47-2B
37 Sloane St. SW1 ↔Knightsbridge ☎020-7235-6232 Ⓕ020-7823-1342 ◎10.00-18.00(Wed 19.00) ⊗Sun

Hackett 53-1B
136/138 Sloane St. SW1 ↔Sloane Square ☎020-7730-3331 Ⓕ020-7730-3525 ◎9.30-18.00(Wed 19.00) ⊗Sun

114 FASHION

⑦③ Mackenzie's 30P 2B

169 Piccadilly W1
☎020-7495-5514 Ⓕ020-7495-6306
⊖Green Park
9.30-18.15(Sun 11.00-17.30) ⊗No
VISA M/C AMEX JCB

Classic British tailoring for men and women, from fine English brand name cloth to Cashmere knitwear and Pashmina. Old English atmosphere. The special express tailoring service takes 3 days. Japanese spoken.

⑦④ Pallant 48-1A

19A Motcomb St. SW1
☎020-7259-6046
⊖Knightsbridge
10.00-18.00 ⊗Sat,Sun
VISA M/C AMEX

Behind the white Doric columns of the Pantechnicon building lies Pallant, a stylish shop housing a unique couture collection. Choose from a range of exquisite clothes designed to meet your individual requirements.

⑦⑤ Paul Smith 36-2B

40/44 Floral St. WC2
☎020-7379-7133 Ⓕ020-7379-4836
Ⓗwww.paulsmith.co.uk
⊖Covent Garden
10.30(Sat 10.00, Sun 13.00)-18.30 (Thur, Sun 19.00, Sat 18.00) ⊗No
VISA M/C AMEX HD JCB

A huge and extremely popular range of urban chic, for men, women and kids. The bold, simple designs fuse modern looks with retro ideas. The brand also includes a footwear collection.

⑦⑥ Vivienne Westwood 30-1A

44 Conduit St. W1
☎020-7439-1109 Ⓕ020-7734-6074
⊖Oxford Circus
10.00-18.00(Thur 19.00) ⊗Sun
VISA M/C AMEX HD JCB

Platform shoes by this notoriously outrageous designer are already enshrined in the Victoria & Albert Museum, but the collections go from strength to strength. Daring menswear and made-to-order womenswear.

FASHION 115

Herbie Frogg — 47-1A
42 Hans Crescent SW1 ⊖ Knightsbridge ☎ 020-7584-2115 Ⓕ 020-7629-0423
◎ 9.30-18.00(Wed 19.00, Sun by appointment only) ⊗ No

Jaeger — 34-2B
200/206 Regent St. W1 ⊖ Oxford Circus ☎ 020-7200-4000 Ⓕ 020-7200-4063
◎ 10.00-18.30(Thur 19.30, Sun 12.00-17.00) ⊗ No

Jones — 36-2A
13 Floral St. WC2 ⊖ Covent Garden ☎ 020-7240-8312 Ⓕ 020-7240-8310
◎ 10.00-18.30(Sun 13.00-17.00) ⊗ No

Joseph at Old Bond Street — 30-2B
23 Old Bond St. W1 ⊖ Green Park ☎ 020-7629-3713 Ⓕ 020-7491-8092
◎ 10.00-18.30 ⊗ Sun

Laura Ashley → See p112 — 34-2A
256/258 Regent St. W1 ⊖ Oxford Circus ☎ 020-7437-9760 Ⓕ 020-7437-0640
◎ 10.00(Sat 9.30-Sun 12.00)-18.30(Wed, Fri 19.00, Thur 20.00, Sun 18.00) ⊗ No

Mackenzie's → See p114 — 30-2B
169 Piccadilly W1 ⊖ Green Park ☎ 020-7495-5514 Ⓕ 020-7495-6306
◎ 9.30-18.15 (Sun 11.00-17.30) ⊗ No

MaxMara — 47-1B
32 Sloane St. SW1 ⊖ Knightsbridge ☎ 020-7235-7941 Ⓕ 020-7235-6940
◎ 10.00-18.00(Wed 19.00) ⊗ Sun

Pallant → See p114 — 48-1A
19A Motcomb St. SW1 ⊖ Sloane Square ☎ 020-7259-6046 ◎ 10.00-18.00 ⊗ Sat,Sun

Paul Smith → See p114 — 36-2B
40-44 Floral St. WC2 ⊖ Covent Garden ☎ 020-7379-7133 Ⓕ 020-7379-0241
◎ 10.30-18.30(Thur 19.00, Sat 18.00) ⊗ No

Question Air — 36-2B
38 Floral St. WC2 ⊖ Covent Garden ☎ 020-7836-8220 ◎ 11.00-19.00 (Sun 12.00-17.30) ⊗ No

Reiss — 53-1A
The Reiss Bldg. 114 Kings Rd. SW3 ⊖ Sloane Square ☎ 020-7225-4900 Ⓕ 020-7225-4901 ◎ 10.00-18.30(Wed, Thur, Fri 10.30-19.00, Sun 12.00-18.00) ⊗ No

Tokio — 52-1B
309 Brompton Rd. SW3 ⊖ South Kensington ☎ 020-7823-7310 Ⓕ 020-7823-7426 ◎ 10.00-18.30(Sun 12.30-17.30) ⊗ No

Vivienne Westwood → See p114 — 30-1A
44 Conduit St. W1 ⊖ Oxford Circus ☎ 020-7439-1109 Ⓕ 020-7734-6074
◎ 10.00-18.00(Thur 19.00) ⊗ Sun

116 FASHION

77 Alain Figaret — 30-1A

Shirts, Blouses

30 New Bond St. W1
☎ 020-7491-8589
⊖ Bond Street / Green Park
9.30-18.30 ⊗ Sun
VISA M/C AMEX JCB

Specialist French shirtmaker designing the finest shirts for 30 years. Offers a stunning choice of over 600 fabrics for men and 200 for women with different collar styles, sleeve and cuff design and impeccable finishings.

78 Coles — 31-2B

101 Jermyn St. SW1
☎ 020-7930-6448 F 020-7839-5196
E info@coles-shirtmakers.com
H www.coles-shirtmakers.com
⊖ Piccadilly Circus
9.30-18.00 (Thur 19.00, Sat 17.30) ⊗ Sun
VISA M/C AMEX JCB

Founded in 1878, Coles specialises in the very highest quality shirts for gentlemen and ladies. A wide selection of fabrics and ready-made shirts is always available, Tax free shopping is also offered.

79 Shirin Cashmere — 47-2A

Cashmere

11 Beauchamp Pl. SW3
☎ 020-7581-1936 F 020-7584-6657
⊖ Knightsbridge
10.00 (Sat 10.30)-18.00 ⊗ Sun
VISA M/C AMEX D JCB

A co-ordinated range of cashmere knitwear from classic styles to contemporary designs. Luxurious clothes, high quality and helpful staff.

80 The Highlands — 31-2B

Outdoor Clothing

73/77 Regent St. W1
☎ 020-7434-0880 F 020-7434-0881
E highlandsuk@aol.com
⊖ Piccadilly Circus
10.00-19.00 (Sun 13.00-18.00) ⊗ No
VISA M/C AMEX D JCB

Established in 1991, this specialist store is renowned for Barbour clothing. Discerning customers can also choose from tartan kilts, Arans, cashmere jumpers, and capes, plus a wide range of hats.

FASHION 117

SHIRTS

Alain Figaret → See p116 — 30-1A
30 New Bond St. W1 ⊖ Bond Street/Green Park ☎ 020-7491-8589 ◎ 9.30-18.30 ⊗ Sun

Coles → See p116 — 31-2B
101 Jermyn St. SW1 ⊖ Piccadilly Circus ☎ 020-7930-6448 ⒻF 020-7839-5196 ◎ 9.30-18.00(Thur 19.00, Sat 17.30) ⊗ Sun

Hervie & Hudson — 31-2B
97 Jermyn St. SW1 ⊖ Green Park ☎ 020-7839-3578 Ⓕ 020-7839-7020 ◎ 9.00-17.30 ⊗ Sun

Thomas Pink — 31-2A
85 Jermyn St. SW1 ⊖ Green Park/Piccadilly Circus ☎ 020-7930-6364 Ⓕ 020-7839-5481 ◎ 9.30-18.30(Thur 19.00, Sat 18.00, Sun 12.00-17.00) ⊗ No

Turnbull & Asser — 31-2A
71/72 Jermyn St. SW1 ⊖ Green Park ☎ 020-7808-3000 Ⓕ 020-7808-3001 ◎ 9.00(Sat 9.30)-18.00 ⊗ Sun

TAILOR

Gieves & Hawkes — 30-1B
1 Savile Row W1 ⊖ Piccadilly Circus ☎ 020-7434-2001 Ⓕ 020-7437-1092 ◎ 9.30-18.30(Fri 9.00-18.00, Sat 10.00-18.00) ⊗ Sun

Richard James — 30-1B
31 Savile Row W1 ⊖ Green Park ☎ 020-7434-0605 Ⓕ 020-7287-2265 ◎ 10.00(Sat 11.00)-18.00 ⊗ Sun

CASHMERE / KNITWEAR

Ballantyne Cashmere — 30-1B
4-6 Savile Row W1 ⊖ Green Park ☎ 020-7734-2861 Ⓕ 020-7794-1613 ◎ 10.00-18.30 ⊗ Sun

Shirin Cashmere → See p116 — 47-2A
11 Beauchamp Pl. SW3 ⊖ Knightsbridge ☎ 020-7581-1936 Ⓕ 020-7584-6657 ◎ 10.00 (Sat 10.30)-18.00 ⊗ Sun

The Cashmere Gallery — 47-1B
25 Brompton Rd. SW1 ○ Knightsbridge ☎ 020-7038-0048 Ⓕ 020 7838 0203 ◎ 9.30-18.00(Sun 10.00-16.00) ⊗ No

KNITWEAR, KILT, OUTDOOR FASHION

The Scotch House — 47-1A
2 Brompton Rd. SW1 ⊖ Knightsbridge ☎ 020-7581-2151 Ⓕ 020-7589-1583 ◎ 9.30(Wed 10.00, Sat 9.00, Sun 12.00)-18.00(Wed 19.00) ⊗ No

Ellis Bringham — 36-2B
30-32 Southampton St. WC2 ⊖ Covent Garden/Embankment ☎ 020-7240-9577 ◎ 10.00-19.00(Thur 19.30, Sat 9.30-18.30, Sun 11.30-17.30) ⊗ No

The Highlands → See p116 — 31-2B
73/77 Regent St. W1 ⊖ Piccadilly Circus ☎ 020-7434-0880 Ⓕ 020-7434-0881 ◎ 10.00-19.00(Sun 13.00-18.00) ⊗ No

118 LEATHER, SHOES

⑧¹ Mulberry　　　　　　　　　　　　　　30-1A

41/42 New Bond St. W1
☎ 020-7491-3900
● 11/12 Gees Court, St Christopher's Pl. W1 :　　33-2A
☎ 020-7493-2546
⊖ Bond Street
10.00-18.00 (Thur 19.00)　⊗ Sun
VISA M/C AMEX D JCB

Esteemed worldwide for classic British styling - a unique blend of heritage and contemporary living. Excellence in design and exacting craftmanship ensure Mulberry fashion and interior collections complement any lifestyle.

⑧² Tanner Krolle　　　　　　　　　　　30-2B

38 Old Bond St. W1
☎ 020-7491-2243　Ⓕ 020-7491-8702
⊖ Green Park / Bond Street
10.00-18.00　⊗ Sun
VISA M/C AMEX

This contemporary collection of day and evening bags, luggage and accessories in beautiful calf, English bridle and exotic leathers, reflects the company's 140-year tradition for fine craftsmanship and luxury with style.

⑧³ Paraboot　　　　　　　　　　　　　30-1B

37 Savile Row W1
☎ 020-7494-3233　Ⓕ 020-7494-2322
Ⓔ parabootsr@aol.com
⊖ Oxford Circus / Piccadilly Circus
10.00-18.00 (Sat 17.00)　⊗ Sun
VISA M/C AMEX

Located in the heart of Mayfair. The French leader in top of the range. Hand stitched footwear for men and women. Almost 100 years of tradition and elegance for the discerning customer.

⑧⁴ Tricker's　　　　　　　　　　　　　30-2B

67 Jermyn St. SW1
☎ 020-7930-6395　Ⓕ 020-7930-6395
Ⓔ jermynst@trickers.com　Ⓗ www.trickers.com
⊖ Green Park / Piccadilly Circus
9.30-17.30 (Sat 17.00)　⊗ Sun　VISA M/C AMEX D JCB

Famous English shoemaker established 1829, offer a comprehensive collection of quality Bench-made shoes from stock. Bespoke hand-made shoes a speciality. A unique shopping experience.

LEATHER, SHOES 119

Anya Hindmarch   47-2B
15/17 Pont St. SW1 ⊖Sloane Square ☎020-7838-9177 ⓕ020-7838-9111 ◎10.00-18.00 ⊗Sun

The Bridge   47-2A
53 Beauchamp Pl. SW3 ⊖Knightsbridge ☎020-7589-8055 ⓕ020-7589-8052 ◎10.00-18.00(Wed 19.00) ⊗Sun

Coach   47-1B
8 Sloane St. SW1 ⊖Sloane Square ☎020-7235-1507 ◎10.00-18.00 (Wed 19.00) ⊗Sun

Mulberry ➜See p118   30-1A
41/42 New Bond St. W1 ⊖Bond Street ☎020-7491-3900 ◎10.00-18.00(Thur 19.00) ⊗Sun

Pickett   30-2B
41 Burlingdton Arcade W1 ⊖Piccadilly Circus/Green Park ☎020-7493-8939 ⓕ020-7730-0299 ◎9.00-18.00 ⊗Sun

Tanner Krolle ➜See p118   30-2B
38 Old Bond St. ⊖Green Park/Bond Street ☎020-7491-2243 ⓕ020-7491-8702 ◎10.00-18.00(Thur 19.00) ⊗Sun

Church's   30-1B
201 Regent St. W1 ⊖Oxford Circus ☎020-7734-2438 ◎10.00-18.30 (Thur 19.30) ⊗Sun

Fratelli Rosetti   30-2A
177 New Bond St. W1 ⊖Green Park ☎020-7491-7066 ⓕ020-7235-5291 ◎10.00-18.00 ⊗Sun

Paraboot ➜See p118   30-1B
37 Savile Row W1 ⊖Oxford Circus / Piccadilly Circus ☎020-7494-3233 ⓕ020-7494-2322 ◎10.00-18.00 (Sat 17.00) ⊗Sun

Patrick Cox   53-1B
129 Sloane St. SW1 ⊖Sloane Square ☎020-7730-8886 ⓕ020-7235-9552 ◎10.00-18.00(Wed 19.00, Sun 11.00-17.00) ⊗No

Russell & Bromley   30-1A
24-25 New Bond St. W1 ⊖Bond Street ☎020-7629-6903 ◎10.00-18.30 (Thur 19.30) ⊗Sun

Shellys   34-2A
266/270 Regent St. W1 ⊖Oxford Street ☎020-7287-0939 ⓕ020-7287-0942 ◎10.00-19.00(Thur 20.00, Sun 12.00-18.00) ⊗No

Tricker's ➜See p118   30-2B
67 Jermyn St. SW1 ⊖Green Park / Piccadilly Circus ☎020-7930-6395 ⓕ020-7930-6395 ◎9.30-17.30(Sat 17.00) ⊗Sun

120 CERAMICS, CHINA, GLASS, SILVERWARE

⑧⑤ Contemporary Ceramics 34-2B

Handmade Ceramics

7 Marshall St. W1
☎ 020-7437-7605 (F) 020-7437-7605
(E) contemporary.ceramics@virgin.net
⊖ Oxford Circus
10.00-17.30 (Thur 19.00) ⊗ Sun
[visa] [M/C] [AMEX]

The only shop in London specialising exclusively in British studio pottery, with the work of more than 100 potters from the British Isles on show. The works include top quality tableware and exceptional ceramic sculpture.

⑧⑥ Von Posch 31-2B

Porcelain

100 Jermyn St. SW1
☎ 020-7930-2211 (F) 020-7930-2211
⊖ Piccadilly Circus
10.00-18.00 (Sat 17.00) ⊗ Sun
[visa] [M/C] [AMEX] [JCB]

An elegant store in a lovely location with a nice relaxed atmosphere where the staff are very helpful, and are always happy to assist the customer as much as posssible. If required, the shop will arrange for goods to be shipped anywhere in the world.

⑧⑦ Thomas Goode & Co. 27-1A

China

19 South Audley St. W1
☎ 020-7499-2823 (F) 020-7629-4230
⊖ Bond Street / Green Park
10.00-18.00 ⊗ Sun
[visa] [M/C] [AMEX] [JCB]

A treasure house of fine crystal, delicate porcelain and bone china. Baccarat, Lalique and Fabergé are all represented. Hand painting is carried out on the premises, which include a museum of the company's history.

⑧⑧ Mappin & Webb 30-1B

Silverware

170 Regent St. W1
☎ 020-7734-3801 (F) 020-7494-3766
⊖ Oxford Circus
10.00-18.00 (Thur 19.00) ⊗ Sun
[visa] [M/C] [AMEX] [JCB]

Silversmiths and jewellers renowned for craftsmanship for over 200 years. High quality silverware, fine gem-set jewellery and branded watches. Appointed by the Royal Family.

CERAMICS, CHINA, GLASS, SILVERWARE 121

Bridgewater 52-2A
739 Fulham Rd. SW6 ⊖Parsons Green ☎020-7371-5264 ◎10.00-17.30(Sat 17.00) ⊗Sun

Ceramica Blue 24-2A
10 Blenheim Cres. W11 ⊖Ladbroke Grove ☎020-7727-0288 ◎10.00-18.30(Mon 11.00-17.00) ⊗Sun

Contemporary Ceramics → See p120 34-2B
7 Marshall St. W1 ⊖Oxford Circus ☎020-7437-7605 Ⓕ020-7437-7605 ◎10.00-17.30 (Thur 19.00) ⊗Sun

Portmeirion 44-1B
13 Kensington Church St. W8 ⊖High Street Kensington ☎020-7938-1891 Ⓕ020-7376-1770 ◎10.00-18.00 ⊗Sun

Royal Doulton 30-2B
167 Piccadilly, W1 ⊖Green Park ☎020-7493-9121 Ⓕ020-7499-3561 ◎9.30-18.00 ⊗Sun

Von Posch → See p120 31-2B
100 Jermyn St. SW1 ⊖Piccadilly Circus/Green Park ☎020-7930-2211 Ⓕ020-7930-2211 ◎10.00-18.00(Sat 17.00) ⊗Sun

Zelli 30-2A
30A Dover St. W1 ⊖Green Park ☎020-7493-0203 ◎9.30-18.00 (Sat 10.00-16.00) ⊗Sun

Thomas Goode & Co. → See p120 27-1A
19 South Audley St. W1 ⊖Bond Street/Green Park ☎020-7499-2823 Ⓕ020-7629-4230 ◎10.00-18.00 ⊗Sun

Waterford Wedgewood 30-1B
158 Regent St. W1 ⊖Oxford Circus ☎020-7734-7262 ◎9.30-18.30 (Thur 19.00, Sun 12.00-18.00) ⊗No

Baccarat 30-2B
37 Old Bond St. W1 ⊖Green Park ☎020 7409-7767 Ⓕ020-7409-7177 ◎10.00-18.00(Sat 17.00) ⊗Sun

Pavillon Christfle 34-2A
10 Hanover St. W1 ⊖Oxford Street ☎020-7491-4004 Ⓕ020-7491-3003 ◎10.00-18.00(Sat 17.00) ⊗Sun

David Richards & Sons 33-1A
12 New Cavendish St. W1 ⊖Bond Street/Baker Street ☎020-7935-3206 Ⓕ020-7224-4423 ◎9.30-17.30 ⊗Sat, Sun

Mappin & Webb → See p120 30-1B
170 Regent St. W1 ⊖Oxford Circus ☎020-7734-3801 Ⓕ020-7494-3766 ◎10.00-18.00(Thur 19.00) ⊗Sun

122 JEWELLERY

Jewellery

⑧⑨ Asprey 30-2A

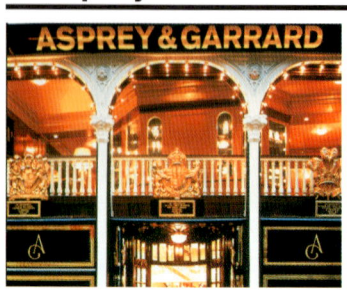

167 New Bond St. W1
☎020-7493-6767 📠020-7491-0384
🚇Green Park/Bond Street
10.00-18.00(Sat 17.00) ⊗Sun
VISA M/C AMEX D

With over 200 years of expertise, Asprey respresents the pinnacle of English style, with the finest jewellery and watches, magnificent silver, elegant china, glass and leather goods.

⑨⓪ Cartier Ltd. 30-2B

175/176 New Bond St. W1
☎020-7408-5700 📠020-7355-3011
🚇Green Park
10.00-18.00(Sat 17.00) ⊗Sun
VISA M/C AMEX D JCB

Since the first store opened in Paris, 1847, the name has been synonymous worldwide with high quality jewellery, watches and leather goods. Cartier's designs are all original, the style forever elegant and classical.

Watches & Clocks

⑨① K.Mozer 47-1B

40 Knightsbridge SW1
☎020-7245-9077 📠020-7245-6077
✉paedsall@kmozer.demon.co.uk
🌐www.kmozer.com
🚇Knightsbridge
10.00-20.00 ⊗Sun
VISA M/C JCB

Fine handmade clocks, long-case grandfather, wall and table clocks and a range of brass mantle clocks. K. Mozer also make a range of automatic and chronograph, hour jump, regulator watches and pocket watches.

Fashion Jewellery

⑨② Folli Follie 47-1B

207 Sloane St. SW1
☎020-7235-1681 📠020-7259-5545
🚇Knightsbridge 10.30-18.30 ⊗Sun
●120 New Bond St. W1 : 28-1A
🚇Bond Street
●80/82 Regent St. W1
🚇Piccadilly Circus : 31-2A
VISA M/C AMEX D JCB

Exclusively designed jewellery, watches and accessories. Fashion orientated, high quality goods with two collections of luxury items produced each year.

JEWELLERY | 123

Asprey → See p122   **30-2A**
167 New Bond St. W1 ⊖ Green Park/Bond Street ☎ 020-7493-6767
Ⓕ 020-7491-0384 ◎ 10.00-18.00(Sat 17:00) ⊗ Sun

Cartier Ltd. → See p122   **30-2B**
175/176 New Bond St. W1 ⊖ Green Park ☎ 020-7408-5700 Ⓕ 020-7355-3011
◎ 10.00-18.00(Sat 17.00) ⊗ Sun

Bvlgari   **30-2A**
172 New Bond St. W1 ⊖ Green Park/Piccadilly Circus ☎ 020-7872-9969
Ⓕ 020-7872-9869 ◎ 10.00(Sun 12.00)-18.00(Sat 17.00) ⊗ No

Cox & Power   **52-1B**
92 Walton St. SW3 ⊖ South Kensington/Knightsbridge ☎ 020-7589-6335
Ⓕ 020-7589-6334 ◎ 10.00-18.00 ⊗ Sun

Dower & Hall   **46-2B**
60 Beauchamp Pl. SW3 ⊖ Knightsbridge ☎ 020-7589-8474 Ⓕ 020-7589-8491 ◎ 10.30-18.30 ⊗ Sun

Hennel   **30-2A**
12 New Bond St. W1 ⊖ Green Park ☎ 020-7629-6888 Ⓕ 020-7493-8158
◎ 9.30-17.30 ⊗ Sun

Tiffany & Co.   **30-2B**
25 Old Bond St. W1 ⊖ Green Park ☎ 020-7409-2790 Ⓕ 020-7491-3110
◎ 10.00-17.30(Sat. 18.00) ⊗ Sun

C R Frost & Son   **25-1A**
60/62 Clerkenwell Rd. EC1 ⊖ Farringdon ☎ 020-7253-0315 ◎ 9.30-17.30
(Sat 10.00-17.00) ⊗ Sun

K.Mozer → See p122   **47-1B**
40 Knightsbridge SW1 ⊖ Knightsbridge ☎ 020-7245-9077 Ⓕ 020-7245-6077
◎ 10.00-20.00 ⊗ Sun

Watches of Switzerland   **30-1A**
16 New Bond St. W1 ⊖ Green Park ☎ 020-7493-5916 ◎ 9.30(Tue, Sat 10.00)-17.30 ⊗ Sun

925   **31-1A**
11 The Quadrant Arcade, 80 Regent St. W1 ⊖ Oxford Circus/Piccadilly Circus
☎ 020-7437-9925 Ⓕ 020-7437-1925 ◎ 10.30-19.00(Sat 10.00-18.30) ⊗ No

Angela Hale   **30-2B**
5 The Royal Arcade, 28 Old Bond St. W1 ⊖ Green Park/Piccadilly Circus
☎ 020-7495-1920 Ⓕ 020-7495-1245 ◎ 10.00-18.00 ⊗ Sun

Folli Follie → See p122   **47-1B**
207 Sloane St. SW1 ⊖ Knightsbridge ☎ 020-7235-1681 Ⓕ 020-7259-5545
◎ 10.30-18.30 ⊗ Sun

124 ANTIQUES, AUCTIONEERS

⑬ The Silver Fund — 28-2B

Antiques(silver)

40 Bury St. SW1
☎020-7839-7664 (F)020-7839-8935
(E)dealers@thesilverfund.com
(H)www.thesilverfund.com
⊖Green Park 9.00-17.30 ⊗Sat, Sun [VISA] [M/C] [AMEX]

Chic yet informal, The Silver Fund lies in the heart of St.James's, where thousands of items of Georg Jensen silver, including jewellery, holloware and flatware are for sale, incorporating famous designers such as Henning Koppel and Johan Rohde.

⑭ M.C.N. Antiques — 24-1A

Japanese

183 Westbourne Grove W11
☎020-7727-3796 (F)020-7229-8839
⊖Notting Hill Gate
9.30-17.30(Sat 11.00-15.00) ⊗Sun
[JCB]

Japanese antiques, porcelain and works of art from the early Edo to the end of the Meiji period.

⑮ Celadon Art Gallery — 31-2A

Art gallery (Oriental)

2/4 Princes Arcade SW1
☎020-7494-0915 (F)020-7494-0942
(E)juan@jchi.freeserve.co.uk
(H)www.celadonart.co.uk
⊖Green Park / Piccadilly Circus
10.00-17.30 ⊗Sun [VISA] [M/C] [AMEX] [JCB]

The gallery specialises in works from Jingdezhen in Jiangxi province, China, which produces an almost bewildering variety of ceramics in contemporary and traditional styles. They also shows fine Japanese ceramics.

⑯ Sotheby's — 30-1A

Auctioneers

34/35 New Bond St. W1
☎020-7293-5000 (F)020-7293-5989
(H)www.southebys.com
⊖Bond Street
9.00-16.30 ⊗Sat, Sun
[VISA] [M/C]

The famous international auctioneers attract dealers from throughout the world to its frequent specialist sales. Services for the public include valuations, gallery talks and educational courses in fine and decorative art.

ANTIQUES, AUCTIONEERS 125

Tin Tin Collectables　24-1A
Unit G38-42, Alfies Antique Market, 13-25 Chirch St. NW8　⊖Edgware Road
☎020-7258-1305 Ⓕ020-7258-1305 ◎10.00-18.00 ⊗Mon, Sun

Stair & Co.　27-1A
14 Mount St. W1　⊖Bond Street ☎020-7499-1784 Ⓕ020-7629-1050 ◎9.30-17.30 (Sat by appointment only) ⊗Sun

The Silver Fund　→See p124　28-2B
40 Bury St SW1　⊖Green Park ☎020-7839-7664 Ⓕ020-7839-8935 ◎9.00-17.30 ⊗Sat, Sun

M.C.N. Antiques　→See p124　24-1A
183 Westbourne Grove W11　⊖Notting Hill Gate ☎020-7727-3796 Ⓕ020-7229-8839 ◎9.30-17.30(Sat 11.00-15.00) ⊗Sun

J.A.N. Fine Art　44-1B
134 Kensington Church St. W8　⊖Notting Hill Gate ☎020-7792-0736 Ⓕ020-7221-1380 ◎10.00-18.00 ⊗Sat, Sun

Celadon Art Gallery　→See p124　31-2A
2/4 Princes Arcade SW1　⊖Green Park / Piccadilly Circus ☎020-7494-0915 Ⓕ020-7494-0942 ◎10.00-17.30 ⊗Sun

Contemporary Applied Arts　35-1A
2 Percy St. W1　⊖Tottenham Court Road/Goodge Street ☎020-7436-2344 Ⓕ020-7436-2446 ◎10.30-17.30 ⊗Sun

Fine Art Society　30-1A
148 New Bond St. W1　⊖Bond Street/Green Park ☎020-7629-5116 Ⓕ020-7491-9454 ◎9.30-17.30(Sat 10.00-13.00) ⊗Sun

Lisson Gallery　24-1A
67 Lisson St. NW1　⊖Edgware Road ☎020-7724-2739 Ⓕ020-7724-7124 ◎10.00-18.00(Sat 17.00) ⊗Sun

Bonhams　46-2B
Montpelier St. SW7　○Knightsbridge ☎020-7393-3900 Ⓕ020-7393-3905 ◎9.00-17.00 ⊗Sat, Sun

Christie's　28-2B
8 King St. SW1　⊖Green Park ☎020-7839-9060 Ⓕ020-7839-1611 ◎9.00-16.45 ⊗Sat, Sun

Phillips　33-2B
101 New Bond St. W1　⊖Bond Street ☎020-7629-6602 ◎8.30(Sun 14.00)-17.00 ⊗Sat

Sotheby's　→See p124　30-1A
34/35 New Bond St. W1　⊖Bond Street ☎020-7293-5000 Ⓕ020-7293-5989 ◎9.00-16.30 ⊗Sat, Sun

126 COSMETICS, LINEN ETC.

⑨⑦ Neal's Yard Remedies 36-1A

15 Neal's Yard WC2
☎ 020-7379-7222
Ⓔ cservices@nealsyardremedies.com
⊖ Covent Garden
10.00-19.00 ⊗ No

Founded in 1981, Neal's Yard Remedies was inspired by French Pharmacies and now sells a broad range of herbs, essential oils & homeopathic remedies, as well as the beauty range in their signature blue glass bottles. The products are used by stars such as Uma Thurman & John Malkovitch.

⑨⑧ Space NK Apothecary 27-1B

45/47 Brook St. W1
☎ 020-7355-1727 / Mail Order 0870-607-7060
⊖ Bond Street
10.00-18.00 ⊗ Sun

Beauty industry insiders, flock to this unique collection of the world's best cosmetics and fragrances. Rare and cult brands are a speciality. Branches in Chelsea, City, Knightsbridge and Covent Garden.

⑨⑨ The Irish Linen Company 30-2B

35/36 Burlington Arcade W1
☎ 020-7493-8949 Ⓕ 020-7499-5485
Ⓗ www.irish-linen.com
⊖ Green Park/Piccadilly Circus
9.30-18.00(Sat 17.00) ⊗ Sun

Founded in 1875. Remains London's most luxurious and classic supplier of finest linens. Everything from a sumptuous table setting to a small, beautiful and thoughtful gift is to be found here.

⑩⓪ The Linen Merchant 47-2A

11 Montpelier St. SW7
☎ 020-7584-3654 Ⓕ 020-7584-3671
Ⓗ www.thelinenmerchant.com
⊖ Knightsbridge
9.30-18.00 ⊗ Sun

An excellent collection of beautiful hand-embroidered linens, traditional and contemporary, which make beautiful and prestigious gifts. Well known for children's bedlinen and towels. Mail order service available.

COSMETICS, LINEN ETC. 127

Neal's Yard Remedies →See p126 36-1A
15 Neal's Yard WC2 ⊖Covent Garden ☎020-7379-7222 ◎10.00-19.00 ⊗No

Space NK Apothecary →See p126 27-1B
45/47 Brook St. W1⊖Bond Street ☎020-7355-1727 ◎10.00-18.00 ⊗Sun

D. R. Harris & Co. 28-2B
29 St James's St. SW1 ⊖Green Park ☎020-7930-3915 ⒻO20-7925-2691 ◎8.30-18.00(Sat 9.30-17.00) ⊗Sun

Floris 31-2A
89 Jermyn St. SW1 ⊖Green Park/Piccadilly Circus ☎020-7930-2885 Ⓕ020-7930-1402 ◎9.30-17.30(Sat 10.00-17.00) ⊗Sun

Penhaligon's 36-2B
41 Wellington St. WC2 ⊖Covent Garden ☎020-7836-2150 Ⓕ020-7497-1076 ◎10.00-18.00(Sun 12.00-17.00) ⊗No

Aromatique 46-2B
154 Brompton Rd. SW3 ⊖Knightsbridge ☎020-7591-1950 ◎10.00-18.00(Thur 19.00) ⊗Sun

The Irish Linen Company →See p126 30-2B
35/36 Burlington Arcade W1 ⊖Green Park/Piccadilly Circus ☎020-7493-8949 Ⓕ020-7499-5485 ◎9.15-17.45(Sat 17.00) ⊗Sun

The Linen Merchant →See p126 47-2A
11 Montpelier St. SW7 ⊖Knightsbridge ☎020-7584-3654 Ⓕ020-7584-3671 ◎9.30-18.00 ⊗Sun

Eye to Eye 46-2B
3A Monpelier St. SW7 ⊖Knightsbridge ☎020-7581-8828 Ⓕ020-7581-8848 ◎10.00(Mon 12.00)-10.30(Thur 19.00, Sat 18.00) ⊗Sun

Washin Optical 31-1B
56/58 Regent St. W1 ⊖Piccadilly Circus ☎020-7287-5901 Ⓕ020-7287-5902 ◎10.00 18.00(Sat 19.00) ⊗Sun

The Conran Shop 52-1B
Michelin House, 81 Fulham Rd. SW3 ⊖South Kensington ☎020-7589-7401 Ⓕ020-7823-7015 ◎10.00(Sun 12.00)-18.00(Wed, Thur 19.00, Sat 18.30) ⊗No

Frevd 36-1A
198 Shaftesbury Ave. WC2 ⊖Totthenham Court Road ☎020-7831-1071 ◎10.30-18.30(Sat 11.00-17.00, Sun 12.00-16.00) ⊗No

Sanderson 47-2A
112/120 Brompton Rd. SW3 ⊖Knightsbridge ☎020-7584-3344 Ⓕ020-7584-8404 ◎10.00-18.00 ⊗Sun

128 STATIONARY, GIFTS ETC.

⑩ London Graphic Centre — 36-2A

16/18 Shelton St. WC2
☎ 020-7759-4500 📠 020-7759-4585
✉ mailorder@londongraphics.co.uk
🌐 www.londongraphics.co.uk
🚇 Covent Garden / Leicester Square
9.00 (Sat 10.30) -18.00 ⊗ Sun
[VISA] [M/C] [AMEX]

London Graphic Centre plays host to around 40,000 products catering for the art & design world. Its spacious floor allows easy browsing and the staff are highly trained. There are also branches in Goodge St. & Putney.

⑩ House of Hanover — 34-2A

13/14 Hanover St. W1
☎ 020-7629-1103 📠 020-7491-1909
🚇 Oxford Circus
9.45-18.15(Sun 11.00-17.00) ⊗ No
[VISA] [M/C] [AMEX] [D] [JCB]

The House of Hanover excels in offering collections of world famous labels at exceptionally low prices.

⑩ Halcyon Days — 28-1A

14 Brook St. W1
☎ 020-7629-8811 📠 020-7409-7901
✉ info@halcyondays.co.uk
🌐 www.halcyondays.co.uk
🚇 Bond Street/Oxford Circus
9.30-18.00 ⊗ Sun [VISA] [M/C] [AMEX] [D] [JCB]

Finest English gifts including clocks and musical boxes from this specialist enamel and porcelain shop with four Royal Warrants. Exquisite products and excellent service.

⑩ Ireland in London — 47-2A

5 Montpelier St. SW7
☎ 020-7589-4455 📠 020-7589-5565
✉ irelandinlondon@cwcom.net
🌐 www.irelandinlondon.com
🚇 Knightsbridge 10.00-19.00 (Sun 12.00-17.00) ⊗ No [VISA] [M/C] [AMEX] [D] [JCB]

Well known for its expert assistance, the shop specialises in traditional handknitted Aran wool sweaters; Merino wool & Lambswool; Cashmere; Irish linen; Claddagh gold rings, and traditional Irish music CDs.

STATIONARY, GIFTS ETC. 129

Ordning & Reda 36-2A
21/22 New Row WC2 ⊖Leicester Square ☎020-7240-8090 ⒻO20-7240-6167 ◎10.00(Sun 11.00)-20.00 ⊗No

London Graphic Centre →See p128 36-2A
16/18 Shelton St. WC2 ⊖Covent Garden / Leicester Square ☎020-7759-4500 Ⓕ020-7759-4585 ◎9.00 (Sat 10.30) -18.00 ⊗Sun

House of Hanover →See p128 34-2A
13/14 Hanover St. W1 ⊖Oxford Circus ☎020-7629-1103 Ⓕ020-7491-1909 ◎9.45-18.15(Sun 11.00-17.00) ⊗No

Halcyon Days →See p128 28-1A
14 Brook St. W1 ⊖Bond Street/Oxford Circus ☎020-7629-8811 Ⓕ020-7409-7901 ◎9.15-17.30 ⊗Sun

Hamleys 30-1B
188/196 Regent St. W1 ⊖Oxford Circus ☎020-7734-3161 Ⓕ020-7494-5858 ◎10.00(Sat 9.30)-20.00(Sun 12.00-18.00) ⊗No

Warner Bros. Studio Stores 30-1B
178/182 Regent St. W1 ⊖Oxford Circus/Piccadilly Circus ☎020-7434-3334 Ⓕ020-7134-3336 ◎10.00-19.00(Thur 20.00, Sun 12.00-18.00) ⊗No

Young England 48-2B
47 Elizabeth St. SW1 ⊖Sloane Square/Victoria ☎020-7259-9003 Ⓕ020-7730-5764 ◎10.00-17.30(Sat. 15.00) ⊗Sun

Lillywhite's 31-2B
24/36 Regent St. SW1 ⊖Piccadilly Circus ☎020-7930-3181 Ⓕ020-7930-2330 ◎10.00-20.00(Sun 11.00-18.00) ⊗No

Swaine Adeney 28-2B
54 St James's St. SW1 ⊖Green Park ☎020-7409-7277 Ⓕ020-7629-3114 ◎10.00-18.00 ⊗Sun

Hobgoblin 35-1A
24 Rathbone Pl. W1 ⊖Tottenham Court Road ☎020-7323 9040 ◎10.00-18.00 ⊗Sun

Benson & Hedges 30-2B
13 Old Bond St. W1 ⊖Green Park ☎020-7493-1825 Ⓕ020-7491-2276 ◎9.00-18.00(Sat 10.30-17.30) ⊗Sun

James Smith & Sons 36-1A
Hazelwood House, 53 New Oxford St. WC1 ⊖Tottenham Court Rord/Holborn ☎020-7836-4731 Ⓕ020-7836-4730 ◎9.30(Sat 10.00)-17.25 ⊗Sun

Ireland in London →See p128 47-2A
5 Montpelier St. SW7 ⊖Knightsbridge ☎020-7589-4455 Ⓕ020-7589-5565 ◎10.00-19.00 (Sun 12.00-17.00) ⊗No

FOOD

Tea

⑩⑤ The Tea House — 36-2A

15 Neal St. WC2
☎020-7240-7539 ⒻJ020-7836-4769
⊖Covent Garden
10.00-19.00(Sun 12.00-18.00) ⊗No
visa M/C AMEX JCB

A shop devoted to tea, infusions and connected items: caddies, sieves, mugs, tea cosies, books, tea gifts and a wide selection of plain English and novelty teapots. Over 100 blends of tea stocked. Mail order available.

Chocolate

⑩⑥ A La Reine Astrid — 30-2B

27 Burlington Arcade W1
☎020-7499-8558 Ⓕ020-7499-6393
Ⓗwww.alareineastrid.com
⊖Piccadilly Circus
10.00-18.00 ⊗Sun
visa M/C AMEX

The finest French chocolates created in Paris in 1935. Chocolate lovers can gather around a central table in an art deco atomosphere, and feast their eyes on delicious praline, ganaches, fresh cream truffle, marrons glacés, & marzipan. The staff are connoisseurs.

⑩⑦ Prestat — 31-2A

14 Princes Arcade SW1
☎020-7629-4838 Ⓕ020-7399-9977
Ⓔsales@prestat.co.uk
Ⓗwww.prestat.co.uk
⊖Piccadilly Circus
9.30-18.00 (Sat 10.00-17.30) ⊗Sun
visa M/C AMEX

By Royal Appointment to The Queen and The Queen Mother, the 100 year old shop specialises in the finest handmade English chocolates since 1902. Famous for its beautiful Jewel Box packaging which make perfect gifts.

Gourmet food

⑩⑧ Harvey Nichols Foodmarket — 47-1B

Harvey Nichols, 109/125 Knightsbridge SW1
☎020-7201-8538 Ⓕ020-7235-5020
Ⓔfoodmarket@harveynichols.co.uk
⊖Knightsbridge
10.00 (Sun 12.00)-20.00 (Sat 19.00, Sun 18.00) ⊗No
visa M/C AMEX D JCB

Contemporary foodmarket situated on the fifth floor of Harvey Nichols department store, offering exclusive products from all over the world. Also situated on the fifth floor are the restaurant, bar and café.

FOOD 131

The Tea House →See p130   36-2A
15 Neal St. WC2 ⊖Covent Garden ☎020-7240-7539 Ⓕ020-7836-4769 ◎10.00-19.00(Sun 12.00-18.00) ⊗No

H. R. Higgins   27-1A
79 Duke St. W1 ⊖Bond Street ☎020-7629-3913 ◎8.45-17.30(Thur, Fri 18.00, Sat 10.00-17.00) ⊗Sun

A La Reine Astrid →See p130   30-2B
27 Burlington Arcade W1 ⊖Piccadilly Circus ☎020-7499-8558 Ⓕ020-7499-6393 ◎10.00-18.00 ⊗Sun

Prestat →See p130   31-2A
14 Princes Arcade SW1 ⊖Piccadilly Circus ☎020-7629-4838 Ⓕ020-7399-9977 ◎9.30-18.00 (Sat.10.00-17.30) ⊗Sun

Berry Bros. & Rudd   28-2B
3 St James's St. SW1 ⊖Green Park ☎020-7396-9600 Ⓕ020-7396-9611 ◎9.00-17.30(Sat 10.00-16.00) ⊗Sun

Roberson   44-2A
348 Kensington High St. W14 ⊖Olympia ☎020-7371-2121 Ⓕ020-7371-4010 ◎10.00-20.00 ⊗Sun

The Vintage House   35-2B
42 Old Compton St. W1 ⊖Leicester Square ☎020-7437-2592 ◎9.30-23.00(Sat 22.00, Sun 12.00-14.00, 19.00-22.00) ⊗No

Neal's Yard Dairy   36-1A
17 Shorts Gdns. WC2 ⊖Covent Garden ☎020-7379-7646 ◎9.00-19.00 (Sun 10.00-17.00) ⊗No

Paxton & Whitfield   31-2A
93 Jermyn St. SW1 ⊖Piccadilly Circus ☎020-7930-0259 Ⓕ020-7321-0621 ◎9.30-18.00(Sat 9.00-17.30) ⊗Sun

Caviar House   30-2B
161 Piccadilly W1 ⊖Green Park ☎020-7409-0445 Ⓕ020-7493-1667 ◎10.00-22.00 ⊗Sun

Bluebird   52-2A
The King's Rd. Gastrodome, 350 King's Rd. SW3 ⊖Sloane Square ☎020-7559-1000 Ⓕ020-7559-1111 ◎9.00-20.00(Thur-Sat 21.00, Sun 12.00-18.00) ⊗No

Fortnum & Mason   21-2A
181 Piccadilly W1 ⊖Piccadilly Circus/Green Park ☎020-7734-8040 Ⓕ020-7437-3278 ◎9.30-18.00 ⊗Sun

Harvey Nichols Foodmarket →See p130   47-1B
Harvey Nichols, 109/125 Knightsbridge SW1 ⊖Knightsbridge ☎020-7201-8538 Ⓕ020-7235-5020 ◎10.00(Sun 12.00)-20.00(Sat 19.00, Sun 18.00) ⊗No

うまい! キリン
KIRIN BEER

Kirin started to produce beer in Britain some eight years ago. The company won the Monde Selection Gold Medal for seven consecutive years, and Kirin continues to pursue its high standards globally.

1994~2000 Consecutive 7years
Monde Selection
Gold Prize Winner
金賞受賞

変わらぬうまさ
キリンビール

KIRIN

KIRIN EUROPE GmbH
Louise Dumont Strasse31
D-40211 Düsseldorf, Germany
Tel:+49-(0)211-353-086
Fax:+49-(0)211-363-996

London Theatre and Musicals

If you can't see everything at least catch one of these:
Art, Buddy, Cats, Chicago, Les Misérables,
The Phantom of the Opera, Starlight Express,
Whistle Down the Wind.

134 MUSICALS & PLAYS

⑩⁹ Buddy 37-2A

Strand Theatre, Aldwych WC2
☎ 020-7930-8800
⊖ Covent Garden
20.00(Fri, Sat 20.30), Matinée 17.30(Fri), 17.00(Sat), 16.00(Sun) ⊗ Sun(Mar-Sep), Mon

Recounts the Buddy Holly story from his early days with the Crickets to the rise of a rock legend and the fateful plane journey. Featuring Buddy's memorable numbers Peggy Sue and That'll be the Day.

⑪⁰ Cats 36-1B

New London Theatre, Drury Lane WC2
☎ 020-7405-0072
⊖ Holborn/Covent Garden
19.45, Matinée 15.00(Tue, Sat) ⊗ Sun

Based on T.S.Eliots Old Possum's Book of practical Cats. The audience gets to meet star cats with larger than life personalities. The show includes music chart hit Memories.

⑪¹ Chicago 36-2B

Adelphi Theatre, Strand WC2
☎ 020-7344-0055
⊖ Charing Cross
20.00(Fri 20.30), Matinée 17.00 (Fri), 15.00(Sat) ⊗ Sun

Raunchy kiss-and-tell tale set in a women's jail, as the inmates bid for press attention, fame, fortune and freedom. High energy choreography and riveting drama.

⑪² Les Misérables 35-2B

Palace Theatre, Shaftesbury Av. W1
☎ 020-7434-0909
⊖ Leicester Square
19.30, Matinée 14.30(Thur, Sat) ⊗ Sun

Jean Valjean, having been given a second chance in life, meets with wealth and success. However once his past catches up with him he lives on the run, while trying to keep a promise he made to a dying woman.

MUSICALS & PLAYS | 135

Adelphi Theatre → See p134 — 36-2B
Strand WC2 ⊖ Charing Cross ☎ 020-7344-0055

Albery Theatre — 36-2A
St Martin's Lane WC2 ⊖ Leicester Square ☎ 020-7369-1730

Aldwych Theatre → See p136 — 37-2A
Aldwych WC2 ⊖ Covent Garden/Holborn ☎ 020-7416-6003

Apollo Victoria Theatre → See p136 — 49-2A
17 Wilton Rd. SW1 ⊖ Victoria ☎ 020-7416-6041

Cambridge Theatre — 36-2A
Earlham St. London WC2 ⊖ Covent Garden ☎ 020-7494-5080

Criterion Theatre — 31-2B
Piccadilly Circus W1 ⊖ Piccadilly Circus ☎ 020-7369-1747

Gielgud Theatre — 29-1A
Shaftesbury Av. W1 ⊖ Piccadilly Circus ☎ 020-7494-5065

Her Majesty's Theatre → See p136 — 29-2B
Haymarket SW1 ⊖ Piccadilly Circus ☎ 020-7494-5400

London Palladium — 34-2A
Argyll St. W1 ⊖ Oxford Circus ☎ 020-7494-5020

Lyric Theatre — 29-1A
Shaftesbury Av. W1 ⊖ Piccadilly Circus ☎ 020-7494 5045

New London Theatre → See p134 — 36-1B
Drury Lane WC2 ⊖ Holborn/Covent Garden ☎ 020-7405-0072

Old Vic Theatre — 51-2B
Waterloo Rd. SE1 ⊖ Waterloo ☎ 020-7369-1762

Palace Theatre → See p134 — 35-2B
Shaftesbury Av. W1 ⊖ Leicester Square ☎ 020-7434-0909

136 MUSICALS & PLAYS

⑬ The Phantom of the Opera 29-2B

Her Majesty's Theatre, Haymarket SW1
☎ 020-7494-5400/5000
⊖ Piccadilly Circus
19.45, Matinée 15.00(Wed, Sat) ⊗ Sun
VISA M/C AMEX

Based on a book, with the same title, about the mysterious events that occurred in the Paris Opera house in 1881.

⑭ Starlight Express 49-2A

Apollo Victoria Theatre, Wilton Rd. SW1
☎ 020-7416-6041
⊖ Victoria
19.45, Matinée 15.00(Tue, Sat) ⊗ Sun
VISA M/C AMEX HD JCB

Once the World Championship Railraod Race gets underway, so does this high speed, action packed musical with a touch of romance. An energetic piece of live theatre.

⑮ Whistle Down the Wind 37-2A

Aldwych Theatre, Aldwych WC2
☎ 020-7416-6003
⊖ Holborn/Covent Garden
19.45, Matinée 15.00(Thur, Sat) ⊗ Sun
VISA M/C AMEX HD JCB

Three children help a stranger hide in a barn, convinced he is Jesus Christ. Meanwhile, a mob of locals is hunting an escaped convict. Catchy, emotional tunes from Andrew Lloyd Webber.

⑯ Art 36-2A

Wyndhams Theatre, Charing Cross Rd. WC2
☎ 020-7369-1736
⊖ Leicester Square
20.00(Ex. Sun), Matinée 15.00(Wed), 17.00(Sat, Sun) ⊗ Mon
VISA M/C AMEX

When one friend buys a controversial modern painting - an entirely white canvas - it forces three long-time male friends to reassess their relationships and their values. There's plenty of humour to balance with the play's intensity.

MUSICALS & PLAYS | 137

Phoenix Theatre — 35-2B
Charing Cross Rd. London WC2 ↔ Charing Cross ☎ 020-7369-1733

Playhouse Theatre — 50-1B
Northumberland Av. WC2 ↔ Embankment ☎ 020-7369-1721

Prince Edward Theatre — 35-2B
Old Compton St. W1 ↔ Leicester Square ☎ 020-7447-5400

Prince of Wales Theatre — 29-1B
Coventry St. W1 ↔ Piccadilly Circus ☎ 020-7839-5972/5987

Royal National Theatre — 51-1A
South Bank SE1 ↔ Waterlooo/Embankment ☎ 020-7452-3000

St Martin's Theatre — 36-2A
West St. WC2 ↔ Leicester Square ☎ 020-7836-1443

Savoy Theatre — 36-2B
Savoy Court, Strand WC2 ↔ Charing Cross ☎ 020-7836-8888

Shakespeare's Globe Theatre — 25-2A
New Globe Walk SE1 ↔ Southwark ☎ 020-7401-9919

Strand Theatre → See p134 — 37-2A
Aldwych WC2 ↔ Charing Cross ☎ 020-7930-8800

Theatre Royal Drury Lane — 36-2B
Catherine St. W1 ↔ Covent Garden/Aldwych ☎ 020-7494-5000

Theatre Royal Haymarket — 29-2B
Haymarket SW1 ↔ Piccadilly Circus ☎ 020-7930-8800

Victoria Palace Theatre — 49-2A
Victoria St. SW1 ↔ Victoria ☎ 020-7834-1317

Wyndhams Theatre → See p136 — 36-2A
Charing Cross Rd. WC2 ↔ Leicester Square ☎ 020-7369-1736

日本の古美術

M.C.N. ANTIQUES (UMEZAWA)

Japanese Porcelain & Works of Art

183, Westbourne Grove, London W11 2SB
Tel: 020-7727-3796 Fax: 020-7229-8839
OPEN 9:30~5:30 (Sat 11:00~3:00)

London
Theatre and Musical Synopses

West End Theatre and
Musicals: the backgrounds & story lines.

140 BUDDY

Written by Alan Janes

Background

Brothers Laurie and Max Mansfield began researching the Buddy Holly story during a competition over who had the greater musical knowledge - and found themselves with all the material for a great stage musical. Over 400 actors auditioned for the part of Buddy, the charismatic young rock 'n' roll star who took 1950s America by storm. The fatal plane crash in 1959 cut short a career that had barely begun, but his songs have survived the generations. *Buddy* the musical looks like doing the same.

Synopsis

An unashamedly nostalgic celebration of the the 50s and its music, *Buddy* charts the brief, but sparkling career of the writer of some of rock 'n' roll's most memorable tunes. Born into a musical family in 1936, Buddy formed his first band with schoolfriend Bob Montgomery. They were influenced by Country & Western, but, more controversially, by Blues music - at that time considered to be solely for black musicians and audiences. Being ahead of their time meant they were subject to much prejudice, but their unique blend of musical inspiration proved a blessing when a new kind of music exploded onto the airwaves in 1954. With the birth of rock 'n' roll, the group started appearing as a support act for such famous names as Bill Haley and Elvis Presley, leading to a recording contract for Buddy. 1957 saw the formation of Buddy's new group, The Crickets, whose first single reached No.3 in America and No.1 in Britain. Success led to success for Buddy, and he began touring with artists including Jerry Lee Lewis and Chuck Berry. By August 1958, Buddy and the Crickets had sold more than 10 million records. The story follows Buddy's musical development from struggling schoolboy to superstar and we are treated to hit after hit delivered with tremendous energy and style. From his early material to the best known classics we are led through Buddy's whole repertoire building up to his last tour in 1959. The concert in Iowa marks the finale of the programme. On the same bill were Richie Valens and 'The Big Bopper', both major stars in their own right and, despite the bad weather, they decided to fly together to the next performance. The wreckage of the plane was found the next day. For many, Don Maclean's epitaph is the most fitting - it was 'the day the music died'.

Strand Theatre
Aldwych WC2
☎ 020-7930-8800

37-2A

CATS

Music by Andrew Lloyd Webber
Based on Old Possum's Book of Practical Cats by T.S. Eliot

Background

Known as 'Old Possum' to his godchildren, T.S. Eliot, the Nobel Prize winner and poet, wrote a series of children's verses describing the extraordinary characters and fantastical lives of a group of cats living in London, which were published in 1939. In 1977, Andrew Lloyd Webber, who had loved the poems' lyrical rhythms as a child, decided to set them to music. Originally conceived of as an anthology of songs, the project really took off when a fragment of an unpublished poem, Grizabella the Glamour Cat, was discovered. Although the story is full of humour, it is this sad tale which gives the whole collection of poems the narrative structure and thematic coherence necessary for a full-scale musical. First performed in 1981, *Cats* is now the longest running musical in British theatre history.

Synopsis

It is the night on which the Jellicle cats gather round the rubbish tip for the Jellicle Ball where one of their number will be chosen to go up to the Heaviside Layer - the cats' way of explaining dying and going to heaven. The selection process forms the focus around which the story and the personalities of the different cats unfold. From the madcap adventures of Mungojerrie and Rumpleteazer, to the thespian triumphs of Gus the theatre cat, we glimpse their relationships, their past histories and the follies and vanities which make them individuals with all-too human failings. While we laugh with the cats at the ridiculous behaviour of dogs in the Awful Battle of the Pekes and the Pollicles, and at the crazy antics of the cats themselves, we feel sadness and pity for Grizabella, the heroine, a faded shadow of a once beautiful creature who is rejected by the others. It is her character that is most human and which serves to remind us of the tragic purpose of the Jellicle Ball, but which also serves to underline the energy and vitality of the other parts. Long before the end of the evening we know who is to be chosen, adding poignancy to the final scenes. The overall impression is not one of sadness, however. Through the voices of these characters emerges a picture of a world with the same mixture of tragedy and comedy, clowns and criminals as our own.

CATS

New London Theatre
Drury Lane WC2
☎ 020-7405-0072

142 CHICAGO

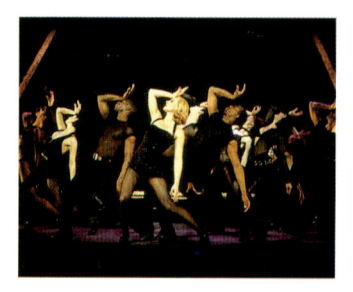

Music by John Kander
Lyrics by Fred Ebb
Book by Fred Ebb and Bob Fosse
Based on the play by Maurine Dallas Watkins

Background

First filmed in 1927 as *Chicago*, then in 1942 as *Roxie Hart* with Ginger Rogers in the title role, the story made it to Broadway in 1975 with a brand new character: Velma. The West End production bursts with the jazzy explosive energy of Fosse's original choreography and a minimal set that defies time and place. A first class entertainment for grown-ups.

Synopsis

The narrative opens at Cook County Jail, where vaudevillian Velma Kelly is serving time for killing her adulterous husband and her sister, who was also her performance partner. Velma tells the story of another broad, Roxie Hart, who murdered her lover Fred Casely after an argument but convinced her gullible husband Amos that the victim was a burglar. The Jail is home to all manners of murderesses accused of crimes of passion. Wearing little more than black fishnet tights and slinky lace bodies, they dazzle with glamour and tartiness. Amongst them, Matron 'Mama' calls the shots and caters for their every whim— for a price. Thanks to Mama, Velma's story has made it into the headlines, and she is basking in the glory of her new-found fame. Her lawyer, flamboyant Billy Flynn, demands US$5,000 to take on Roxie's case. A skilful media manipulator, he rearranges Roxie's story for tabloid columnist Mary Sunshine. The press conference scene with Roxie seated on Billy's lap as a ventriloquist's dummy, mechanically mouthing his words, is original to the West End show and one of its most searing comments on the modern judicial system. With her limelight and lawyer stolen by Roxie, Velma tries to coax her rival into partnership in her old Sister Act. Roxie turns her down. Yet this is Chicago, and celebrity is short-lived – another murderess soon becomes the pet of the media and gains Billy's attention. Hungry for publicity, Roxie contrives a false pregnancy. The date is set for Roxie's trial, at which Billy will exude his razzle-dazzle showmanship and reduce the jury to tears with a new version of the truth. Just as Roxie is about to walk free and into stardom, another sordid crime is committed wiping Roxie's tale into oblivion. Finally Roxie takes up Velma's offer of a vaudeville show. Joined by the whole company, they lament the transient nature of fame and decide to celebrate today while it lasts.

CHICAGO

Adelphi Theatre
Strand WC2
☎ 020-7344-0055

36-2B

LES MISERABLES 143

Written by Alain Boublil & Claude-Michel Schönberg
Music by Claude-Michel Schönberg
Lyrics by Herbert Kretzmer
Based on the novel by Victor Hugo

Background

In his epic novel, Victor Hugo describes the appalling living conditions of *Les Misérables*: the neglected and the poor of 19th century France. With wages below subsistence levels, people were reduced to crime in order to survive. Brought together by desperation, workers' demands for social reform spilled over into violent protest and revolution in the 1830s causing the government to side with the manufacturers in brutally crushing the uprising. While every Frenchman may know Hugo's dramatic novel by heart, musical theatre does not have a strong tradition in France. The current production, however, was originally staged in Paris in 1980 and came to London in 1985.

Synopsis

In 1815, after 19 years in prison, Jean Valjean is released on parole. However, branded as a criminal by his papers, he is treated as an outcast and is unable to find work. Helped by the Bishop of Digne, however, he repays him by stealing. Valjean is captured, but the Bishop lies to save him and Valjean, touched by his kindness, decides to escape from his past by adopting a new identity. Unfortunately, this means breaking his parole and brings Inspector Javert, the policeman who released him from prison, onto his trail again. Eight years later, Valjean has become a factory owner and mayor. One of his employees, Fantine, is thrown out of his factory when it is discovered that she has an illegitimate child, Cosette. To survive, she becomes a whore and, after a violent argument, is flung into prison. Valjean intervenes and orders her to be taken to hospital where he learns from the dying Fantine of her daughter, whom he promises to look after. In 1832 the streets of Paris are in revolutionary turmoil and Valjean and Cosette are attacked by a gang but saved by Inspector Javert, who is still chasing Valjean. Realising that Cosette is in love with one of the students who are manning the barricades, Valjean postpones his escape and becomes embroiled in the fighting. The revolutionaries are overrun, but Valjean manages to save Cosette and her lover and flee Paris. An escaped convict, however, he realises that he is endangering their happiness and that he must leave them, only to be reunited in his final hour.

Les Misérables

The Palace Theatre
Shaftesbury Av. W1
☎ 020-7434-0909

35-2B

144 THE PHANTOM OF THE OPERA

Music by Andrew Lloyd Webber
Lyrics by Charles Hart
Additional lyrics by Richard Stilgoe
Based on the novel Le Fantôme de l'Opéra by Gaston Leroux

Background

The Paris Opera House, with its underground lake and labyrinthine passageways, was the scene of real-life intrigue during the 19th century as jealous rivals fought for theatrical fame. Despite its historical accuracy, however, *The Phantom of the Opera* was not the most successful of Leroux's many books. In fact, the story of the Phantom owes much of its popularity to the decision by Universal Studios to use it as the basis of a film.

Synopsis

Romance and horror are equally mixed in this story of a tragic love triangle between Raoul, Comte de Chagny, Christine, a chorus girl, and the Phantom. It is 1911 and, at an auction at the Paris Opera House, Raoul notices that one of the items on sale is a broken chandelier. This triggers his memory, and we are taken back to the past where we relive with Raoul the unsolved mystery of the Phantom of the Opera: rehearsals of *Hannibal* in 1881 have been plagued by strange happenings causing Carlotta, the prima donna, to walk out. Her place is given to Christine who has been taking singing lessons from an unknown teacher. Raoul, her childhood sweetheart is mesmerised by her performance and, backstage, declares his love for her. Christine, however, is not free. Much as she loves Raoul, she is bound to her mysterious singing master whom she believes is the protective Angel of Music, promised by her dying father. In love with her, this ghostly figure warns the theatre owners that disaster will follow if she is not given the main role in the next opera. Rejected by Christine, who declares her love for Raoul, and ignored by the owners, the Phantom brings down a chandelier in mid-performance and lets loose a torrent of jealous rage. Nor is this the end of his intervention. In Act Two, he presents the theatre with an opera he has written which he insists must be performed with Christine in the lead. The theatre accepts, hoping to trap the Phantom, but he escapes, dragging Christine down into the dark labyrinth under the opera house which is his home. When Raoul discovers them, the Phantom, in despair, forces her to chose between the two men who love her and his tragic fate is sealed.

29-2B

The Phantom of the OPERA

Her Majesty's Theatre
Haymarket SW1
☎ 020-7494-5400/5000

ART 145

Play by Yasmina Reza
Translated by Christopher Hampton

Background

Yasmina Reza's play first hit the canvas in Paris in the mid '90s at the Comedie des Champs-Elysees. It has since been translated into 35 languages, and its raging success has seen it performed all over the globe. Christopher Hampton was the perfect choice as translator, with his own enviable list of writing credits for both theatre and film, and a penchant for triangular relationships. Hampton's own acute human observations and quick wit marry well with Yasmina Reza's incisive writing style. The close relationship between writer, translator and the director of the original West End production, Matthew Warchus, has imbued the play with vibrancy and cohesion, and successive casts have drawn on this great energy. The play has received both the Olivier Award and the London Evening Standard Award for Best Comedy.

Synopsis

When Serge buys an expensive example of modern art, he soon realises that he has not simply made an investment or chosen a feature to decorate his home. What he has done, is sparked off the re-evaluation of his two closest friendships. The white painting, apparently white lines on a white canvas, sets Serge back some 200,000 francs. Serge's friend, Marc dismisses the purchase as wholly ridiculous. Yvan takes the diplomatic line of being open-minded in his judgement of the painting whilst attempting to appease Marc. Things are brought to a head on the evening the three plan to have dinner. Yvan, soon to be married, arrives late to find that the other two are more than disgruntled. He pours out his family problems in a hilarious speech about whose names should be included on the wedding invitations, forcing Marc and Serge to pause in their own complaints. Marc and Serge soon begin using Yvan as their own whipping boy and blame him for creating "conditions of conflict" in his own life and theirs. Insults abound until Serge calls upon Yvan for a marker pen, hands it to Marc inviting him to draw on the painting. He does.

The play puts the nature of modern male friendship under scrutiny, probing at what their friendships now consist of, looking at their individual places in the worlds of work, love, marriage and modern expectation. At the same time it provides a very witty take on 'What is modern art ?' and with the proliferation of artists like Damien Hirst and Tracey Emin, it is a refreshingly honest and unpretentious questioning of art and how much to pay for it. Perhaps it is worth remembering that entrance to the Tate Modern, is free.

ART

36-2A

Wyndhams Theatre
Charing Cross Rd. WC2
☎ 020-7369-1736

Need to email home...?

we NEVER close

When in London contact friends and family instantly by emailing them from the world's largest Internet cafes.

High speed Internet access 24 hours a day, every day, from just **£1**

Tottenham Court Road - Tube Exit 2
Oxford Street - Opposite Bond Street Tube
Trafalgar Square - Opposite Charing X Station
Kensington High Street - Exit Tube, turn left
Victoria - Opposite BR Main Line Station

easyEverything
the world's largest Internet cafés

Open NOW in: Edinburgh . Amsterdam . Rotterdam . Barcelona
Antwerp . Madrid . Munich . Berlin . Brussels . Glasgow . Rom

London's Arts & Places of Interest

Galleries, Museums & Palaces.
From Science to Sherlock Holmes.
Historic Houses to Modern Design.

THE BANQUETING HOUSE

Whitehall, London SW1A 2ER

For a truly prestigious occasion why not suggest the unique setting of the Royal Palace.

The Banqueting House, in Whitehall, is centrally located and so convenient for both City and the West End.

This flexible venue can accommodate anything from 375 for dinner, up to 400 for a concert, and 500 for a reception.

For further information telephone Fiona Thompson on 020-7839-7569.

PLACES OF INTEREST 149

① Bank of England　　　　　　　　　　40-2A

Threadneedle St. London EC2 ⊖ Bank ☎ 020-7601-5545 Museum: ◎ 10.00-17.00 ⊗ Sat, Sun ⓔ Free

The Bank of England has been at the backbone of the British economy since 1694, when it was set up to raise funds for foreign wars. Its work is explained in an excellent museum which has a high-tech display of the world's money markets.

② Banqueting House　　　　　　　　　　50-1B

Whitehall, London SW1 ⊖ Waterloo / Charing Cross / Embankment ☎ 020-7930-4179 ⓗ www.hrp.org.uk ◎ 10.00-17.00 ⊗ Sun ⓔ 3.80(2.30)

Built by Inigo Jones in 1622, it is a perfect example of Palladian architecture. The ceiling, by Rubens, was commissioned by Charles I who was executed outside this building in 1649.

③ British Airways London Eye　　　　　51-1A

Belvedere Rd. London SE1 ⊖ Waterloo / Embankment ☎ 0870-5000600 ⓗ www.ba-londoneye.com ◎ 9.00-22.00(Sep-Mar:10.00-18.00) ⊗ Sun ⓔ 8.50 (5.00)

The world's tallest observation wheel, located in the heart of London. Each enclosed cabin takes 30 minutes to make a complete revolution, with a commentary on the spectacular 25-mile views.

④ Buckingham Palace　　　　　　　　　49-1A

St James's Pk. London SW1 ⊖ Green Park ☎ 020-7930-4832 ⓗ www.royalresidences.com State Rooms: ◎ Aug-Oct: 9.30-16.30(Might vary) ⊗ No ⓔ 10.00

Chosen by Queen Victoria in 1837 as the official home of the monarchy, the palace was built in 1705 for the Duke of Buckingham. Call for the time of the Changing of the Guard.

⑤ Carlyle's House　　　　　　　　　　　52-2B

24 Cheyne Row, London SW3 ⊖ Sloane Square ☎ 020-7352-7007 / 01494-755559 ◎ Apr-Oct: 11.00-17.00 ⊗ Mon, Tue ⓔ 3.50(1.75)

The home of the eminent 19th century historian and polemicist Thomas Carlyle has been preserved just as it was when he died in 1881. The drawing room hosted his many eminent literary visitors.

⑥ Covent Garden　　　　　　　　　　　36-2B

The Piazza, London WC2 ⊖ COVENT GARDEN ☎ 020-7836-9136 ◎ Shopping 10.30-19.00 ⊗ No

In the 1530s this was the vegetable garden of Westminster Abbey; now the 1831 covered market houses jewellery stalls and designer boutiques, string quartets and a mechanical theatre, while cafés and street entertainers fill the Piazza.

150 PLACES OF INTEREST

⑦ Cutty Sark 23-2A

King William Walk, London SE10 ⊖ *Cutty Sark / Greenwich*
☎ 020-8858-3445 ⓗ www.cuttysark.org.com ⓒ 10.00-17.00 ⓧ No ⓔ 3.50(2.50)

A survivor from the majestic days of sailing ships, this tea clipper won the annual race from China to London in 1871. Exhibits detail life at sea in the 19th century and British Pacific trade.

⑧ The Dickens House 24-1B

48 Doughty St. London WC1 ⊖ *Russell Square*
☎ 020-7405-2127 ⓗ www.dickensmuseum.com ⓒ 10.00-17.00 ⓧ Sun ⓔ 4.00(2.00)

Between 1837 & 39 Dickens wrote his most popular works at this address. The house looks as it would have in Dickens' time, with first editions of his works and his personal reading copies on display.

⑨ Dr Johnson's House 38-2A

17 Gough Sq. London EC4 ⊖ *Chancery Lane / Blackfriars* ☎ 020-7353-3745 ⓒ 11.00-17.30 (Oct-Apr: 17.00) ⓧ Sun ⓔ 4.00(1.00)

Dr Johnson, 18th century scholar and wit, compiled the first dictionary in the attic of this house. The restored building contains a collection of furniture and paintings connected with the great man.

⑩ Guildhall 40-2A

Gresham St. London EC2 ⊖ *Bank / St Paul's*
☎ 020-7606-3030 ⓒ 9.00-17.00 ⓧ Sun(Oct-Apr)

Built in 1441, it has since acted continuously as the administrative centre of the City. For many centuries the hall functioned as a court and many people were condemned to death here. Now it is where the Lord Mayor is appointed and installed.

⑪ Hampton Court Palace 22-2B

East Molesey, Surrey KT8 ⇌ *Hampton Court*
☎ 020-8781-9500 ⓗ www.hrp.org.uk ⓒ 9.30(Mon 10.15)-18.00(Nov-Apr: 16.30) ⓧ No ⓔ 10.50(7.00 Under 5yrs Free)

This magnificent Tudor palace was taken from Cardinal Wolsey by Henry VIII. Full of superb paintings and decorations, the complex is set in an ornamental park with a famous 18th century maze.

⑫ HMS Belfast 43-2A

Morgan's Lane, London SE1 ⊖ *London Bridge*
☎ 020-7940-6300 ⓗ www.hmsbelfast.org.uk ⓒ 10.00-18.00(Nov-Feb:17.00) ⓧ No ⓔ 5.00(Under 16yrs Free)

Rescued from the scrapyard in 1971, this WWII warship is the largest surviving from the period. Displays portray life on board during the war and general Royal Navy history.

PLACES OF INTEREST 151

⑬ Houses of Parliament & Big Ben 50-2B

Palace of Westminster, London SW1 ↔ *Westminster* ☎ *020-7219-4272 (Reservation necessary for tours)* ⓗ *www.parliament.uk* ⓒ *14.30-22.30 (Mon-Wed), 11.30-19.30 (Thur), 9.30-15.00 (Fri)* ⓧ *Sat, Sun*

Edward the Confessor's palace became the seat of English administrative power in the 13th century. Of the original, only Westminster Hall remains.

⑭ Kensington Palace 45-1A

Kensington Gardens, London W8 ↔ *High Street Kensington / Queens way* ☎ *020-7937-9561* ⓗ *www.hrp.org.uk* ⓒ *10.00-17.00 (16.00 Oct-Mar)* ⓧ *No* ⓔ *8.50 (6.10)*

Converted into a royal palace by Christopher Wren in 1689 and more recently home of Diana, Princess of Wales. Highlights of the royal apartments are portraits, sculpture and a collection of royal clothing.

⑮ London Aquarium 51-2A

County Hall, Riverside Bldg. Westminster Bridge Rd. London SE1 ↔ *Wwaterloo / Westminster* ☎ *020-7967-8000* ⓗ *www.londonaquarium.co.uk* ⓒ *10.00-18.00* ⓧ *No* ⓔ *8.00 (5.00)*

Europe's largest aquarium is set in London's former County Hall. The Edwardian building is now home to sharks, piranhas, seahorses and friendly rays which can be stroked.

⑯ London Zoo 24-1B

Regent's Pk. London NW1 ↔ *Camden Town* ☎ *020-7722-3333* ⓗ *www.londonzoo.co.uk* ⓒ *10.00-17.30 (Nov-Mar: 16.00)* ⓧ *No* ⓔ *9.00 (7.00)*

The zoo now concentrates on conservation, education and the breeding of endangered species. Architectural highlights include a Brutalist Rhino Pavilion and the Modernist Penguin Pool.

⑰ Madame Tussaud's 32-1B

Marylebone Rd. London NW1 ↔ *Baker Street* ☎ *0870-400-3000* ⓗ *www.madame-tussauds.com* ⓒ *10.00 (Sat, Sun 9.30, Jun-Arg 9.00-17.30)-17.30* ⓧ *No* ⓔ *11.50 (8.00)*

Mme Tussaud modelled royal death masks during the French Revolution. Now current celebrities mix with historical figures. Includes popular Chamber of Horrors. Planetarium extra charge.

⑱ Mansion House 42-1A

Mansion House, London EC4 ↔ *Bank* ☎ *020-7626-2500*

The Lord Mayor's official residence is open only to groups of 15-40 people, booked a month in advance. The mid-18th century Palladian façade is by George Dance and the most splendid of the state rooms is the stunning Egyptian Hall.

PLACES OF INTEREST

⑲ The Monument
42-1B

Monument St. London EC3 ⊖ Monument ☎ 020-7626-2717 ◎ 10.00-17.40 ⊗ No ⓔ 1.50(0.50)

Designed by Wren to commemorate the Great Fire of 1666 which destroyed much of the City. It is the tallest isolated stone column in the world at 62m, and there are good views from the top.

⑳ Nelson's Column
50-1A

Trafalgar Sq. London WC2 ⊖ Charing Cross

Sharing the square with thousands of pigeons, is E.H. Baily's 1843 statue of Admiral Lord Horatio Nelson, the one-armed English naval hero, who was fatally wounded at the Battle of Trafalgar against Napoleon in 1805. Fourteen people dined on the top before the statue was added.

㉑ Royal Botanical Gardens Kew
22-2B

Richmond, Surrey TW9 ⊖ Kew Gardens ☎ 020-8940-1171 ⊕ www.kew.org ◎ 9.30-18.30(Sat,Sun19.30) ⊗ No ⓔ 5.00(2.50 Under 5yrs Free)

A global botanical resource, Kew has the largest living plant collection in the world. Tropical plants are housed in architecturally fascinating glasshouses and hardy species decorate the park. Gardens were landscaped by Capability Brown.

㉒ The Royal Mews
49-1A

Buckingham Palace Rd. London SW1 ⊖ Victoria ☎ 020-7839-1377 ⊕ www.royalresidences.com ◎ 12.00-16.00(Aug-Sep:10.30-16.30) ● Mon-Thur ⓔ 4.30(2.10)

Designed by Nash in 1825, the Mews houses the magnificent royal carriages and Rolls Royces used on formal occasions. The most spectacular exhibit is the gold state coach built in 1761 for George III.

㉓ St James's Palace
49-1B

Pall Mall, London SW1 ⊖ Green Park

Standing on the site of a former leper hospital, this palace was built by Henry VIII in 1532. It was used as a royal residence by Elizabeth I, and Queen Elizabeth II gave her first speech from here. Members of the public can only view the red-brick, Tudor façade.

㉔ St Margaret's Church
50-2A

Parliament Sq. London SW1 ⊖ Westminster ☎ 020-7222-5152 ⊕ www.westminster-abbey.org ◎ 9.30-16.00 ⊗ Sun

Next to Westminster Abbey is St Margaret's, first built in the 11th century and completely rebuilt 1480-1523. The Tudor stained glass celebrates the first marriage of Catherine of Aragon, to Henry VIII's elder brother, Arthur.

PLACES OF INTEREST 153

㉕ St Paul's Cathedral 39-2A

St Paul's Churchyard, London EC4 ⊖ St Paul's ☎ 020-7246-8348 ⓗ www.stpauls.co.uk ◎ 8.30-16.30 ⊗ Sun ⓔ 5.00(2.50)

Christopher Wren's masterpiece replaced the old medieval cathedral burnt down in the Great Fire. High Renaissance in design, it has the world's third largest dome. It was completed in 1708.

㉖ Tower Bridge 43-2B

Tower Bridge, London SE1 ⊖ Tower Hill ☎ 020-7403-3761 ⓗ www.towerbridge.org.uk ◎ 10.00-18.00(Nov-Mar: 9.30-18.00) ⊗ No ⓔ 6.25(4.25)

Built in 1894 in Gothic style to complement its neighbour, the Tower of London. The museum inside houses the original Victorian steam engines which raised and lowered the bridge.

㉗ The Tower of London 43-2B

Tower Hill, London EC3 ⊖ Tower Hill ☎ 020-7709-0765 ◎ 9.00(Sun 10.00)-17.00(Nov-Feb: 9.00(Sun, Mon 10.00)-16.00) ⊗ No ⓔ 11.00(7.30)

At one time a palace, gaol, torture and execution place. The Crown Jewels, housed here, form the most valuable and beautiful collection of gemstones anywhere in the world.

㉘ Westminster Abbey 50-2A

Broad Sanctuary, London SW1 ⊖ WESTMINSTER ☎ 020-7222-5152 ⓗ www.westminster-abbey.org ◎ 9.00-16.45(Sat 9.00-14.45) ⊗ Sun ⓔ 5.00 (2.00)

Built in 1050 it is the setting for coronations and the final resting place of monarchs, public figures and famous poets.

㉙ Westminster Cathedral 49-2A

Victoria St. London SW1 ⊖ Victoria ☎ 020-7798-9055 ⓗ www.westminstercathedral.org.uk ◎ 7.00(Sat 8.00)-19.00(Sun 19.45) ⊗ No ⓔ Free

This stunningly rich, Italianate Catholic cathedral was begun in 1895 by John Francis Bentley but remains unfinished. Inside, sculptor Eric Gill's 14 Stations of the Cross decorate the nave's piers. The main attraction for most is the campanile.

㉚ Whitehall 50-1A

Whitehall, London SW1 ⊖ Charing Cross

This street is at the centre of British political and public life. It runs from Trafalgar Square to the Houses of Parliament and the Prime Minister lives just off it at 10 Downing Street. Other interesting sights along here are the Cenotaph, commemorating the dead of WWI, and Richmond House.

154 GALLERIES, MUSEUMS

㉛ Accadeimia Italiana 48-1B

8 Grosvenor Pl. London SW1 ⊖ Hyde Park Corner
☎ 020-7235-0303 ◎ 10.00(Sun 14.00)-18.00(Wed 20.00) ⊗ Mon ⓒ 5.00

Home of the Accademia Italiana, the Academy also promotes the visual arts from all over Europe through exhibitions, lectures and educational events.

㉜ Bethnal Green Museum of Childhood 25-1B

Cambridge Heath Rd. London E2 ⊖ Bethnal Green
☎ 020-8983-5200 ◎ 10.00-18.00 ⊗ Fri ⓒ Free

Fascinating collection from 16th century onwards. Includes dolls' houses, teddy bears, train sets and early jigsaw puzzles. Also clothing and baby equipment, with a 17th century nappy.

㉝ Bramah Tea & Coffee Museum 25-2A

The Clove Building, Maguire St. London SE1 ⊖ Tower Hill ☎ 020-7378-0222 ⓗ www.bramahmuseum.co.uk ◎ 10.00-18.00 ⊗ No ⓒ 4.00

The story of two drinks, from the coffee shops of 17th century London to the rise of tea as the British national brew. Sample the wares at the shop and cafe; book for afternoon tea seminars.

㉞ British Museum 36-1A

Great Russell St. London WC1 ⊖ Russell Square ☎ 020-7636-1555 ⓗ www.british-museum.ac.uk ◎ 10.00-17.00 (Sun 12.00-18.00) ⊗ No ⓒ Free(Special exhibition prices vary)

Founded in 1753 it is one of the world's premiere museums. The enormous range of exhibits results from the acquisitive nature of the British Empire and its once vast economic and political power.

㉟ Cabinet War Rooms 50-2A

Clive Steps, King Charles St. London SW1 ⊖ Westminster
☎ 020-7930-6961 ⓗ www.iwm.org.uk ◎ 9.30-17.15, 10.00-17.15(Oct-Mar) ⊗ No ⓒ 4.80(Under 15yrs Free)

This labyrinth of underground rooms protected the British Government during the worst bombing of WWII. The rooms are preserved exactly as they were when Churchill planned strategy here.

㊱ Design Museum 25-2A

Butlers Wharf, 28 Shad Thames, London SE1 ⊖ Tower Hill ☎ 020-7403-6933 ⓗ www.designmuseum.org
◎ 11.30-18.00 ⊗ No ⓒ 5.50(4.00)

One of London's most inspiring attractions. Capturing the excitement of design evolution and ingenuity, exhibitions encompass furniture, fashion, architecture, engineering and technology.

GALLERIES, MUSEUMS 155

㊲ Hayward Gallery 51-1A

South Bank Centre, Belvedere Rd. London SE1 ⊖ Waterloo / Embankment ☎ 020-7928-3144 ◎ 10.00-18.00(Tue, Wed 20.00) ⊗ No ⓒ 6.00 (4.00, Under 12yrs Free)

One of London's major art galleries. Exhibitions range from classical to modern works, but contemporary British artists are strongly represented.

㊳ Imperial War Museum 51-2B

Lambeth Rd. London SE1 ⊖ Lambeth North ☎ 020-7416-5000 ⊕ www. iwm.org.uk ◎ 10.00-18.00 ⊗ No ⓒ 5.50(Under 16yrs Free), After 16.30 Free

Interactive exhibits and modern techniques bring 20th century warfare alive. Not only tanks, planes and military equipment, but poetry, art and documentary film footage can be seen.

㊴ Kenwood House 24-1A

Hampstead Lane, London NW3 ⊖ Archway / Golders Green ☎ 020-8348-1286 ◎ 10.00-18.00(Nov-Mar 16.00) ⊗ No ⓒ Free(Special exhibition prices vary)

Situated on Hampstead Heath in landscaped grounds, the 17th century house was remodelled by Robert Adam. Paintings by Rembrant, Vermeer and Van Dyck. Lakeside concerts in summer.

㊵ Leighton House 44-2A

12 Holland Park Rd. London W14 ⊖ High Street Kensington ☎ 020-7602-3316 ◎ 11.00-17.30 ⊗ Tue

Built by Frederic Leighton, the Pre-Raphaelite painter favoured by Queen Victoria. Superb collection of paintings and Islamic tiles gathered on his travels. Exhibitions and concerts held in the artist's studio.

㊶ London Dungeon 42-2B

28/34 Tooley St. London SE1 ⊖ London Bridge ☎ 020-7403-7221 ⊕ www. thedungeons.com ◎ 10.00-20.00(Sep-Mar: 10.30-17.00) ⊗ No ⓒ 10.95(6.95)

One of London's most popular tourist venues, it illustrates the bloody aspects of British history. Realistic martyrdom, torture and plague scenes are punctuated by beheadings and human sacrifice.

㊷ London Transport Museum 36-2B

The Piazza, London WC2 ⊖ Covent Garden ☎ 020-7379-6344 ⊕ www. ltmuseum.co.uk ◎ 10.00(Fri 11.00)-18.00 ⊗ No ⓒ 5.50(2.95)

Children can enjoy pretending to drive an historical bus or modern tube train and adults can marvel at a transport system which carries over 6 million people a day on journeys totalling 800,000 kms.

GALLERIES, MUSEUMS

㊸ Museum of Garden History — 51-2A

Lambeth Palace Rd. London SE1 ⊖ Waterloo ☎ 020-7401-8865 ⓗ www. museumgardenhistory.org ◎ 10.30-17.00(Mid Dec-Jan: Closed) ⓧ Sat £ Free

Gardeners to Charles 1 and 11, John Tradescant and son were adventurous plant collectors; a trust in the gardeners' name set up this Museum of Garden History in 1977. It is a visionary centre for gardening lectures, exhibitions, and courses.

㊹ Museum of London — 39-1B

150 London Wall, London EC2 ⊖ Barbican / St Paul's ☎ 020-7600-3699 ⓗ www.museumoflondon. org.uk ◎ 10.00(Sun 12.00)-17.50 ⓧ No £ One year ticket 5.00 (Under 16 yrs Free), After 16.30 Free

From pre-history to the present day the museum charts the city's development. Archaeological finds used to recreate Roman London. Also good 20th century displays.

㊺ National Army Museum — 53-2B

Royal Hospital Rd. London SW3 ⊖ Sloane Square ☎ 020-7730-0717 ⓗ www.national-army-museum. ac.uk ◎ 10.00-17.30 ⓧ No £ Free

From Tudor Yeomen in 1485 to the UN peacekeeping work of today, exhibits depict life for those fighting a war. Displays chronicle famous campaigns and the development of weapons. Also on show are medals, uniforms and paintings.

㊻ National Gallery — 50-1A

Trafalgar Sq. London WC2 ⊖ Charing Cross ☎ 020-7839-3321 ⓗ www.nationalgallery.org.uk ◎ 10.00-18.00 (Wed 21.00) ⓧ No £ Free (Special exhibition prices vary)

One of the world's richest art collections. Renaissance works by Botticelli, Uccello and da Vinci; also major works by Raphael, Rembrandt and Van Dyck. Takes several days to view.

㊼ National Maritime Museum — 23-2A

Romney Rd. London SE10 ⊖ Greenwich ☎ 020-8858-4422 ⓗ www.nmm.ac.uk ◎ 10.00-17.00 ⓧ No £ 7.50(Under 16yrs Free)

Britain's seafaring heritage in beautiful Inigo Jones building. Exhibition sections on trade, the explorations of Captain Cook and a special Nelson exhibition. Includes the Royal Observatory and the Greenwich 0° Meridian Line.

㊽ National Portrait Gallery — 50-1A

St Martin's Pl. London WC2 ⊖ Charing Cross / Leicester Square ☎ 020-7306-0055 ⓗ www. npg. org.uk ◎ 10.00-18.00(Sat,Sun 21.00) ⓧ No £ Free (Special exhibition prices vary)

Britain's history through famous faces. Portraits by Holbein, Van Dyck and Rembrandt contrast with the modern work of Henry Moore.

㊾ The Natural History Museum 45-2B

Cromwell Rd. London SW7 ⊖ South Kensington ☎ 020-7938-9123 Ⓗ www.nhm.ac.uk ◎ 10.00(Sun 11.00)-17.50 ⊗ No Ⓔ 7.50(Under 16yrs Free), After 16.30(Sat,Sun 17.00) Free

A celebration of the planet's biodiversity from extinct dinosaurs to modern man. Beautifully illustrates the concepts of ecology, evolution and genetics. Educational and entrancing.

㊿ The Photographers' Gallery 36-2A

5 & 8 Great Newport St. London WC2 ⊖ Leisecter Square ☎ 020-7831-1772 Ⓗ www.Photonet.org.uk ◎ 11.00(Sun 12.00)-18.00 ⊗ No

Britain's primary venue for contemporary photography. Exhibitions change regularly. Gallery also has café, library and shop selling original prints. Occasional lectures and theatrical events.

(51) Pollock's Toy Museum 35-1A

1 Scala St. London W1 ⊖ Goodge Street ☎ 020-7636-3452 Ⓗ www.pollocks.cwc.net ◎ 10.00-17.00 ⊗ Sun Ⓔ 3.00(1.50)

Pollock was a toy-theatre-maker in the late 19th-early 20th centuries. The museum is crammed not only with his puppets and theatres but also with toys from around the world. Ideal for children.

(52) Royal Academy of Arts 30-2B

Burlington House, Piccadilly, London W1 ⊖ Piccadilly Circus / Green Park ☎ 020-7439-7438 Ⓗ www. royalacademy.org.uk ◎ 10.00-18.00 (Fri 20.30) ⊗ No Ⓔ Prices vary

A superb permanent collection and visiting exhibitions of masterpieces on loan from abroad make the RA hugely popular. Not to be missed is Michaelangelo's *Madonna and Child.*

(53) Royal Air Force Museum 22-1B

Grahame Park Way, London NW9 ⊖ Colidale ☎ 020-8205-2266 Ⓗ www.rafmuseum.org.uk ◎ 10.00-18.00 ⊗ No Ⓔ 7.00(4.50)

Aircraft from the dawn of flight to modern high-tech jets are on display. Particular emphasis is placed on the RAF's role in preserving Britain's freedom in the two world wars.

(54) Science Museum 45-2B

Exhibition Rd. London SW7 ⊖ South Kensington ☎ 020-7942-4455 Ⓗ www.sciencemuseum.org.uk ◎ 10.00-18.00 ⊗ No Ⓔ 6.50(Under 16yrs Free), After 16.30 Free

This interactive museum was intended to celebrate the machines of the industrial revolution. It now illuminates every field of scientific endeavour from food preservation to space exploration.

158 GALLERIES, MUSEUMS

⑤⑤ Serpentine Gallery　　　　　　　　　　45-1B

Kensington Gardens, London W2 ⊖ South Kensington / Lancaster Gate ☎ 020-7402-6075 ◎ 10.00-18.00 ⊗ No ⓒ Free

Avant-garde, 20th century art gallery which specializes in the provocative. Housed in an old tea pavilion, the exhibition often spills out of the building into the surrounding park.

⑤⑥ Shakespeare's Globe Exhibition　　　25-2A

New Globe Walk, London SE1 ⊖ Mansion House ☎ 020-7902-1500 ⓗ www.shakespeares-globe.org ◎ 9.00-12.00(Oct-Apr: 10.00-17.00) ⊗ No ⓒ 7.50(5.00)

Exhibition about the 29-year project to build an exact, functioning replica of Shakespeare's open-roofed theatre, using authentic materials and skills. Includes theatre tour (except during performances).

⑤⑦ The Sherlock Holmes Museum　　　　32-1A

239 Baker St. London NW1 ⊖ Baker Street ☎ 020-7935-8866 ⓗ www.sherlock-holmes.co.uk ◎ 9.30-18.00 ⊗ No ⓒ 6.00 (4.00)

This small museum, dedicated to Conan Doyle's fictional character, re-creates the Victorian rooms in which Holmes is described as living. Personal items and mementos of his famous cases line the walls.

⑤⑧ Sir John Soane's Museum　　　　　　37-1A

13 Lincoln's Inn Fields, London WC2 ⊖ Holborn ☎ 020-7405-2107 ⓗ www.soane.org ◎ 10.00-17.00,(First Tue in the month 18.00-21.00) ⊗ Mon, Sun ⓒ Free(Special exhibition prices vary)

The eclectic architect who designed the Bank of England was also a painter, sculptor and collector. His home, which he remodelled to contain his artistic treasures, is a fascinating work in itself.

⑤⑨ Tate Britain　　　　　　　　　　　　　24-2B

Millbank, London SW1 ⊖ Pimlico ☎ 020-7887-8008 ⓗ www.tate.org.uk ◎ 10.00-18.00 ⊗ No ⓒ Free(Special exhibition prices vary)

Brilliant collection of 16th to 20th century art ranging from Pre-Raphaelites to Van Gogh, Matisse and Picasso. The modern Clore Gallery houses the definitive Turner collection.

⑥⓪ Tate Modern　　　　　　　　　　　　　25-2A

Bankside, London SE1 ⊖ Blackfriars / Southwark ☎ 020-7887-8008 ⓗ www.tate.org.uk ◎ 10.00-18.00(Fri, Sat 22.00) ⊗ No ⓒ Free(Special exhibition prices vary)

Converted by architects Herzog & de Meuron, the Tate Modern displays the Tate Collection of International Modern Art from 1900 to the present day including: Matisse, Warhol, Bacon, Picasso & Rothko.

GALLERIES, MUSEUMS 159

⑥¹ Theatre Museum   36-2B

Russell St. London WC2 ⊖ Covent Garden ☎ 020-7943-4700 ⓗ theatremuseum.vam.ac.uk ◎ 10.00-18.00 ⊗ Mon ⓔ 4.50(Under 16yrs Free)

Interactive displays use models, props and costumes to portray the development of theatre since the 16th century. Children can dress up and adults can admire Mick Jagger's jump-suits.

⑥² Victoria & Albert Museum   46-2A

Cromwell Rd. London SW7 ⊖ South Kensington ☎ 020-7938-8500 ⓗ www.vam.ac.uk ◎ 10.00-17.45 ⊗ No ⓔ 5.00(Under 18yrs Free), After 16.30 Free

One of the world's greatest decorative art museums. Highlights include history of fashion, Raphael cartoons and Italian sculpture. Superb collection of works from India and the Far East.

⑥³ The Wallace Collection   33-2A

Hertford House, Manchester Sq. London W1 ⊖ Bond Street ☎ 020-7935-0687 ⓗ www.the-wallace-collection.org.uk ◎ 10.00(Sun 14.00)-17.00 ⊗ No ⓔ Free

This wonderful collection includes *The Laughing Cavalier* by Frans Hals and works by Rembrandt, Titian and Poussin. Also contains English portraits and a collection of Sèvres porcelain.

⑥⁴ Wellington Museum   48-1A

Apsley House, 149 Piccadilly, London W1 ⊖ Hyde PArk Corner ☎ 020-7499-5676 ◎ 11.00-17.00 ⊗ Mon ⓔ 4.50(Under 18yrs Free)

An intriguing glimpse into an 18th century aristocratic home, the museum houses the art collection and many of the possessions of the Duke of Wellington who defeated Napoleon in 1815.

⑥⁵ William Morris Gallery   23-1A

Lloyd Pk. Forest Rd. London E17 ⊖ Walthamstow Central ☎ 020 8527-3782 ⓗ www.lbwf.gov.uk/wmg ◎ 10.00-13.00, 14.00-17.00 ⊗ Mon, Sun (Ex. first Sun in the month) ⓔ Free

This Georgian house contains a collection of Morris' textiles, wallpaper, stained glass and poetry as well as work by his contemporaries.

⑥⁶ Wimbledon Lawn Tennis Museum   22-2B

Church Rd. London SW19 ⊖ Southfields ☎ 020-8946-6131 ◎ 10.30-17.00 ⊗ No ⓔ 5.00(4.00)

The game's development from its invention as a diversion for the rich in the 1860s to the professional sport of today is charted in paintings, ornaments and video.

New Mayflower

Chinese Restaurant

FULL LICENSED · AIR CONDITIONED
7 DAYS A WEEK   5:00 PM - 4:00 AM

68-70 SHAFTESBURY AVENUE LONDON W1
TELEPHONE : 020-7734-9207

The splendours of Chinese cuisine
by one of Chinatown's best known chefs.
Relax and enjoy dinner till late in our
comfortable dining room.
Excellent service and reasonable prices.

London's Entertainment Lists

Cinema, Art Centres, Classical Music,
Opera, Ballet, Jazz, Rock, Nightclubs, Casinos,
Department Stores, Shopping Centres, Arcades,
Markets, Pubs, Wine Bars, Cafes, Internet Cafes,
Tea Rooms, Sports & Exhibition Centres

162 CINEMAS

CINEMAS

[MAINSTREAM]

ABC Shaftesbury Avenue   36-2A
135 Shaftesbury Av. London W1 ⊖Tottenham Court Road / Leicester Square
☎020-7836-8861 ⒽWww.abccinemas.co.uk

ABC Tottenham Court Road   35-1B
30 Tottenham Court Rd. London W1 ⊖Tottenham Court Road ☎020-8795-6400
Ⓗwww.abccinemas.co.uk

Chelsea Cinema   53-2A
206 King's Rd. London SW3 ⊖Sloane Square ☎020-7351-3742

Clapham Picture House   24-2B
76 Venn St. London SW4 ⊖Clapham Common ☎020-7498-2242
Ⓗwww.picturehouse-cinemas.co.uk

Curzon Mayfair   27-2B
38 Curzon St. London W1 ⊖Green Park ☎020-7369-1720

Curzon Soho   29-1B
93/107 Shaftesbury Av. London W1 ⊖Leicester Square ☎020-7439-4805

Finchley Road Warner Village   24-1A
241/279 Finchley Rd. London NW3 ⊖Finchley Road ☎020-7604-3066 Ⓗwww.warnervillage.co.uk

Gate   44-1A
87 Notting Hill Gate, London W11 ⊖Notting Hill Gate ☎020-7727-4043

Greenwich Cinema   25-2B
180 Greenwich High Rd. London SE10 ⊖Greenwich ☎020-8293-0101
Ⓗwww.networkcinemas.com

Notting Hill Coronet   44-1A
103 Notting Hill Gate, London W11 ⊖Notting Hill Gate ☎020-7727-6705

Odeon Camden Town   24-1B
14 Parkway, London NW1 ⊖Camden Town ☎0870-5050007 Ⓗwww.odeon.co.uk

Odeon Kensington   44-2A
263 Kensington High St. London W8 ⊖High Street Kensington ☎0870-5050007
Ⓗwww.odeon.co.uk

Odeon Leicester Square   29-1B
22/24 Leicester Sq. London WC2 ⊖Leicester Square ☎020-7930-6111 Ⓗwww.odeon.co.uk

Odeon Marble Arch   32-2A
10 Edgware Rd. London W2 ⊖Marble Arch ☎0870-5050007 Ⓗwww.odeon.co.uk

Odeon Swiss Cottage   24-1A
96 Finchley Rd. London NW6 ⊖Swiss Cottage ☎0870-5050007 Ⓗwww.odeon.co.uk

Ritzy   25-2A
Brixton Oval, Coldharbour Lane, London SW2 ⊖Brixton ☎020-7737-2121

CINEMAS 163

Screen on Baker Street — 32-1B
96/98 Baker St. London NW1 ⊖ Piccadilly Circus ☎ 020-7486-0036 ⓗ www.screencinemas.co.uk

Screen on the Green — 25-1A
83 Upper St. London N1 ⊖ Angel ☎ 020-7226-3520

Screen on the Hill — 24-1A
203 Haverstock Hill, London NW3 ⊖ Belsize Park ☎ 020-7435-3366

UCI Whiteleys — 45-1A
Whiteleys Shopping Centre, Queensway, London W2 ⊖ Queensway ☎ 0870-010-2030

UGC Chelsea — 52-2A
279 King's Rd. London SW3 ⊖ Sloane Square ☎ 0870-907-0710

UGC Fulham Road — 52-2A
142 Fulham Rd. London SW10 ⊖ South Kensington ☎ 0870-907-0711

UGC Haymarket — 29-2B
63/65 Haymarket, London SW1 ⊖ Piccadilly Circus ☎ 0870-907-0712

Warner Village West End — 29-1B
Leicester Sq. London WC2 ⊖ Leicester Square ☎ 020-7437-4343 ⓗ www.warnervillage.co.uk

[ART-HOUSE]

BFI London IMAX Cinema — 51-1B
Waterloo Bullring, South Bank, London SE1 ⊖ Waterloo ☎ 020-7902-1234 ⓗ www.bfi.org.uk/about/guide/imax.html   British Film Institute shows a board range of world cinema and supports many film festivals.

Ciné Lumière — 45-2B
17 Queensberry Pl. London SW7 ⊖ South Kensington ☎ 020-7838-2144 ⓗ www.institut.ambafrance.org.uk   Foreign and art-house films shown in beautiful, well-equipped auditorium. One of the finest cinemas in England.

The Everyman Cinema — 24-1A
1 Holly Bush Vale, London NW3 ⊖ Hampstead ☎ 020-7431-1818 ⓗ www.everymancinema.com   London's longest running repertory cinema. Screens Hollywood classics.

Goethe Institute — 46-1A
50 Prince Gate, Exhibition Rd. London SW7 ⊖ South Kensington ☎ 020-7596-4000 ⓗ www.goethe.de/gr/lon   Screens films related to Germany.

ICA Cinema — 29-2B
Nash House, The Mall, London SW1 ⊖ Charing Cross / Piccadilly Circus ☎ 020-7930-3647 ⓗ www.ica.org.uk   Two cinemas showing contemporary, foreign and art-house films.

Lux Cinema — 25-1A
2/4 Hoxton Sq. London N1 ⊖ Old Street ☎ 020-7684-0201 ⓗ www.lux.org.uk   Shows art house and independent films, backed with talks, exhibitions and foyer installations.

CINEMAS, ARTS CENTRES, CLASSICAL MUSIC

The Metro — 29-1B
11 Rupert St. London W1 ⊖ Piccadilly Circus ☎ 020-7734-1506 Two screens, one very small, showing independent and foreign films.

NFT (National Film Theatre) — 51-1A
South Bank, London SE1 ⊖ Waterloo / Embankment ☎ 020-7928-3535 ⊕ www.bfi.org.uk/showing/nft Two cinemas showing a diverse range of foreign films and classic revivals. Rare and restored films also shown. A great place for movie enthusiasts.

Phoenix — 22-1B
52 High Rd. London N2 ⊖ East Finchely ☎ 020-8444-6789 The Phoenix opened with Noël Coward's *Private Lives* in 1930, and maintained a close association with this most English of playwrights. The Coward bar was opened in 1969.

Riverside Studios Cinema — 22-2B
Crisp Rd. London W6 ⊖ Hammersmith ☎ 020-8237-1111 ⊕ www.riversidestudios.co.uk Shows an eclectic programme of international films.

ARTS CENTRES

Barbican Centre — 39-1B
Silk St. London EC2 ⊖ Moorgate / Barbican ☎ 020-7638-8891 ⊕ www.barbican.org.uk A large arts centre which has regular music festivals and exhibitions. Begun in the 1960s but not completed until 1982, the building contains a concert hall, three cinemas, two theatres and an art gallery.

ICA (Institute of Contemporary Arts) — 29-2B
Nash House, The Mall, London SW1 ⊖ Charing Cross / Piccadilly Circus ☎ 020-7930-3647 ⊕ www.ica.org.uk With two cinemas, a new media (internet) centre and multiple spaces for talks and exhibitions, the ICA prides itself on being a venue for provocative and avant-garde art.

Riverside Studios — 22-2B
Crisp Rd. London W6 ⊖ Hammersmith ☎ 020-8237-1111 ⊕ www.riversidestudios.co.uk Variety of events from dance, theatre and films to lectures, workshops and dance classes.

The South Bank Centre — 51-1A
South Bank, London SE1 ⊖ Waterloo / Embankment ☎ 020-7960-4242 ⊕ www.sbc.org.uk An immense arts complex with museums and galleries, three concert halls (Royal Festival Hall, Purcell Room and Queen Elizabeth Hall), the National Theatre and National Film Theatre. The Festival Hall was built in 1951 for the Festival of Britain, and the centre has been growing since. Drinks from bars and cafés inside can be taken out onto the riverside walk, and the indoor spaces are light and inviting, with plenty of seating. One of London's great views is to be had at dusk from the gallery at the top of the RFH.

CLASSICAL MUSIC

Barbican Hall — 39-1B
Barbican Centre, Silk St. London EC2 ⊖ Moorgate / Barbican ☎ 020-7638-8891 ⊕ www.barbican.org.uk Home to the London Symphony Orchestra. One of London's two large acoustically designed classical music venues.

Blackheath Halls — 25-2B
23 Lee Rd. Blackheath, London SE3 ⇌ Blackheath ☎ 020-8463-0100 ⊕ www.blackheathhalls.com A convivial atmosphere for classical or world music.

CLASSICAL MUSIC, OPERA, BALLET   165

Purcell Room   51-1A
South Bank, London SE1 ⊖ Waterloo / Embankment ☎ 020-7960-4242 ⓗwww.sbc.org.uk   The most intimate concert space on the South Bank, for chamber music, solo recitals and readings.

Queen Elizabeth Hall   51-1A
South Bank, London SE1 ⊖ Waterloo / Embankment ☎ 020-7960-4242 ⓗwww.sbc.org.uk   Specializes in small orchestral and chamber music concerts, including experimental contemporary performances.

Royal Albert Hall   45-2B
Kensington Gore, London SW7 ⊖South Kensington ☎020-7589-8212   Built in 1871, the hall has hosted the famous Promenade Concerts for more than a century. From July to September, the Proms continue to premiere new music.

Royal College of Music   45-2B
Prince Consort Rd. London SW7 ⊖ Gloucester Road ☎ 020-7960-4242 ⓗwww.rcm.ac.uk   Chamber concerts staged every day Mon-Fri throughout termtime.

Royal Festival Hall   51-1A
South Bank, London SE1 ⊖ Waterloo / Embankment ☎ 020-7960-4242 ⓗwww.sbc.org.uk   Showcase for the world's top orchestras, the building also houses an arts bookshop, music shop, bar, restaurant and exhibition spaces.

St James's Church Piccadilly   31-2A
197 Piccadilly, London W1 ⊖Piccadilly Circus ☎020-7734-4511   A lovely setting for a lunchtime concert.

St John's Smith Square   50-2B
Smith Sq. London SW1 ⊖Westminster ☎020-7222-1061 ⓗwww.sjss.org.uk 18th century church providing a superb setting for chamber, orchestral and choral works.

St Martin-in-the-Fields   50-1A
Trafalgar Sq. London WC2 ⊖Charing Cross / Leicester Square ☎020-7839-8362 ⓗwww.stmartin-in-the-fields.org ◯8.00(Sat 9.00)-18.00(Sun 19.45)   Excellent acoustics for chamber works and choral recitals.

Wigmore Hall   33-2B
36 Wigmore St. London W1 ⊖ Bond Street ☎ 020-7935-2141   Excellent acoustics for chamber works and choral recitals. Very popular on Sunday morning when performance includes sherry or coffee.

OPERA, BALLET

Almeida Theatre   25-1A
Almeida St. Off Upper St. London N1 ⊖Angel ☎020-7359-4404   A good venue for the smaller scale operas and concerts.

The London Coliseum   36-2A
St Martin's Lane, London WC2 ⊖ Leicester Square ☎ 020-7632-8300 Home to the English National Opera and the place to see visiting dance and ballet companies during the summer. All operas are sung in English.

Peacock Theatre   37-1A
Portugal St. London WC2 ⊖Holborn ☎020-7863-8222   Offers a full programme of innovative dance with exciting modern companies from around the world.

The Place Theatre   24-1B
17 Duke's Rd. London WC1 ⊖Euston ☎020-7387-0031 ⓗwww.theplace.org.uk One of the best modern dance venues in London, The Place has four resident companies, including the Shobana Jeyasingh Dance Company.

OPERA, BALLET, JAZZ

Royal Opera House   36-2B
Bow St. London WC2 ⊖ Covent Garden ☎ 020-7304-4000 ⊕ www.royaloperahouse.org   Houses grand presentations by its resident companies-the Royal Opera and Royal Ballet.

Sadler's Wells Theatre   24-1B
Rosebery Av. London EC1 ⊖ Angel ☎ 020-7863-8000 ⊕ www.sadlers-wells.com   Theatres and music halls have been built and re-built on this site since 1683. The most recent refurbishment finished in 1998, allowing the return of the Sadler's Wells company and its innovative dance, opera and ballet productions.

JAZZ

100 Club   35-2A
100 Oxford St. London W1 ⊖ Tottenham Court Road ☎ 020-7636-0933 ◎19.30(Fri 20.30)-1.00(Fri, Sat 2.00, Sun 23.30) ⊗No   Famed venue for jazz, New Orleans, and R&B. Café, and free lunchtime jazz on Fridays.

606 Club   24-2A
90 Lots Rd. London SW10 ⊖ Fulham Broadway ☎ 020-7352-5953 ⊕www.606club.co.uk ◎19.30(Fri-Sun 20.15)-1.00(Thur 1.30, Fri, Sat 2.00, Sun 23.30) ⊗No   R & B and jazz are favourites here with frequent live performances. They also have a reasonable menu.

Boisdale   48-2B
13/15 Eccleston St. London SW1 ⊖Victoria ☎020-7730-6922 ⓕ020-7730-0548 ⊕ www.boisdale.uk.com ◎12.00-1.00(Sun 23.00) ⊗No   The choice of - wait for it - more than two hundred whiskies, wonderful haggis here too.

Bull's Head   22-2B
373 Lonsdale Rd. London SW13 ⊖Hammersmith ☎020-8876-5241 ◎11.00-23.00(Sun 12.00-22.30) ⊗No   Large Victorian pub by the riverside featuring top international jazz musicians every night.

Dover Street Restaurant & Bar   30-2B
8/9 Dover St. London W1 ⊖Green Park ☎020-7629-9813 ⊕www.doverst.co.uk ◎17.30(Fri,Sat 19.00)-3.00 ⊗Sun   A basement bar and restaurant with an à la carte menu. Live music and dancing until 3am. Capacity 450. Jazz and R&B.

Jazz After Dark   35-2B
9 Greek St. London W1 ⊖ Leicester Square ☎ 020-7734-0545 ⊕www.jazzafterdark.co.uk ◎12.00-2.00(Fri, Sat 3.00) ⊗Sun   A good place for larger parties, somewhere for late night drinking and comfortable easy-jazz sounds.

Jazz Café   24-1B
5/7 Parkway, London NW1 ⊖ Camden Town ☎ 020-7916-6060 ⊕www.jazzcafe.co.uk ◎19.00-1.00(Fri, Sat 2.00) ⊗No   Live mainstream and crossover jazz in Art Deco converted bank. Café and restaurant serving modern British cuisine.

Mezzo   35-2A
100 Wardour St. London W1 ⊖Tottenham Court Road ☎ 020-7314-4000 ◎18.00-1.00(Fri, Sat 3.00) ⊗Sun   A Conran menu accompanied by jazz musicians at this huge restaurant - seafood and jazz seems like a good option as they usually have a good list of caviar and oysters.

Pizza Express   35-2A
10 Dean St. London W1 ⊖Tottenham Court Road / Oxford Circus ☎020-7439-8722(restaurant)/7437-9595(jazz) ⊕www.pizzaexpress.co.uk/index_jazz.htm ◎11.00-0.00(restaurant)/21.00-0.00 (jazz) ⊗No   Resident band and guests in cellar of restaurant. One of the main London venues for modern jazz.

JAZZ, ROCK 167

Pizza on the Park   48-1A
11 Knightsbridge, London SW1 ↔ Hyde Park Corner ☎ 020-7235-5273 ⓒ8.15(Sat,Sun 9.15)-0.00 ⊗No An elegantly designed restaurant featuring mainstream and traditional jazz bands.

Quaglino's   28-2B
16 Bury St. London SW1 ↔ Green Park / Piccadilly Circus ☎020-7930-6767 ⓒ12.00-0.00(Sun 22.30) ⊗No Large, glamourous brasserie designed by Terence Conran. French, Italian and Oriental dishes. Live jazz Fri and Sat, piano music Mon-Thur. Reservations advisable.

Ronnie Scott's   35-2B
47 Frith St. London W1 ↔Leicester Square / Piccadilly Circus ☎020-7439-0747 Ⓗwww.ronniescotts.co.uk ⓒ20.30-3.00(Sun 19.30-23.00) ⊗No Legendary jazz club opened by the saxophonist Ronnie Scott in the 60s. All the biggest names play here.

St Giles Jazz Club   25-2A
St. Giles Church, Camberwell Church St. London SE5 ↔Oval ☎020-7701-1016 ⓒ20.00-2.00 ●Fri Live jazz by top artists, good restaurant serving a wide range of dishes.

Smollensky's on the Strand   36-2B
105 Strand, London WC2 ↔ Charing Cross ☎020-7497-2101 Ⓗwww.smollenskys.co.uk ⓒ12.00-0.00(Sun 23.00) ⊗No Jazz played Thurs-Sat. Easy listening atmosphere with resident pianist.

The Spitz   25-1A
Old Spitalfields Market, 109 Commercial St. London E1 ↔Liverpool Street ☎020-7392-9032 Ⓗwww.spitz.co.uk ⓒ11.00(Sun 12.00)-0.00(Fri, Sat 1.00, Sun 22.30) ⊗No Cool jazz every Fri for free; special performance nights.

Victorian Oven   41-1B
51 Brushfield St. London E1 ↔Liverpool Street ☎020-7377-6227 ⓒ11.30-22.30(Sun9.30 17.00) ⊗Sat Live jazz every Wednesday.

Vortex Jazz Bar   25-1B
139/141 Stoke Newington Church St. London N16 ⇌ Stoke Newington ☎020-7254-6516 Ⓗwww.palay.ndirect.co.uk/vortex.jazz ⓒ10.00(Sun 11.00)-23.30(Fri, Sat 0.00, Sun 23.00) ⊗No Nothing too special, but that said, it is an unpretentious setting of old furniture, fun coloured decor and has a reasonable menu - an easy atmosphere for lazy dining or for music events.

The Wenlock Arms   25-1A
26 Wenlock Rd. London N1 ↔ Old Street ☎ 020-7608-3406 Ⓗwww.wenlock-arms.co.uk ⓒ12.00-23.00(Sun 22.30) ⊗No At the weekends they offer live jazz here, and this coupled with their range of real ales and decent cider make it well worth a visit.

ROCK

Astoria   35-2B
157 Charing Cross Rd. London WC2 ↔ Tottenham Court Road Ⓗwww.meanfiddler.com ☎020-7434-0403 ⓒ22.30-5.30 ⊗Sun Large, central venue for live music holding a total of 3000 people. Clubs and special events.

168 ROCK

Borderline 35-2B
Orange Yard, London W1 ⊖ Tottenham Court Road ☎ 020-7734-2095 ⓗwww.borderline.co.uk ◎20.00-2.00 ⊗Sun Stages gigs of all kinds including rock and pop .

Break for the Border 34-2A
8/9 Argyll St. London W1 ⊖ Oxford Circus ☎ 020-7734-5776 ◎17.00-23.00(Wed, Thur 1.00, Fri, Sat 3.00) ⊗Sun Restaurant serves Tex-Mex food: burgers, fajitas and cocktails. Tue-Sat DJs and dancing until 3am.

Brixton Academy 24-2B
211 Stockwell Rd. London SW9 ⊖ Brixton ☎ 020-7771-3000 ◎Box Office 13.00(Sat 12.00)-15.00/020-7771-2000 (24h telephone booking) ⊗Sun Huge venue for rock and alternative bands. Also has R&B and jazz funk on occasion.

Bull & Gate 24-1B
389 Kentish Town Rd. London NW5 ⊖Kentish Town ☎020-7485-5358 ◎11.00-0.00 ⊗No Small venue staging up-and-coming indie and rock bands. Serves real ale.

Camden Falcon 24-1B
234 Royal College St. London NW1 ⊖ Camden Town ☎ 020-7485-3834 ◎14.00-23.00(Sun 16.00-22.30) ⊗No A very young atmosphere for rock fans, bands play regularly.

Dublin Castle 24-1B
94 Parkway, London NW1 ⊖Camden Town ☎020-7485-1773 ◎11.00-0.00 ⊗No Young venue with a cramped back room where the bands play.

Forum 24-1B
9/17 Highgate Rd. London NW5 ⊖ Kentish Town ☎ 020-7284-1001 ⓗwww.meanfiddler.com ◎⊗Depends on show This place has a dedicated following with popular live bands.

Garage 25-1A
20/22 Highbury Corner, London N5 ⊖Highbury & Islington ☎020-7607-1818 ⓗwww.meanfiddler.com ◎20.00-23.30(Fri, Sat 3.00) ⊗Sun Alternative rock and indie played on two floors. Many up-coming bands have gone from here to fame.

Hammersmith Apollo 22-2B
Queen Caroline St. London W6 ⊖ Hammersmith ☎ 020-7416-6080 ◎⊗*Depends on show.* A major venue for top, mainstream bands.

Hope & Anchor 25-1A
207 Upper St. London N1 ⊖Highbury & Islington ☎020-7354-1312 ◎12.00-1.00 ⊗No A good venue for bands just starting out, 30 year history of introducing the up-and-coming.

LA2 35-2B
157 Charing Cross Rd. Lodon WC2 ⊖Tottenham Court Road ☎020-7434-0403 ◎19.00-4.00 ⊗No Good sound system, average rock band venue.

Leisure Lounge 38-1A
121 Holborn, London EC1 ⊖Chancery Lane ☎020-7242-1345 ◎22.00-3.00(Fri 5.00, Sat 6.00) ●Thur-Sat Air conditioned basement bars, with free FM on Saturday nights.

ROCK, NIGHTCLUBS

Mean Fiddler   22-1B
28 High St. Harlesden, London NW3 ⊖Willesden Green ☎020-8961-5490 Ⓗwww.meanfiddler.com ⒸSat 23.00-3.00, Sun 14.00-23.00 Once a venue for Irish music, now mostly stages classic rock.

The Roadhouse   36-2B
The Piazza, London WC2 ⊖Covent Garden ☎020-7240-6001 Ⓗwww.roadhouse.co.uk Ⓒ17.30-2.30 ⊗Sun American-style venue playing R&B and soul music. Bar and Tex-Mex restaurant.

Rock Garden   36-2B
Bedford Chambers, The Piazza, London WC2 ⊖Covent Garden ☎020-7240-3961 Ⓗwww.rockgarden.co.uk Ⓒ17.00-3.00(Fri, Sat 4.00, Sun 2.00) ⊗No Once a vegetable warehouse, now a rock venue featuring new and up-coming groups. U2 and The Smiths played here before fame beckoned. Tex-Mex restaurant.

Shepherd's Bush Empire   22-1B
Shepherd's Bush Green, London W12 ⊖Shepherd's Bush ☎020-7771-2000 Ⓒ⊗Depends on show. Used to be a BBC TV studio, now a major venue for big US and British bands. Seating on three levels ensures good views.

The Social Bar   34-1A
5 Little Portland St. London W1 ⊖Oxford Circus ☎020-7636-4992 Ⓗwww.thesocial.co.uk Ⓒ12.00-0.00(Sun 17.00-22.30) ⊗No OK it's small, but's that's true of too many London rock venues, this is an impressive new gig.

Sound Republic   29-1B
10 Wardour St. London W1 ⊖Leicester Square ☎020-7287-1010 Ⓒ12.00-1.00(Fri 3.00, Sat 4.00) ⊗No This place is really beginning to improve as they add more live gigs to their programme.

WAG   29-1B
33/37 Wardour St. London W1 ⊖Leicester Sqaure ☎020-7437-5534 Ⓒ22.00-3.00(Fri 4.00, Sat 5.00) ⊗Sun, Mon Indie, rock and retro music. Snack bar, bars and dance areas on two floors.

Water Rats   24-1B
328 Gray's Inn Rd. London WC1 ⊖King's Cross ☎020-7837-7269 Ⓒ20.00-0.00 ⊗Sun A decent pub venue, with bands that have at least some claim to fame.

NIGHTCLUBS

333   25-1A
333 Old St. London EC1 ⊖Old Street ☎020-7739-5949 Ⓒ22.00-5.00 ●Fri, Sat ⓔ5-10 Trend-setters' nightclub.

AKA   36-1A
18 West Central St. London WC1 ⊖Tottenham Court Road ☎020-7836-0110 Ⓗwww.the-end.co.uk Ⓒ18.00(Sat 19.00)-3.00(Tue 1.00) ⊗Sun, Mon Ground floor club where the under 30's band out; upstairs fashionable restaurant with a surprisingly good menu.

Bar Rumba   29-1A
36 Shaftesbury Av. London W1 ⊖Piccadilly Circus ☎020-7287-2715 Ⓗwww.barrumba.co.uk Ⓒ17.00(Sat 19.00, Sun 20.00)-3.30(Fri 4.00, Sat 6.00, Sun 1.00) ⊗No ⓔ3-12 The best Latin dance DJ in London, fabulous salsa.

NIGHTCLUBS

Bug Bar — 24-2B
The Crypt, St Matthew's Peace Garden, Brixton Hill, London SW2 ⊖Brixton ☎020-7738-3184 ◎19.00-1.00(Sat 3.00, Sun 23.00) ⊗No ⓒ3.00(21.00-), 5.00(23.00-) Hosts stand-up comics, gigs and DJ's, a buzzy place worth checking out.

Café de Paris — 29-1B
3 Coventry St. London W1 ⊖Leicester Square ☎020-7734-7700 ⓗwww.cafedeparis.com ◎10.30-4.00 ⊗Sun, Mon, Tue ⓒ15 Cramped, crowded nightclub with a rather eclectic choice of sounds.

Camden Palace — 24-1B
1A Camden High St. London NW1 ⊖Camden Town ☎020-7387-0428 ⓗwww.camdenpalace.com ◎22.00(Thur 20.00)-2.30(Thur 3.00, fri 6.00, Sat 7.00) ⊗Sun, Mon ⓒ5-15 This place still has its appeal and seems to be a reliably good night out.

The Clinic — 29-1B
13 Gerrard St. London W1 ⊖Leicester Square ☎020-7734-9836 ◎17.00(Thur 22.00)-2.00(Mon 23.00, Thur 3.00, Fri, Sat 4.00) ⊗Sun ⓒ3-7 Although one of the smaller dance venues, this boasts great music nights including reggae evenings.

Crazy Larry's — 24-2A
533 King's Rd. London SW10 ⊖Fulham Broadway ☎020-7376-5555 ◎22.00-2.30 ●Thur-Sat Club with 70s, 80s, 90s music and club mixes.

The Cross — 24-1B
Goods Way Depot, off York Way, London N1 ⊖King's Cross ☎020-7837-0828 ◎22.30-4.30(Sat 6.00) ●Fri, Sat This intimate space attracts quite a young crowd with its top house sounds.

Dust — 38-1A
27 Clerkenwell Rd. Lndon EC1 ⊖Farringdon ☎020-7490-5120 ◎11.00(Sat 20.00, Sun 12.00)-23.00(Thur-Sat 2.00, Sun 19.00) ⊗No Sophisticated ambience, well designed wood and copper-look interior, DJ and bar.

Electric Ballroom — 24-1B
184 Camden High St. London NW1 ⊖Camden Town ☎020-7485-9006 ◎22.30-3.00 ●Fri, Sat Large club with two floors playing a range of music from Rock, Technogoth to Country & Western.

The Emporium — 31-1A
62 Kingly St. London W1 ⊖Oxford Circus ☎020-7734-3190 ⓗwww.emporiumlondon.com ◎22.00-4.00 ⊗Sun A dance place where you can go celebrity spotting.

The End — 36-1A
18A West Central St. London WC1 ⊖Tottenham Court Road ☎020-7419-9199 ⓗwww.the-end.co.uk ◎Thur 19.00-1.00, Fri 22.00-5.00, Sat 22.00-6.00, Sun 20.00-3.00 ⊗Mon-Wed A really great club - good sounds - especially if you are a drum and bass fan - very cool interior.

Equinox — 29-1B
4 Leicester Sq. London WC2 ⊖Leicester Square ☎020-7437-1446 ◎21.00-3.00(Fri, Sat 4.00) ⊗Sun Large dance venue playing mainstream chart and dance music. Plenty of bars and a spectacular laser system.

NIGHTCLUBS 171

Fabric 38-1B
77A Charterhouse St. London EC1 ⊖Farringdon ☎020-7490-0444 ⓗwww.fabric-london.com ◎22.00-5.00(Sat 7.00, Sun: Depends on show) ●Fri, Sat, Sun £10-15 Unpretentious dance club with top DJs and great sounds.

The Fridge 25-2A
Town Hall Parade, Brixton Hill, London SW2 ⊖Brixton ☎020-7326-5100 ⓗwww.fridge.co.uk ◎22.00-6.00 ●Fri, Sat £6-12 An important club especially for those interested in Brixton's music scene.

Gossips 35-2B
69 Dean St. London W1 ⊖Piccadilly Circus ☎020-7434-4480 ◎17.00-3.00 ⊗Sun Rock, reggae and soul.

Hammersmith Palais 22-1B
240 Sheperd's Bush Rd. London W6 ⊖Hammersmith ☎0800-783-7485 ⓗwww.leopardclubs.com ◎22.00-3.00 ●Fri, Sat £5-10 A great place for nights that celebrate the 70's, 80's and 90's music scenes.

Hanover Grand 34-2A
6 Haover St. London W1 ⊖Oxford Circus ☎020-7499-7977 ⓗwww.hanovergrand.com ◎22.30-4.00(Wed 3.30, Sat 5.00) ⊗Sun, Mon, Tue This club takes up the interior of what was previously a theatre, it makes a lavish setting for rather glamorous clubbing.

Heaven 50-1B
Under the Arches, off Villiers St. London WC2 ⊖Embankment / Charing Cross ☎020-7930-2020 ⓗwww.heaven-london.com ◎22.30(Sat 22.00)-3.00 (Fri6.00, Sat 5.00) ⊗Thur,Sun London's premiere gay club situated under Charing Cross station. Four bars, three dance floors, and straight or mixed events every night except Sat and Tues.

Hippodrome 36-2A
Cranbourn St. London WC2 ⊖Leicester Square ☎020-7437-4311 ◎21.00-3.00(Fri, Sat 3.30) ⊗Sun Smart, up-market club. A London landmark, but more popular with young European tourists than with Londoners.

Home 29-1B
1 Leicester Sq. London WC2 ⊖Leicester Square ☎020-8964-1999 ⓗwww.homecorp.co.uk ◎22.00(Sat 21.00)-3.00 ●Thur, Fri, Sat £5-15 Top club, gorgeously designed interior, super sound, great DJ.

Iceni 27-2B
11 White Horse St. London W1 ⊖Green Park ☎020-7495-5333 ◎23.00-3.30 ●Fri,Sat Five rooms on three floors playing a variety of music. Also has films, jam sessions and board games. Very popular with smart, trendy Londoners.

Legends 30-1B
29 Old Burlington St. London W1 ⊖Oxford Circus / Piccadilly Circus / Green Park ☎020-7437-9933 ◎22.00-4.00(Thur 3.00) ●Thur-Sat Chrome and steel decor attracts a smart but mixed crowd. Well stocked bar.

Limelight 29P 1B
136 Shaftesbury Av. London W1 ⊖Leicester Square ☎020-7434-0572 ◎22.00-3.00(Fri, Sat 21.00-3.30, Sun 18.00-23.00) ⊗No Two dance floors where funk, garage and house predominate. This converted church now deals in Soul not souls and the only Saint you'll find is a San Miguel.

NIGHTCLUBS, CASINOS

The Los Locos Tejas — 36-2B
24/26 Russell St. London WC2 ⊖Covent Garden ☎020-7379-0220 ⓗwww.los-locos.co.uk ◎17.00-3.00 ⊗Sun Very laid back drinking, dining and dining atmosphere, with music ranging from the 60's to current sounds.

Madame JoJo's — 31-1B
8 Brewer St. London W1 ⊖Piccadilly Circus ☎020-7734-3040 ⓗwww.madamejojos.com ◎21.00(Tue 21.30, Fri 22.30, Sat 22.00)-3.00(Sun 2.00) ⊗Mon Rather racy atmosphere with nights of deep funk, groove and nu-jazz and much, much more.

Ministry of Sound — 25-2A
103 Gaunt St. London SE1 ⊖Elephant & Castle ☎020-7378-6528 ◎22.00-6.00 ●Fri, Sat Big name DJs and a great sound system pack in the crowds all weekend. A must for house and garage fans. Also features an all-night cinema.

Motcombs — 47-2B
5 Halkin Arcade, West Halkin St. London SW1 ⊖Hyde Park Corner ☎020-7235-5532 ⓗwww.motcombs.co.uk ◎21.00-3.00 ⊗Sun Dance, chart and classic pop sounds here, parties catered for.

Notting Hill Arts Club — 44-1B
21 Notting Hill Gate, London W11 ⊖Notting Hill Gate ☎020-7460-4459 ◎17.00-1.00(Sun 16.00-23.00) ⊗Mon Pretty good DJ, good place to hang out if you are giving the hard clubbing scene a miss.

Samantha's — 30-1B
2 New Burlington St. London W1 ⊖Piccadilly Circus / Oxford Circus ☎020-7734-6249 ◎Depends on show ⊗Sun, Mon Popular split-level disco with two dance floors, cocktail bar and a fish pond. Good for older club-goers. Smart dress required.

Scala — 24-1B
278 Pentonville Rd. London N1 ⊖King's Cross ☎020-7833-2022 ⓗwww.scala-london.co.uk ◎21.00-3.00(Fri, Sat 5.00) ⊗Sun, Mon, Tue (Depends on show) ⓒ6-12 This club is built inside the former cinema, it's now quite a dazzling addition to clubland with the accent on hip-hop.

Stringfellows — 36-2A
16/19 Upper St Martin's Lane, London WC2 ⊖Covent Garden / Leicester Square ☎020-7240-5534 ◎20.00-3.30 ⊗Sun This hang-out of the stars has pulsating lights and a glitzy, mirrored interior. À la carte restaurant, smart dress only. Table dancing Mon-Thur.

Subterania — 24-1A
12 Acklam Rd. London W10 ⊖Ladbroak Grove ☎020-8960-4590 ⓗwww.meanfiddler.com ◎22.00-3.00(Wed 2.00) ●Wed, Fri, Sat Features mainly techno dance music with some rap, soul and funk. European atmosphere and a great sound system.

WKD Café — 25-1A
18 Kentish Town Rd. London NW1 ⊖Camden Town ☎020-7267-1869 ◎12.00-2.00(Fri,Sat 3.00, Sun 1.00) ⊗No A small club with different music every day, from funk and fusion to indie and experimental. Capacity 300 people.

CASINOS

By law all casinos require membership which takes 24 hours to obtain.

50 St James — 30-2B
50 St. James's St. London SW1 ⊖Green Park ☎020-7491-4678 ⓕ020-7318-6616 ⓔ50stjames@clublci.com ⓗwww.clublci.com ◎12.30-4.00 ⊗No ⓒ500 Full membership (12.30-21.00 Complimentary)

CASINOS, DEPARTMENT STORES

Les Ambassadeurs — 27-2A
5 Hamilton Pl. London W1 ↔Hyde Park Corner ☎020-7495-5555 Ⓕ020-7318-6620 Ⓔlesambassadeurs@clublci.com Ⓗwww.clublci.com Ⓞ12.30-4.00 ⊗No £500 membership fee and an introduction required. Roulette, punto banco and black-jack are the main games.

Barracuda Club — 32-2B
1 Baker St. London W1 ↔Baker Street ☎020-7935-5013 Ⓕ020-7224-6768 Ⓞ14.00-6.00 ⊗No Complimentary

Connoisseur Club — 45-1A
2 Kensington High St. London W8 ↔High Street Kensington ☎020-7603-1155 Ⓕ020-7937-5335 Ⓞ13.00-4.00 ⊗No Complimentary

Crockfords Club — 27-2B
30 Curzon St. London W1 ↔Green Park ☎020-7493-7771 Ⓞ12.00-4.00 ⊗No Established 150 years ago, with a reputation as one of the more civilised clubs. £300 membership fee, plus introduction preferred.

Golden Nugget — 29-1A
22/32 Shaftesbury Av. London W1 ↔Piccadilly Circus ☎020-7439-0099 Ⓕ020-7318-6625 Ⓔgoldennugget@clublci.com Ⓗwww.clublci.com Ⓞ14.00-4.00 ⊗No A large casino with black-jack, roulette and punto banco. £10 membership fee.

Grosvenor Victoria Casino — 32-2A
150/166 Edgware Rd. London W2 ↔Marble Arch ☎020-7262-7777 Ⓕ020-7724-1214 Ⓞ12.30-4.00 ⊗No Complimentary

London Park Tower Casino — 47-1B
101 Knightsbridge, London SW1 ↔Knightsbridge ☎020-7235-9595 Ⓕ020-7235-9784 Ⓞ12.00-4.00 ⊗No Complimentary

Palm Beach Casino Club — 30-2A
30 Berkeley St. London W1 ↔Green Park ☎020-7493-6585 Ⓕ020-7318-6617 Ⓔpalmbeach@clublci.com Ⓗwww.clublci.com Ⓞ13.30-4.00 ⊗No Once the old ballroom of the Mayfair Hotel and now an exciting club. Complimantary.

The Rendezvous Casino Club — 27-2B
14 Old Park Lane, London W1 ↔Hyde Park Corner ☎020-7491-8586 Ⓕ020-7318-6623 Ⓔrendezvous@clublci.com Ⓗwww.clublci.com Ⓞ12.00-4.00 ⊗No Dress code: smart casual with jacket after 7.30pm. Games: black jack, punto banco, casino stud poker, roulette and slot machines. Complimentary.

Sportsman Club — 32-2A
40 Bryanston St. London W1 ↔Marble Arch ☎020-7414 0061 Ⓕ020-7318-6616 Ⓔsportsman@clublci.com Ⓗwww.clublci.com Ⓞ12.30-4.00 ⊗No Complimentary

DEPARTMENT STORES

Army & Navy — 49-1B
101 Victoria St. London SW1 ↔St James's Park ☎020-7834-1234 Ⓗwww.houseoffraser.co.uk Ⓞ9.30(Sun 11.00)-18.00(Thur 19.00, Sun 17.00) ⊗No Large department store selling everything from fashion to furniture.

Barkers — 44-2B
63 Kensington High St. London W8 ↔High Street Kensington ☎020-7937-5432 Ⓗwww.houseoffraser.co.uk Ⓞ10.00(Sat 9.30, Sun 12.00)-19.00(Thur 20.00, Sun 18.00) ⊗No Department store with everything from designer bags to kids clothing, it also has a new Clarins beauty section.

DEPARTMENT STORES

Bhs 34-2A
252/258 Oxford St. London W1 ⊖Oxford Circus ☎020-7629-2011 ◎9.30-19.00(Thur 20.00) ⊗No Reasonably priced department store, especially good for adult clothing and home furnishing.

D.H. Evans 33-2B
318 Oxford St. London W1 ⊖Oxford Circus ☎020-7629-8800 ◎10.00(Sat 9.30, Sun 12.00)-19.00(Thur 20.00, Sun 18.00) ⊗No Unpretentious store with quality fashion and lingerie departments. Also has furniture and electrical goods.

Debenhams 33-2B
334/348 Oxford St. London W1 ⊖Bond Street ☎020-7580-3000 ⓗwww.debenhams.com ◎9.30(Wed 10.00, Sat 9.00, Sun 12.00)-20.00(Mon, Tue 19.00, Thur 21.00, Sun 18.00) ⊗No Reasonably priced clothes. Also kitchenware and cosmetics.

Dickins & Jones 34-2A
224/244 Regent St. London W1 ⊖Oxford Circus ☎020-7734-7070 ◎10.00(Sun 12.00)-19.00(Mon, Tue 18.30, Thur 20.00, Sun18.00) ⊗No Fashionable store with an accent on quality clothing and accessories. Fabulous dress fabrics. Designers available include Ghost, Nicole Farhi and MaxMara.

Fortnum & Mason 31-2A
181 Piccadilly, London W1 ⊖Piccadilly Circus/Green Park ☎020-7734-8040 ⓗwww.fortnumandmason.co.uk ◎9.30-18.00 ⊗Sun Old-fashioned and atmospheric shop famous for its food hampers. Menswear includes Fortnum & Mason Collections and womenswear is by Missoni, Jean Muir, MaxMara, etc.

Harrods 47-1A
87/135 Brompton Rd. London SW1 ⊖Knightsbridge ☎020-7730-1234 ⓗwww.harrods.com ◎10.00-18.00(Wed-Fri 19.00) ⊗Sun 'Everything for everyone everywhere' is the motto of what is undoubtedly the most famous store in the world. Superb food halls.

Harvey Nichols 47-1B
109/125 Knightsbridge, London SW1 ⊖Knightsbridge ☎020-7235-5000 ◎10.00(Sun 12.00)-19.00(Wed-Fri 20.00, Sun 18.00) ⊗No Artistic window displays and top fashions from world famous designers such as Calvin Klein, Dolce & Gabbana and John Rocha.

John Lewis 33-2B
278/306 Oxford St. London W1 ⊖Oxford Circus / Bond Street ☎020-7629-7711 ⓗwww.johnlewis.co.uk ◎9.30(Thur 10.00, Sat 9.00)-18.00(Thur 20.00) ⊗Sun Large fabric department. Fashionable, inexpensive clothes. Own brands as well as Aquascutum, Jaeger and Liz Claiborne.

Liberty 34-2A
210/220 Regent St. London W1 ⊖Oxford Circus ☎020-7734-1234 ⓗwww.liberty-of-london.com ◎10.00(Sun 12.00)-18.30(Thur 20.00, Fri, Sat 19.00, Sun 18.00) ⊗No Famed for its stunning window displays, fabrics and Oriental department.

Marks & Spencer 34-2B
173 Oxford St. London W1 ⊖Oxford Circus ☎020-7437-7722 ⓗwww.marks-and-spencer.com ◎9.30-19.00(Thur, Fri 20.00, Sun 12.00-18.00) ⊗No Renowned for its good quality knitwear, underwear and range of ready-to-eat foods.

Peter Jones 53-1B
Sloane Sq. London SW1 ⊖Sloane Square ☎020-7730-3434 ⓗwww.john-lewis.com ◎9.30-18.00(Wed 19.00) ⊗Sun Many floors of delightful shopping on offer, catering for just about any and every taste and desire; wonderful textile and fabrics department.

DEPARTMENT STORES, SHOPPING CENTRES, ARCADES, MARKETS — 175

Selfridges   33-2A
400 Oxford St. London W1 ⊖Bond Street / Marble Arch ☎020-7629-1234 ⓗwww.selfridges.com ⓒ10.00(Sat 9.30, Sun 12.00)-19.00(Thur, Fri 20.00, Sun 18.00) ⓧNo Outstanding international food hall and cosmetics department.

SHOPPING CENTRES, ARCADES

Brent Cross Shopping Centre   22-1B
Hendon, London NW4 ⊖Hendon Central ☎020-8202-8095 ⓗwww.brentcross-london.com ⓒ10.00(Sat 9.00 Sun 11.00)-20.00(Sat 19.00 Sun 17.00) ⓧNo Huge shopping centre with over 100 shops including great fashion, gifts and restaurants.

Burlington Arcade   30-2B
51 Piccadilly, London W1 ⊖Green Park / Piccadilly Circus ⓒArcade Gates: 9.00-18.00 ⓧSun Built in 1819. It is prohibited to whistle or eat while walking. A guard dressed in period costume, patrols.

Hay's Galleria   42-2B
London Bridge City, Tooley St. London SE1 ⊖London Bridge ☎020-7940-7770 ⓗwww.haysgalleria.co.uk ⓒⓧDepends on shops Situated on the river promenade between London Bridge and Tower Bridge. Fashionable shops and cafés, unique galleries, a tourist information centre and even a weekend fair.

Piccadilly Arcade   31-2A
Piccadilly, London W1 ⊖Green Park/Piccadilly Circus ⓒArcade Gates: 8.00-20.00 ⓧSun Specialist stores exhibit a high degree of craftsmanship. Stores include a shirtmakers, shoemakers, photographers and pottery showroom.

Plaza   35-2A
116/128 Oxford St. London ⊖Oxford Circus ⓒ10.00(Sun 12.00)-19.00(Thur 20.00, Sun 18.00) ⓧNo Shopping centre that houses various high street fashion shops, W.H.Smith and food gallery for coffees and snacks.

Thomas Neal's   36-2A
Earlham St. London WC2 ⊖Covent Garden ⓒArcade Gates: 10.00-23.00 ⓧNo Close to Covent Garden. A shopping world with unique and fashionable outlets.

MARKETS

[STREET MARKETS]

Berwick Street Market   29-1A
Berwick St. London W1 ⊖Piccadilly Circus ⓒ8.00-18.00 ⓧSun Good cheese and fish stalls, and considering it's the centre of London - very reasonable fruit and veg.

Borough Market   42-2A
Borough High St./ Stoney St. London, SE10 ⊖London Bridge ⓗwww.londonslarder.org.uk ⓒFri 12.00-18.00, Sat 9.00-16.00 ●Fri, Sat A wonderful food market, check out the olive and dairy stalls in particular.

Brick Lane Market   25-1A
Brick Lane, London E1 ⊖Aldgate East ⓒ8.00-13.00 ●Sun Very good for all manner of second hand goods, a super array of stalls; one of the best London market atmospheres.

MARKETS

Camden Lock — 24-1B
Chalk Farm Rd. London NW1 ⊖Camden Town / Chalk Farm ◎10.00-18.00 ⊗Mon Every inch of space from Chalk Farm to Camden Town tube is occupied by a shop or café selling new and second-hand clothes, crafts, antiques, furniture or ethnic fare.

Camden Passage — 25-1A
Camden Passage, off Upper St. London N1 ⊖Angel ◎10.00(Wed 8.00)-17.00(Wed 14.00, Sat 16.00) ⊗Mon, Sun Numerous stalls are situated along this quaint street filled with restaurants and bookshops. Silverware, jewellery, prints and toys are among the items on offer.

Columbia Road Flower Market — 25-1A
Columbia Rd. London E2 ⊖Old Street ◎8.00-13.00 ●Sun Gourmet gardening.... Horticultural bliss...cut flowers, bedding plants and a fabulous selection of shrubs.

Jubilee Market — 36-2B
Jubilee Hall, The Piazza, London WC2 ⊖Covent Garden ◎9.00-17.00 ⊗No Stalls vary each day: antiques on Mon, general goods Tue-Fri, and crafts Sat-Sun. The place to see some of the best buskers in London.

Leather Lane Market — 38-1A
Leather Lane, London EC1 ⊖Farringdon / Chancery Lane ◎10.30-14.00 ⊗Sat, Sun A lively market with a wide selection of goods. Originally had nothing to do with the leather trade but now you can buy some leather goods here.

New Caledonian Market — 25-2A
Bermondsey Sq. London SE1 ⊖London Bridge / Borough ◎5.00-13.00 ●Fri Reputed to be the best outdoor antique market in London. Valuable paintings, silver and old jewellery are quickly sold to collectors before ordinary buyers arrive. Remember to haggle over the price and get there very early.

Petticoat Lane Market — 41-1B
Middlesex St. London E1 ⊖Liverpool Street / Aldgate East ◎9.00-14.00 ●Sun London's largest market sells everything from leather jackets and watches to CDs and socks.

Portobello Road Market — 24-1A
Portobello Rd. London W11 ⊖Ladbroke Grove / Notting Hill Gate ◎8.00-18.00 ⊗No Antiques and bric-à-brac on Saturdays and a food market during the week. Good cafés and restaurants attract a young crowd.

Shepherd's Bush Market — 24-2A
Goldhawk Rd. London W12 ⊖Shepherd's Bush ◎9.30-17.00(Thur 14.30) ⊗Sun Fantastic place to pick up ingredients for African, Caribbean and Arabic cooking, also very good for linen and curtain material.

Spitalfields Market — 25-1A
Commercial St. London E1 ⊖Liverpool Street ◎9.00-18.00(店により異なる) ⊗Sat Especially good for organic produce, as well as stalls with crafts, antiques and clothing.

St James's Crafts Market — 31-2A
197 Piccadilly, London W1 ⊖Green Park ◎10.00-18.00 ⊗Sun, Mon Situated in St. James's Churchyard near Piccadilly. Great antique market on Tuesdays.

Walthamstow Market — 25-1B
Walthmstow High St. London, E17 ⊖Walthamstow Central ◎8.00-18.00 ⊗Sun One of Europe's biggest markets, selling everything from fruit and veg. to fashion and hardware goods.

MARKETS, PUBS

[ANTIQUE MARKETS]

Alfie's Antique Market   24-1A
13/25 Church St. London NW8 ⊖Edgware Road ☎020-7723-6066 ◎10.00-18.00 ⊗Sun, Mon Two hundred antique dealers spread over three floors, plus a rooftop restaurant to relax in.

Antiquarius   53-2A
Chenil House, 181/183 King's Rd. London SW3 ⊖Sloane Square ☎020-7351-5353 ◎10.00-18.00 ⊗Sun Indoor antique market with over 200 stalls selling, among other things, a wide variety of brooches, silverware and antique clothing.

Gray's Antique Market   33-2B
58 Davies St. London W1 ⊖Bond Street ☎020-7629-7034 ◎10.00-18.00 ⊗Sat, Sun Sells a large range of high quality antiques, such as Chippendale furniture and Sheffield plate.

PUBS

The Albert   49-1B
52 Victoria St. London SW1 ⊖St James's Park ☎020-7222-5577 ◎11.00-23.00(Sun 12.00-22.30) ⊗No A Grade II listed Victorian pub with wooden floors and original gas lamps. Serves traditional English breakfast and roasts. Extensive wine list.

The Albion   25-1A
10 Thornhill Rd. London N1 ⊖Angel / Highbury & Islington ☎020-7607-7450 ◎12.00-23.00(Sun 22.30) ⊗No Once a coaching inn, now an elegant pub with a country theme. Award winning beer garden with picnic tables for the summer months. Cosy, open fire in the winter.

Anchor Bankside   42-2A
34 Park St. London SE1 ⊖London Bridge ☎020-7407-1577 ◎11.00-23.00(Sun 12.00-22.30) ⊗No Once frequented by smugglers, a ghost and Dr Johnson, this historical pub has good food, a beer garden and a summer barbecue. Also displays a model of Shakespeare's Globe and upstairs celebrates the Financial Times, published nearby. Excellent view of the river.

Argyll Arms   34-2A
18 Argyll St. London W1 ⊖Oxford Circus ☎020-7494-0557 ◎11.00-23.00(Sun 12.00-21.00) ⊗No Victorian smoked-glass pub. Ideal stop-off for tired shoppers right at Oxford Circus. Serves real ale and a wide selection of wines.

The Atlas   24-2A
16 Seagrave Rd. London SW6 ⊖West Brompton ☎020-7385-9129 ◎12.00-23.00(Sun 22.30) ⊗No Good food on offer at this friendly pub.

The Blackfriar   38-2B
174 Queen Victoria St. London EC4 ⊖Blackfriars ☎020-7236-5474 ◎11.30-23.00(Sat 12.00-16.30) ⊗Sun Stunning Art Deco interior of wood carvings, stained glass and marble pillars. Lunch menu.

Builders Arms   52-1B
13 Britten St. London SW3 ⊖South Kensington ☎020-7349-9040 ◎11.00-23.00(Sun 12.00-22.30) ⊗No Great beers, reasonable wine list, super food - Cumberland sausage, homemade pies and dishes to suit vegetarians.

Bunch of Grapes   46-2B
207 Brompton Rd. London SW3 ⊖South Kensigton / Knightsbridge ☎020-7589-4944 ◎11.00-23.00 (Sun 12.00-22.30) ⊗No Grade II listed pub. The four bars have snob screens to separate Victorian gentlemen from the working class, and food is traditional British.

PUBS

Cartoonist 38-1A
International Press Centre, 76 Shoe Lane, London EC4 ⊖Chancery Lane / Blackfriars ☎020-7353-2828 ◎11.00-23.00 ⊗Sat, Sun The headquarters of the International Cartoonist Club is practically wallpapered with cartoons. Great names have visited here to receive the Cartoon Club Award.

The Chapel 24-1A
48 Chapel St. London NW1 ⊖Edgware Road ☎020-7402-9220 ◎12.00-23.00(Sun 22.30) ⊗No Simple but sophisticated interior, seating outside, friendly local atmosphere.

Cheshire Cheese 38-2A
5 Little Essex St. London WC2 ⊖Temple ☎020-7836-2347 ◎11.00-23.00 ⊗Sat, Sun Intimate, oak-beamed Jacobean pub frequented by members of the legal profession. Three bars and a ghost.

Cittie of York 37-1B
22 High Holborn, London WC1 ⊖Chancery Lane ☎020-7242-7670 ◎11.30(Sat 12.00)-23.00 ⊗Sun This original 1430 inn has been rebuilt many times, but has always been a pub or coffee house. Cozy cubicles, ancient stove, medieval roof.

Coat & Badge 24-2A
8 Lacy Rd. London SW15 ⊖East Putney ☎020-8788-4900 ◎11.00-23.00(Sun 12.00-22.30) ⊗No Fair number of decent beers on offer, the food's OK with desserts fairing best. Occasional jazz singer.

The Crown 25-1A
116 Cloudesley Rd. London N1 ⊖Angel ☎020-7837-7107 ◎12.00-23.00(Sun 22.30) ⊗No A super place to dine with a very relaxing mood and friendly service, welcoming Victorian bar.

Dawny Boys 24-1B
63 Lamb's Conduit St. London WC1 ⊖Russell Square ☎020-7405-8278 ◎11.00-23.00(Sun 12.00-22.30) ⊗No Famous for its real ales.

Dickens Inn 43-2B
St Katharine's Way, London E1 ⊖Tower Hill ☎020-7488-2208 ◎11.00-23.00(Sun 12.00-22.30) ⊗No This converted 18th century spice warehouse located by the marina is very lively, especially during summer. There are five separate bars and a good restaurant.

Dog & Duck 35-2B
18 Bateman St. London W1 ⊖Tottenham Court Road ☎020-7437-4447 ◎12.00(Sat 18.00, Sun 19.00)-23.00(Sun 22.30) ⊗No Warm Edwardian interior, a really inviting, if small, friendly pub.

The Dove 22-1B
19 Upper Mall, London W6 ⊖Ravenscourt Park ☎020-8748-5405 ◎11.00-23.00(Sun 12.00-22.30) ⊗No It has the smallest bar room in the world and former patrons include George Orwell and Ernest Hemingway. Serves Thai food.

Duke of York 37-1B
7 Roger St. London WC1 ⊖Farringdon ☎020-7242-7230 ◎12.00(Sat 18.00)-23.00 ⊗Sun Convivial atmosphere, with strong main courses but a lack of desserts.

The Engineer 24-1B
65 Gloucester Av. London NW1 ⊖Chalk Farm ☎020-7722-0950 ◎9.00-23.00 (Sun 22.30) ⊗No Very hearty and often spicy fare on offer, with choice ingredients and fresh herbs...a truly mouth watering menu with enough wine and beer options to quench any remaining thirst.

Flask   24-1A
14 Flask Walk, London NW3 ⊖ Hampstead ☎ 020-7435-4580 ◌ 11.00-23.00(Sun 12.00-22.30) ⊗ No A popular haunt for thesbians, you can rub shoulders with famous writers and actors, or stick to drinking and darts with the numerous unknown.

Fox & Anchor   38-1B
115 Charterhouse St. London EC1 ⊖ Farringdon ☎ 020-7253-4838 ◌ 7.00-23.00 ⊗ Sat, Sun Good beers and homely cooking or sandwiches to snack on.

George Inn   42-2A
77 Borough High St. London SE1 ⊖ London Bridge ☎ 020-7407-2056 ◌ 11.00-23.30(Sun 12.00-22.30) ⊗ No London's only remaining galleried coaching inn, featured in Dickens' *Little Dorritt*. Entertainments include medieval jousts, morris dancing and jazz. À la carte restaurant.

The Grenadier   48-1A
18 Wilton Row, London SW1 ⊖ Hyde Park Corner ☎ 020-7235-3074 ◌ 12.00-23.00(Sun 12.00-22.30) ⊗ No Used as an officers' mess by the Duke of Wellington and his soldiers. Famous for Bloody Marys served on Sundays in specially opened bar. English restaurant.

Guinea   27-1B
30 Bruton Pl. London W1 ⊖ Green Park / Bond Street ☎ 020-7409-1728 ◌ 12.30(Sat 18.30)-23.00 ⊗ Sun The 'new' pub was built in 1675, replacing the 1423 original inn. Award winning restaurant serving Aberdeen Angus steak.

Island Queen   25-1A
87 Noel Rd. London N1 ⊖ Angel ☎ 020-7704-7631 ◌ 12.00-23.00(Sun 22.30) ⊗ No One room, Victorian pub decorated with pirates as a theme. Restaurant specializes in Mexican food.

Jerusalem Tavern   25-1A
55 Britton St. London EC1 ⊖ Farringdon ☎ 020-7490-4281 ◌ 9.00-23.00 ⊗ Sat, Sun A super place for some real flavoursome draught beers, specialising in Suffolk bitter and beers.

The Lamb   24-1B
94 Lamb's Conduit St. London WC1 ⊖ Russell Square ☎ 020-7405-0713 ◌ 11.00-23.00(Sun 12.00-16.00, 19.00-22.30) ⊗ No Sumptuous, Grade II listed Victorian building retaining many original features. Patio at rear.

Lamb & Flag   36-2A
33 Rose St. London WC2 ⊖ Covent Garden / Leicester Square ☎ 020-7497-9504 ◌ 11.00-23.00(Sun 12.00-22.30) ⊗ No Once called The Bucket of Blood because bare-fist fighting took place upstairs. Jazz on Sundays. Serves real ale.

Lansdowne   24-1B
90 Gloucester Av. London NW1 ⊖ Chalk Farm ☎ 020-7483-0409 ◌ 12.00(Mon 18.00, Sun 12.30)-23.00(Sun 22.30) ⊗ No Fuller's London Pride is but one of the cheery beers on offer here. The place is child friendly and has a rather sumptuous menu.

Museum Tavern   36-1A
49 Great Russell St. London WC1 ⊖ Tottenham Court Road / Holborn ☎ 020-7242-8987 ◌ 11.00-23.00(Sun 12.00-22.30) ⊗ No Located opposite the British Museum - an ideal spot to rest tired feet. Karl Marx also rested here after a stint in the library. Cream teas served in the afternoon.

180 PUBS

Nag's Head   47-1B
53 Kinnerton St. London SW1 ⊖Hyde Park Corner ☎020-7235-1135 ◎11.00-23.00(Sun 12.00-22.30) ⊗No A very sociable pub where anyone would feel at ease.

O'Hanlon   25-1A
8 Tysoe St. London EC1 ⊖Angel ☎020-7837-4112 ◎12.00-23.00(Sun 22.30) ⊗No Excellent kegged beers, dry stout and port stout, the food here is wholesome Irish fare.

Peasant   25-1A
240 St John St. London EC1 ⊖Angel ☎020-7336-7726 ◎12.00(Sat 18.00)-23.00 ⊗Sun Excellent kegged beers, dry stout and port stout, the food here is wholesome Irish fare.

Pineapple   24-1B
51 Leverton St. London NW5 ⊖Kentish Town ☎020-7485-6422 ◎12.30(Sat, Sun 12.00)-23.00(Sun 22.30) ⊗No A lively local pub with a very welcoming atmosphere, some fine beers on offer including Brakspear's Special.

Princess Louise   36-1B
208 High Holborn, London WC1 ⊖Holborn ☎020-7405-8816 ◎11.00(Sat 12.00)-23.00 ⊗Sun Very impressive Victorian interior, marvellous cask bitter and beers.

Printer's Devil   38-1A
98/99 Fetter Lane, London EC4 ⊖Chancery Lane ☎020-7242-2239 ◎11.00-23.00 ⊗Sat, Sun A printers' and journalists' pub, so called because of the traditional name given to a printer's apprentice. Collection of pictures illustrates the history of printing.

Prospect of Whitby   25-2B
57 Wapping Wall, London E1 ⊖Wapping ☎020-7481-1317 ◎11.00-15.00, 17.30-23.00(Sun 12.00-22.30) ⊗No Once called the Devil's Tavern because it was popular with thieves and smugglers. Restaurant overlooking the Thames and beer garden open in the summer. Nautical decorations.

Royal Oak   42-2A
44 Tabard St. London SE1 ⊖Borough ☎020-7357-7173 ◎11.00-23.00 ⊗Sat, Sun Sells the entire range of beers from Harvey's of Lewes....heaven to the beer connoiseur.

Running Footman   27-1B
5 Charles St. London W1 ⊖Green Park ☎020-7499-2988 ◎11.00-23.00(Sat, Sun 11.30-15.00, 19.00-23.00) ⊗No À la carte restaurant upstairs serves traditional English food. Real ales available.

The Salisbury   36-2A
90 St Martin's Lane, London WC2 ⊖Leicester Square ☎020-7836-5863 ◎11.00-23.00(Sun 12.00-22.30) ⊗No Frequented by actors from nearby theatreland. Stunning interior with cut-glass mirrors, acid-etched windows and Art Nouveau fittings.

Seven Stars   37-1B
53/54 Carey St. London WC2 ⊖Holborn / Chancery Lane / Temple ☎020-7242-8521 ◎11.00-23.00 ⊗Sat, Sun One of the smallest in London, this 17th century pub survived the Great Fire. Dickens was a patron. Now popular with members of the legal profession.

PUBS, WINE BARS | 181

Sherlock Holmes 50-1B
10/11 Northumberland St. London WC2 ⊖Charing Cross / Embankment ☎020-7930-2644 ◎11.00-23.00(Sun 12.00-22.30) ⊗No Conan Doyle arranged for Sherlock Holmes and Sir Henry Baskerville to meet here, giving the pub its name. Holmes memorabilia and cream teas.

Spaniard's Inn 24-1A
Hampstead Lane, London NW3 ⊖Hampstead / Golders Green ☎020-8731-6571 ◎11.00-23.00(Sun 12.00-22.30) ⊗No Dick Turpin robbed travellers through Hampstead Heath from this 16th century inn, and Charles Dickens had Mrs Bardell arrested in its rose garden, in *The Pickwick Papers*. Take the 210 bus between Archway and Golders Green.

Spread Eagle 24-1B
141 Albert St. London NW1 ⊖Camden Town ☎020-7267-1410 ◎11.00-23.00(Sun 12.00-22.30) ⊗No A real mix of customers here, suited, casual, street fashioned...very Camden at any rate.

Star Tavern 48-1A
6 Belgrave Mews West, London SW1 ⊖Hyde Park Corner / Sloane Square / Knightsbridge ☎020-7235-3019 ◎11.30-23.00(Sat 11.30-15.00, 18.30-23.00, Sun 12.00-15.00, 19.00-22.30) ⊗No Traditional pub in Good Beer Guide situated in a cobbled mews. Food on weekdays only. Real fire in winter.

Tattershall Castle 50-1B
Kings Reach, Victoria Embankment, London SW1 ⊖Embankment ☎020-7839-6548 ◎11.00(Sat, Sun 12.00)-23.00(Thur-Sat 3.00, Sun 22.30) ⊗No London's only paddle steamer functions as a pub and, at weekends, a nightclub. There is a buffet, snack bar and a barbecue in the summer, when you can also drink on deck.

White Horse 24-2A
1 Parson's Green, London SW6 ⊖Parsons Green ☎020-7736-2115 ◎11.00-23.00(Sun 22.30) ⊗No A spacious pub serving Trappist-brewed beer, European lagers, real ales and a wide selection of food. Occasional beer festivals.

Windsor Castle 44-1A
114 Campden Hill Rd. London W8 ⊖Notting Hill Gate ☎020-7243-9551 ◎12.00-23.00(Sun 22.30) ⊗No Traditional pub serving excellent quality food from English standards to European cuisine. Sunday lunches are extremely popular. Open fires in winter.

Ye Grapes 27-2B
16 Shepherd Market, London W1 ⊖Green Park ☎020-7499-1563 ◎11.00-23.00(Sun 12.00-22.30) ⊗No One of the few Mayfair pubs that isn't dominated by city professionals, a comfortable, welcoming drinking house.

Ye Olde Mitre 38-1A
1 Ely Court, Ely Pl. London EC1 ⊖Chancery Lane ☎020-7405-4751 ◎11.00-23.00 ⊗Sat, Sun Built in 1546, it still retains its Tudor charm. Elizabeth I is said to have danced round the cherry tree in the courtyard.

WINE BARS

The Actor's Retreat 25-1A
326 St John St. London EC1 ⊖Angel ☎020-7837-0722 ◎12.00-14.30(Ex. Sat), 18.00-23.00 ⊗Sun Family-owned wine bar with a selection of Italian wines.

Albertine 22-1B
1 Wood Lane, London W12 ⊖Shepherd's Bush ☎020-8743-9593 ◎12.00(Sat 18.30)-23.00 ⊗Sun Small, candlelit bar with an excellent wine list. Good food and a wide selection of cheeses.

WINE BARS

Andrew Edmonds — 35-2A
46 Lexington St. London W1 ↔Oxford Circus / Piccadilly Circus ☎020-7437-5708 ◎12.30(Sat, Sun 13.00)-15.00, 18.00-22.45(Sun 22.30) ⊗No Intimate restaurant/bar in Soho. Serves excellent wine and a variety of inventive dishes.

Archduke — 51-1A
Concert Hall Approach, London SE1 ↔Waterloo ☎020-7928-9370 ◎8.30-23.00(Sun 12.00-22.30) ⊗No Specializes in sausages from around the world, but excellent food in general. Good range of wines and nightly jazz.

Balls Brothers Bishopsgate — 41-2B
158 Bishopsgate, London EC2 ↔Liverpool Street ☎020-7426-0567 ⓗwww.ballsbrothers.co.uk ◎11.00-22.00 ⊗Sat, Sun Serves food all day, great soup, salads and plenty of sandwich and baguette options.

Bar des Amis — 36-2B
11/14 Hanover Pl. London WC2 ↔Covent Garden ☎020-7379-3444 ◎11.30-23.00 ⊗Sun Interesting wine list plus monthly special. Award winning cheeseboard.

Bleeding Heart — 38-1A
Bleeding Heart Yard, London EC1 ↔Chancery Lane / Ferringdon ☎020-7242-8238/2056 ⒻO20-7831-1402 ◎12.00-22.30 ⊗Sat, Sun Some 400 wines are served at this French bistro and wine bar. Terrace tables available during summer.

Bow Wine Vaults — 39-2B
10 Bow Churchyard, London EC4 ↔Mansion House / Bank ☎020-7248-1121 ◎11.00-23.00 ⊗Sat, Sun Over 100 wines from France, Spain, Germany and California. Hot and cold dishes and excellent cheeses served.

Cellar Gascon — 39-1A
59 West Smithfield, London EC1 ↔Barbican ☎020-7796-0600 ◎12.00-0.00 ⊗Sun Absolutely swinging French bar with an air of sophisticated frivolity and a bar list to happily drown in...superb wine list.

City Litten Tree — 43-1A
1 Seething Lane, London EC3 ↔Tower Hill ☎020-7488-4224 ◎11.30-21.00(Wed 23.00, Thur 23.30, Fri 0.00) ⊗Sat, Sun Good, cheap food: steak, vegetarian, pasta. Italian and Australian wines.

Cork & Bottle — 36-2A
44/46 Cranbourn St. London WC2 ↔Leicester Square ☎020-7734-7807 ◎11.00-23.30(Sun 12.00-22.30) ⊗No Crowded but enjoyable cellar bar off Leicester Square. Great selection of wines and bar snacks. Decorated with wine posters and information for the uninitiated.

Corney & Barrow — 36-2A
116 St Martin's Lane, London WC2 ↔Charing Cross ☎020-7655-9800 ◎12.00-0.00(Thur-Sat 2.00) ⊗Sun You can choose between their restaurant, wine bar or champagne bar - positioned well for theatre goers.

The Crescent — 52-1B
99 Fulham Rd. London SW3 ↔South Kensington ☎020-7225-2244 ◎10.00(Sun, Mon 11.00)-23.00 ⊗No Wine lovers heaven with some 225 wines on its list.

The Ebury Wine Bar — 48-2B
139 Ebury St. London SW1 ↔Victoria ☎020-7730-5447 ◎12.00-22.00 (Sun 21.30) ⊗No Crowded and lively place after office hours. There's an extensive wine list with good quality, mostly British food at reasonable prices.

WINE BARS 183

Gordon's   50-1B
47 Villiers St. London WC2 ⊖Embankment ☎020-7930-1408 ⊙11.00-23.00 ⊗Sun   Situated in a 300-year-old cellar, this is one of the most atmospheric wine bars in London. Offers a selection of quality wines, ports and sherries.

The Hanover Square Wine Bar & Grill   34-2A
25 Hanover Sq. London W1 ⊖Oxford Circus ☎020-7408-0935 ⊕www.donhewitsonlondonwinebars.com ⊙11.00-23.00 ⊗Sat, Sun   Very strong on New Zealand and Australian wines...the dining is candle lit with easy jazz sounds.

Hardy's   32-1B
53 Dorset St. London W1 ⊖Baker Street ☎020-7935-5929 ⊙12.00-15.00, 17.30-22.30 ⊗Sat, Sun   Orange walls and mirrors create a dazzling interior. High quality but expensive food and wine.

Jamie's   34-1B
74 Charlotte St. London W1 ⊖Goodge Street ☎020-7636-7556 ⊕www.jamiesbars.co.uk ⊙11.00-23.00 ⊗Sat, Sun   European un-fussy menu accompanied by bold and festive wines, and a strong champagne list.

No.77 Wine Bar   24-1A
77 Mill Lane, London NW6 ⊖Hampstead ☎020-7435-7787 ⊙12.00-0.00(Mon, Tue 23.00, Sun 22.30) ⊗No   Relaxing wine bar with a good lunch and dinner menu; popular with families most weekends, a suitably child friendly atmosphere with gentle jazz tones playing in the background. Great wine list.

Odette's Wine Bar   24-1B
130 Regent's Park Rd. London NW1 ⊖Chalk Farm ☎020-7722-5388 ⊙12.30-22.30(Sun 15.00) ⊗No   Candle light, about 30 wines served by the glass, and good modern European menu.

Oriel   48-2A
50/51 Sloane Sq. London SW1 ⊖Sloane Square ☎020-7730-2804 ⊙8.30-23.00(Sun 9.00-22.30) ⊗No   Located in fashionable Sloane Square. Serves chicken steaks, salads and Mediterranean cuisine. Young crowd.

Osteria d'Isola   47-1B
145 Knightsbridge, London SW1 ⊖Knightsbridge ☎020-7838-1044 ⊙12.00-22.30(Sun 21.30) ⊗No   Great if posey gastrobar...amazing number of wines on offer by the glass and fun cocktail list. Their artichokes also make it definitely worth a visit.

Shiraz   36-2A
12 Upper St Martin's Lane, London WC2 ⊖Leicester Square ☎020-7379-7811 ⊕www.donhewitsonlondonwinebars.com ⊙11.00(Sat 17.00)-23.00 ⊗Sun   A calming environment in the heart of the capital, jazz plays smoothly whilst you sample their reasonable wine list and enjoy quite an exotic menu.

Tiles   49-1A
36 Buckingham Palace Rd. London SW1 ⊖Victoria ☎020-7834-7761 ⊙12.00-23.00 ⊗Sat, Sun   Very active lunchtime atmosphere and rather more laid back in the evenings, a sturdy wine list and delicious dessert selection.

Trader Vic's   27-2A
London Hilton Hotel, 22 Park Lane, London W1 ⊖Hyde Park Corner ☎020-7208-4113 ⊙17.00-0.30(Sun 22.30) ⊗No   Great choice of superbly mixed cocktails served in super-kitsch, South Sea island surroundings.

El Vino   38-2A
47 Fleet St. London EC4 ⊖Blackfriars / Temple ☎020-7353-6786 ⊙11.30-20.00(Thur, Fri 21.00) ⊗Sat, Sun   To enter here women must wear a skirt and men a shirt and tie. Has a good selection of French and German wines, spirits and champagnes.

WINE BARS, CAFES

Vinopolis Wine Wharf 42-2A
Stoney St, London SE1 ⊖London Bridge ☎020-7940-8335 ⓗwww.vinopolis.co.uk ◎11.00-23.00(Sat, Sun 21.00) ⊗No Steel and wood modern interior, strong menu and devilishly fun wine tasting... a place full of temptation.

CAFES

Amato 35-2B
14 Old Compton St. London W1 ⊖Tottenham Court Road ☎020-7734-5733 ⓗwww.amato.co.uk ◎8.00(Sat, Sun 10.00)-22.00(Sun 20.00) ⊗No Very convivial atmosphere, tasty homemade omelettes or quiches, light lunches and heavily delicious pastries and desserts.

Aroma 36-2A
36A St Martin's Lane, London WC2 ⊖Charing Cross / Leicester Square ☎020-7836-5110 ◎8.00(Sat 9.00, Sun 11.00)-20.00(Sun 19.00) ⊗No The bright decor is as eye-catching as the dessert and cake selection. Ready-made sandwiches and salads, plus six choices of great tasting coffee.

Boulevard 36-2B
40 Wellington St. London WC2 ⊖Covent Garden ☎020-7240-2992 ◎12.00-0.00 ⊗No Light, sunny interior, interesting menu and good service. A convenient place to drop in after shopping.

Café Bagatelle 33-2A
The Wallace Collection, Manchester Sq. London W1 ⊖Bond Street ☎020-7563-9505 ◎10.00-16.45 ⊗No A glass covered courtyard at the Wallace Collection, an exciting modern European menu and an air of sophistication.

Café Bohème 29-1B
13/17 Old Compton St. London W1 ⊖Leicester Square / Tottenham Court Road ☎020-7734-0623 ◎8.00(Sun 9.00)-0.00(Sat 4.00) ⊗No French-style café serving beer, capuccino, snacks, omelettes and good French food. Situated in the centre of Soho. Attracts a young crowd.

Café Delancey 24-1B
3 Delancey St. London NW1 ⊖Camden Town ☎020-7387-1985 ◎9.00-23.30(Sun 22.00) ⊗No Spacious, relaxed café with a distinctly Bohemian feel. Meals are served all day. Good steaks, salads and unusual daily specials.

Café Libre 34-2B
22 Great Marlborough St. London W1 ⊖Oxford Circus ☎020-7437-4106 ◎8.00(Sun10.00)-22.00(Thur, Fri, Sat 23.00, Sun 21.30) ⊗No North side of Liberty's. Convenient resting place after shopping along Oxford St.

Carluccio's Caffè 34-2B
8 Market Pl. London W1 ⊖Oxford Circus ☎020-7636-2228 ◎8.00(Sat 10.00, Sun 11.00)-23.00(Sun 13.00) ⊗No Italian cafe/restaurant, the cakes, pastries and desserts are the real winners here.

The Coffee Gallery 36-1A
23 Museum St. London WC1 ⊖Tottenham Court Road ☎020-7436-0455 ◎8.00(Sat 10.00, Sun 12.00)-17.30 ⊗No Charming cafe, with contemporary art to admire whilst you dive into their huge coffees.

Crowbar Coffee 25-1A
406 St. John St. London EC1 ⊖Angel ☎020-7713-1463 ◎8.00(Sun 9.00)-20.00 ⊗No Minimalist cafe with wonderful coffees and good snack options.

CAFES

Dôme   52-2A
354 King's Rd. London SW3 ⊖ South Kensington / Sloane Square ☎ 020-7352-2828 ◎8.00-23.00(Sun 9.00-22.30) ⊗No Parisian chain famous throughout London. Renowned for its lively and friendly atmosphere and good value brasserie fare.

Eat   35-2B
16A Soho Sq. London W1 ⊖ Tottenham Court Road ☎ 020-7287-7702 ⒽWww.eatcafe.co.uk ◎7.00-18.00(Sat 10.00-17.00) ⊗Sun A scrumptious selection of takeaway eats, with good sandwiches and cookie fillers for those eating in.

Fifth Floor Café   47-1B
Harvey Nichols, 109/125 Knightsbridge, London SW1 ⊖ Knightsbridge ☎ 020-7235-5000 ◎10.00-22.30(Sun 12.00-18.00) ⊗No Designer café with bright and airy interior. Evening jazz and full restaurant.

The Garden Café   34-2B
4 Newburgh St. London W1 ⊖ Oxford Circus ☎ 020-7494-0044 ◎8.00(Sat 9.00, Sun 11.00)-19.00(Sun 18.00) ⊗No A varied menu with veggie options, sandwiches or meals served with chips, good desserts. A very friendly atmosphere.

Giraffe   24-1A
46 Rosslyn Hill, London NW3 ⊖ Hampstead ☎ 020-7435-0343 ◎8.00(Sat, Sun 9.00)-0.00(Sun 12.00) ⊗No A place for exceptional and unusual teas and coffees and riotous cakes, trifles and other desirable desserts... spoil yourself.

The Green Café   24-2A
60 New King's Rd. London SW6 ⊖ Parsons Green ☎ 020-7371-5763 ◎8.00(Sat 9.00, Sun 10.00)-18.00(Sun 16.00) ⊗No Worth checking out, 10min walk from Parsons Green Station.

ICA Café   29-2B
The Mall, London SW1 ⊖ Piccadilly Circus ☎ 020-7930-8619 ◎12.00-1.00(Mon 23.00, Sun 22.30) ⊗No A rather smoky atmosphere with a menu influenced by Japan and Brazil, plenty of wines and cocktails.

Jamaica Blue   34-2A
18a Maddox St. London W1 ⊖ Oxford Circus ☎ 020-7408-2272 Ⓗwww.jamaicablue.co.uk ◎10.00(Sat, Sun 12.00)-22.00(Fri, Sat 23.00) ⊗No So laid back, rather like the Jamaican TV ads. The desserts make more statements than the other dishes, but Bob Marley fans will relish all the Jamaican mementoes, decor and music.

Lisboa Pâtisserie   24-1A
57 Golborne Rd. London W10 ⊖ Westbourne Park / Ladbroke Grove ☎ 020-8968-5242 ◎8.00-20.00 ⊗No Attracts coffee connoisseurs from across London. Traditional Portuguese delicacies, such as pasteis de nata, are also much in demand.

Lunch   25-1A
60 Exmouth Market, London EC1 ⊖ Angel ☎ 020-7278-2420 Ⓗwww.lunch.uk.com ◎8.30(Sat 10.00)-16.00 ⊗Sun Get there early, their popular lunch time menu is soon running out after 1pm....a sure sign of just how good their grub is.

La Madeleine   31-1A
5 Vigo St. London W1 ⊖ Piccadilly Circus / Oxford Circus ☎ 020-7734-8353 ◎8.00-20.00 ⊗Sun Very French café just off Regent St. Delicious pâtisseries and reasonable meals.

Maison Bertaux   35-2B
28 Greek St. London W1 ⊖ Leicester Square ☎ 020-7437-6007 ◎9.00-20.00 ⊗No Wonderful cakes, pastries and snacks in a friendly French atmosphere.

CAFES, INTERNET CAFES

Maison Blanc — 24-1A
37 St John's High St. London NW8 ⊖St John's Wood ☎020-7586-1982 ◎8.30-18.30(Sun 9.00-18.00) ⊗No Authentic French patisserie offering the obvious goodies, and tasting rather better than most.

Monmouth Coffee Company — 36-2A
27 Monmouth St. London WC2 ⊖Covent Garden / Leicester Square ☎020-7379-3516 ◎9.00-18.30 ⊗Sun For genuine coffee enthusiasts this café is paradise. Menu is restricted. Coffee tasting area and coffee equipment sold.

Neal's Yard Café Society — 36-1A
13 Neal's Yard, London WC2 ⊖Covent Garden ☎020-7240-1168 ◎10.30-20.00 ⊗No The menu is mainly pasta and pizza here, and they specialise in making a variety of exciting smoothies for those healthy-drink-junkies.

The Orangery — 45-1A
Kensington Palace, Kensington Gardens, London W8 ⊖Queensway ☎020-7376-0239 ◎10.00-17.00(18.00 May-Sep) ⊗No The grounds of Kensington Palace provide the perfect setting for tea lovers, here you can choose from an exemplary range of teas and cakes and enjoy views of the orangery and the stunning floral arrangements.

Pâtisserie Valerie — 33-1A
105 Marylebone High St. London W1 ⊖Baker Street / Bond Street ☎020-7935-6240 ◎7.30(Sat 8.00)-19.00(Sun 9.00-18.00) ⊗No Enchanting spot for cake lovers. Handmade chocolates, tarts, gâteaux and éclairs, plus a choice of main meals. Very busy at lunch time.

Portrait Café — 50-1A
National Portrait Gallery, 2 St Martin's Pl. London WC2 ⊖Leicester Square ☎020-7312-2465 ◎10.00-17.30(Thur, Fri 20.30) ⊗No A health concious menu here, organic and fresh are the order of the day with plenty of fruit drinks, decent salads, breads and cakes.

Raoul's — 24-1A
13 Clifton Rd. London W9 ⊖Warwick Avenue / Maida Vale ☎020-7289-7313 ◎8.30(Sun 9.00)-23.00 ⊗No Continental café serving interesting hot dishes, savouries and more than 30 types of bought-in pastries.

Table Café — 35-1A
Habitat, Tottenham Court Rd. London W1 ⊖Goodge Street ☎020-7636-8330 ◎10.00(Sun 12.00)-17.30(Thur 19.30) ⊗No A good place for pasta dishes, particularly if you have children as its a perfectly friendly environment for little ones. Good cakes, snacks and shakes (milk).

Victory Café — 33-2B
South Molton Lane, London W1 ⊖Bond Street ☎020-7495-1587 ◎10.00-17.30 ⊗Sat, Sun Easy-listening music in the background, a palatable brunch and snack selection.

INTERNET CAFES

Buzzbar — 44-1A
95 Portobello Rd. London W11 ⊖Notting Hill Gate ☎020-7460-4906 Ⓔmike@portobellogold.com Ⓗwww.buzzbar.co.uk ◎10.00(Sun 12.00)-21.00(Sat, Sun 19.00) ⊗No The internet boasts more buzz than the menu but this is one of the more relaxing net-cafe environments, usally full of local thesbians.

INTERNET CAFES, TEA ROOMS 187

Café Internet   49-1A
22/24 Buckingham Palace Rd. London SW1 ↔Victoria ☎020-7289-7313 Ⓔcafe@cafeinternet.co.uk Ⓗwww.cafeinternet.co.uk ⊘9.00(Sat, Sun 10.00)-22.00(Sat, Sun 21.00) ⊗No Bar and cafe and clintele that have each lived: The Beach.

Cyberia Cyber Café   35-1A
39 Whitfield St. London W1 ↔Goodge Street ☎020-7681-4200 Ⓔcyberia@easynet.co.uk Ⓗwww.cyberiacafe.net ⊘9.00(Sat, Sun 11.00)-21.00(Sat 19.00, Sun 18.00) ⊗No The first internet cafe to open in London, now established enough to offer web design courses.

dot com   44-1A
3/5 Thorpe Close, London W10 ↔Ladbroke Grove ☎020-8964-5484 Ⓔdotcom@dotcom.uk.com Ⓗwww.dotcom.uk.com ⊘11.00(Sun 12.00)-23.00(Sat, Sun 19.00) ⊗No Good net place especially if you're in need of a quick lesson in a web application, they offer resonable tuition in web design and the food here is OK.

easyEverything   44-2B
160/165 Kensington High St. London W8 ↔High Street Kensington ☎020-7938-1841 Ⓗwww.easyEverything.com ⊘24h ⊗No 24-hour a day net access.

Global Café   31-1A
15 Golden Sq. London W1 ↔Piccadilly Circus ☎020-7287-2242 Ⓔdbcox@hotmail.com Ⓗwww.globalcafe.net ⊘8.00(Sat 10.00, Sun 12.00)-23.00 ⊗No Relaxed, friendly atmosphere, often filled with thesbians good coffee.

Intercafé   34-2A
25 Great Portland St. London W1 ↔Oxford Circus ☎020-7631-0063 Ⓗwww.intercafe.co.uk ⊘7.30-19.00(Sat 9.30-17.00) ⊗Sun Coffee and surfing, just be careful not to spill it!

Internet Exchange   45-1A
Whiteleys Shopping Centre, Bayswater, London W1 ↔Queensway ☎020-792-0619 Ⓔadmin@internet-exchange.co.uk Ⓗwww.cafe.co.uk ⊘9.00-23.00 ⊗No Coffee and net access.

The Vibe Bar   25-1A
91 Brick Lane, London E1 ↔Aldgate East ☎020-7419-1183 Ⓔclaudine@vibe-bar.co.uk Ⓗwww.vibe-bar.co.uk ⊘11.00-23.00 ⊗No A very chilled out atmosphere for a drink and chance to check out your e-mail.

Webshack   35-2A
15 Dean Street, London W1 ↔Tottenham Court Road ☎020-7439-8000 Ⓔwebmaster@webshack-cafe.com Ⓗwww.webshack-cafe.com ⊘10.00-23.00(Sun 13.00-21.00) ⊗No Sofas to collapse into between your net-update and your next smoothie.

TEA ROOMS

Chinoiserie   47-2B
Hyatt Carlton Tower, 2 Cadogan Pl. London SW1 ↔Knightsbridge ☎020-7235-1234 ⊘7.00(Sat, Sun 8.00)-23.45, Tea Time: 15.00-18.00 ⊗No Close to Harvey Nichols and Harrods. Oriental interior with relaxing background harp music.

TEA ROOMS

Claridge's   27-1B
Brook St. London W1 ⊖Bond Street ☎020-7629-8860 ⊕www.claridge-hotel.com ©7.00(Sun 8.00)-23.00 Tea Time: 15.00-17.30 ⊗No Booking is advisable for afternoon tea in what was once Lady Claridge's reading room. Choice of 21 varieties of tea. The hotel itself celebrated its centenary in 1998.

The Conservatory   48-1A
The Lanesborough, Hyde Park Corner, London SW1 ⊖Hyde Park Corner ☎020-7259-5599 ⊕www.lanesborough.com ©7.00(Sun 7.30)-23.30(Fri-Sun 0.00),Tea Time: 15.30-18.00 ⊗No Full set tea with piano accompaniment. Weekend dinner and dancing. Open for lunch and dinner during the week. Has excellent vegetarian food.

The Fountain Restaurant   31-2A
Fortnum & Mason, 181 Piccadilly, London W1 ⊖Piccadilly Circus ☎020-7734-8040(Ext. 492) ⊕www.fortnumandmason.co.uk ©8.30-20.00, Tea Time:15.00-17.45 ⊗Sun Old fashioned but delicious. Selection of teas, ice-creams, sorbets, sundaes and savouries.

Jane Asher's Tea Room   53-1A
22/24 Cale St. London SW3 ⊖South Kensington / Sloane Square ☎020-7584-6177 ©9.30-17.30 ⊗Sun Small, charming shop owned by actress Jane Asher. Serves cakes, quiches and croissants. Modern European cuisine.

Julie's Wine Bar   24-2A
135 Portland Rd. London W11 ⊖Holland Park ☎020-7229-8331 ©11.30-23.30 ⊗No Afternoon teas served in popular restaurant. Antiques, Indian furniture and candles.

Palm Court   37-2A
Le Meridien Waldorf, Aldwych, London WC2 ⊖Holborn ☎020-7836-2400 ©7.00-23.00 Tea Time:15.00(Sat 14.30, Sun16.00)-17.30(Sat17.00, Sun18.30) ⊗No Edwardian, marbled elegance with big band dancing at weekends. Good service and full set tea.

The Palm Court   28-2A
The Ritz, 150 Piccadilly, London W1 ⊖Green Park ☎020-7493-8181 ⊕www.theritzhotel.co.uk ©7.00-23.00 ⊗No Reservations are necessary, as are jacket and tie. Combination finger sandwiches, scones with jam and clotted cream.

Palm Court Lounge   27-2B
Park Lane Hotel, Piccadilly, London W1 ⊖Green Park ☎020-7499-6321 ⊕www.sheraton.com/parklane ©7.00-3.00 Tea Time:15.00-18.00 ⊗No Traditional English or Devon cream teas in Art Deco lounge. Pianist or harpist. Reservations necessary.

Pâtisserie Valerie   35-2B
44 Old Compton St. London W1 ⊖Leicester Square / Piccadilly Circus / Tottenham Court Road ☎020-7437-3466 ⊕www.patisserie-valerie.co.uk ©7.30(Sat 8.00, Sun 9.30)-22.00(Sun19.00) ⊗No Handmade chocolates, tarts and savouries.

Primrose Pâtisserie   24-1B
136 Regent's Park Rd. London NW1 ⊖Chalk Farm ☎020-7722-7848 ©8.00-21.00 ⊗No Apple strudel, pastries and cheesecakes are the specialities. A few hot dishes such as beef goulash also served.

TEA ROOMS, SPORTS

Richoux 30-2B
172 Piccadilly, London W1 ⊖Green Park ☎020-7493-2204 ◎8.00(Sun 9.00)-23.00(Sat 23.30) ⊗No Traditional English teas served in an Edwardian setting. Restaurant open for lunch and dinner.

Sotheby's Café 30-1A
34/35 New Bond St. London W1 ⊖Bond Street ☎020-7293-5077 ◎9.30-16.45, Tea Time:15.00-16.45 ⊗Sat, Sun Traditional English tea with strawberries, clotted cream, cucumber sandwiches and old-fashioned cakes, served on Wedgwood tea stands.

Terrace Garden Restaurant 31-2B
Le Meridien Piccadilly, 21 Piccadilly, London W1 ⊖Piccadilly Circus ☎020-7465-1642 ◎7.00-23.00, Tea Time: 15.00-17.30 ⊗No Overlooking Piccadilly, on the second floor of Le Meridien Piccadilly Hotel.

Thames Foyer 36-2B
The Savoy, Strand, London WC2 ⊖Charing Cross / Covent Garden ☎020-7836-4343 ⒽGwww.savoy-group.co.uk ◎8.00-23.00(Sun 0.00) Tea Time: 15.00-17.30(Sun 18.00) ⊗No Homemade pastries, scones and tea with piano accompaniment. Jacket and tie necessary.

SPORTS

[SPORTS STADIUMS]
Crystal Palace National Sports Centre 23-2A
Ledrington Rd. Norwood, London SE19 ⇌Crystal Palace ☎020-8778-0131 Ⓗwww.c-palace.org Hosts a major athletic meeting every summer. It is also possible to participate in 52 different sports from skiing to wall-climbing.

Wembley Stadium 22-1B
Empire Way, Wembley, Middlesex HA9 ⊖Wembley Park ☎020-8900-1234 Ⓗwww.wembleynationalstudium.co.uk The home of world football and where England won the World Cup in 1966. The stadium holds 80,000 for premier sporting events.

[RUGBY]
Rugby Football Union Twickenham 22-2A
Whitton Rd. Twickenham, Middlesex TW1 ⇌Twickenham ☎020-8892-2000 Hosts national and international matches.

[TENNIS]
All England Lawn Tennis & Croquet Club 22-2B
Church Rd. Wimbledon, London SW19 ⊖Southfields ☎020-8944-1066/8946-2244 Eating strawberries and cream at Wimbledon in June is a British institution. One of the four international Grand Slam tennis tournaments.

[CRICKET]
Lord's Cricket Ground 24-1A
St John's Wood Rd. London NW8 ⊖St John's Wood ☎020-7289-1611 County games and International Test matches.

The Oval Cricket Ground 24-2B
Kennington Oval, London SE11 ⊖Oval ☎020-7582-6660 London's second venue for International Test matches and county games.

190 SPORTS, EXHIBITION CENTRES

[HORSE RACING]

Ascot Racecourse — 22-2A
Ascot, Berkshire SL5 ≷ Ascot ☎01344-622211

Epsom Racecourse — 22-2B
Epsom Grandstand, Epsom Downs, Surrey KT18 ≷ Epson ☎01372-726311
Ⓗwww.epsomderby.co.uk Where the Derby is held.

Kempton Park Racecourse — 22-2A
Sunbury-on-Thames, Middlesex TW16 ≷ Kempton Park / Sunbury ☎01932-782292

Sandown Park Racecourse — 22-2A
Esher, Surrey KT10 ≷ Esher ☎01372-463072

[DOG RACING]

Catford Stadium — 23-2A
Adenmore Rd. London SE6 ≷ Catford/Catford Bridge ☎020-8690-8000

Romford Stadium — 23-1B
London Rd. Romford, Essex RM7 ≷ Romford ☎01708-762345

Walthamstow Stadium — 23-1A
Chingford Rd. London E4 ⊖Walthamstow Central ☎020-8531-4255

Wimbledon Stadium — 22-2B
Plough Lane, London SW19 ⊖Wimbledon Park ☎020-8946-8000

[MOTOR RACING]

Brands Hatch Circuit — 23-2B
Fawkham, Longfield, Kent DA3 ≷ Swanley ☎01474-872331 Ⓗwww.brands-hatch.co.uk

Silverstone Circuit — 22-1A
Silverstone, nr. Towcester, Northampton NN12 ≷ Northampton ☎01327-857271 Ⓗwww.silverstone-circuit.co.uk

EXHIBITION CENTRES

Business Design Centre — 25-1A
228A St Paul's Rd. London N1 ⊖Highbury & Islington ☎020-7359-3535
Ⓗwww.businessdesigncentre.co.uk

Earl's Court Exhibition Centre — 24-2A
Warwick Rd. London SW5 ⊖Earl's Court ☎020-7385-1200

Olympia Exhibition Centre — 24-2A
Hammersmith Rd. London W14 ⊖Olympia ☎020-7603-3344 Ⓕ020-7370-8500

Useful Addresses in London

Embassies, Airlines, Consulates,
Tourist Boards, & Useful Information

EMBASSIES, CONSULATES

Australian High Commission 37-2A
Australia House, Strand, London WC2 ⊖ *Temple* ☎ *020-7379-4334/09001-600333* Ⓕ *020-7465-8218* Ⓗ *www.australia.org.uk* ◎ *9.00-12.00* ⊗ *Sat, Sun*

Austrian Embassy 48-1A
18 Belgrave Mews West, London SW1 ⊖ *Hyde Park Corner / Knightsbridge* ☎ *020-7235-3731* Ⓕ *020-7344-0292* Ⓗ *www.bmaa.gv.at/embassy/uk/* ◎ *9.00-12.00* ⊗ *Sat, Sun*

Belgian Embassy 48-2B
103 Eaton Sq. London SW1 ⊖ *Victoria* ☎ *020-7470-3700/09001-600255* Ⓕ *020-7259-6213* Ⓗ *www.belgium-embassy.co.uk* ◎ *9.00-11.30* ⊗ *Sat, Sun*

Canadian High Commission 27-1A
38 Grosvenor St. London W1 ⊖ *Bond Street* ☎ *020-7258-6600* Ⓕ *020-7258-6506* Ⓗ *www.canada.org.uk* ◎ *8.00-11.00* ⊗ *Sat, Sun*

Chinese Embassy 33-1B
31 Portland Pl. London W1 ⊖ *Regent's Park* ☎ *020-7631-1430/0891-880808* Ⓕ *020-7436-9178* Ⓗ *www.chinese-embassy.org.uk* ◎ *9.00-12.00* ⊗ *Sat, Sun*

Embassy of the Czech Republic 44-1B
26 Kensington Palace Gardens, London W8 ⊖ *Notting Hill Gate* ☎ *020-7243-1115* Ⓕ *020-7243-7926* ◎ *10.00-12.30* ⊗ *Sat, Sun*

Royal Danish Embassy 47-2B
55 Sloane St. London SW1 ⊖ *Knightsbridge / Sloane Square* ☎ *020-7333-0265/0900-1600115* Ⓕ *020-7333-0266* Ⓗ *www.denmark.org.uk* ◎ *9.30-12.30(Telephone enquiries: ◎ 9.00-10.00, 15.00-16.00)* ⊗ *Sat, Sun*

Egyptian Consulate 48-1A
2 Lowndes St. London SW1 ⊖ *Knightsbridge* ☎ *020-7235-9777/09001-887777* Ⓕ *0900-1669902* Ⓗ *www.egypt-embassy.org.uk* ◎ *9.30-12.30* ⊗ *Sat, Sun*

Embassy of Finland 48-1A
38 Chesham Pl. London SW1 ⊖ *Hyde Park Corner / Knightsbridge* ☎ *020-7838-6200* Ⓕ *020-7838-9703* Ⓗ *www.finemb.org.uk* ◎ *9.00-12.00* ⊗ *Sat, Sun*

French Consulate General 45-2B
6A Cromwell Pl. London SW7 ⊖ *South Kensington* ☎ *09001-887733* Ⓕ *09001-669932* Ⓗ *www.embafrance.org.uk* ◎ *9.00-10.00, 13.30-14.30* ⊗ *Sat, Sun*

German Embassy 48-1A
23 Belgrave Sq. London SW1 ⊖ *Hyde Park Corner / Knightsbridge* ☎ *020-7824-1300/0906-833-1166* Ⓕ *020-7824-1449* Ⓗ *www.german-embassy.org.uk* ◎ *9.00-12.00* ⊗ *Sat, Sun*

The Consulate General of Greece 24-2A
1A Holland Pk. London W11 ⊖ *Holland Park* ☎ *020-7221-6467/09001-171202* Ⓕ *020-7243-3202* ◎ *10.00-13.00* ⊗ *Sat, Sun*

Hungarian Embassy 48-1A
35 Eaton Pl. London SW1 ⊖ *Victoria / Sloane Square* ☎ *020-7235-2664* Ⓕ *020-7823-1348* Ⓗ *www.huemblon.org.uk* ◎ *10.00-12.00* ⊗ *Sat, Sun*

Irish Embassy 47-1A
106 Brompton Rd. London SW3 ⊖ *Knightsbridge* ☎ *020-7225-7700* Ⓕ *020-7225-7777* ◎ *10.00-12.00, (Telephone enquiries:14.30-16.30)* ⊗ *Sat, Sun*

EMBASSIES, CONSULATES 193

Italian Consulate General 48-2A
38 Eaton Pl. London SW1 ↔ Sloane Square ☎ 020-7235-9371/0891-600340 Ⓕ 020-7823-1609 Ⓗ www.ambitalia.org.uk ◎ 9.00-12.00 ⊗ Sat, Sun

Embassy of Japan 27-2B
101/104 Piccadilly, London W1 ↔ Green Park ☎ 020-7465-6500 Ⓕ 020-7491-9347 Ⓗ www.embjapan.org.uk ◎ 9.30-13.00, 14.30-17.30 ⊗ Sat, Sun

Kenya High Commission 33-1B
45 Portland Pl. London W1 ↔ Regent's Park ☎ 020-7636-2371 Ⓕ 020-7323-6717 ◎ 9.30-12.00 ⊗ Sat, Sun

Embassy of the Republic of Korea 49-1B
60 Buckingham Gate, London SW1 ↔ St James's Park ☎ 020-7227-5500 Ⓕ 020-7227-5503 Ⓗ www.mofat.go.kr/mail/etop.html ◎ 10.00-12.00, 14.00-16.00 ⊗ Sat, Sun

Royal Netherlands Embassy 45-2B
38 Hyde Park Gate, London SW7 ↔ High Street Kensington ☎ 020-7590-3200/09001-171217 Ⓕ 020-7581-3458 ◎ 9.30-11.30 ⊗ Sat, Sun

New Zealand High Commission 29-2B
New Zealand House, 80 Haymarket, London SW1 ↔ Piccadilly Circus ☎ 0991-100100 Ⓕ 020-7973-0370 Ⓗ www.immigration.govt.nz ◎ 10.00-15.45 ⊗ Sat, Sun

Royal Norwegian Embassy 48-1A
25 Belgrave Sq. London SW1 ↔ Hyde Park Corner ☎ 020-7591-5500 Ⓕ 020-7245-6993 Ⓗ www.norway.org.uk ◎ 10.00-12.30 ⊗ Sat, Sun

Polish Consulate General 33-1B
73 New Cavendish St. London W1 ↔ Oxford Circus / Regent's Park ☎ 020-7580-0476 Ⓕ 020-7323-2320 Ⓗ www.poland-embassy.org.uk ◎ 10.00-14.00(Wed 12.00) ⊗ Sat, Sun

Portuguese Consulate General 47-1A
62 Brompton Rd. London SW3 ↔ Knightsbridge ☎ 0891-600202 Ⓕ 020-7581-3085 Ⓗ www.portembassy.gla.ac.uk ◎ 9.00-13.30 ⊗ Sat, Sun

Russian Embassy 44-1B
5 Kensington Palace Gardens, London W8 ↔ Notting Hill Gate ☎ 020-7229-8027 Ⓕ 020-7229-3215 ◎ 10.30-12.00 ⊗ Wed, Sat, Sun

South African High Commission 50-1A
15 Whitehall, London SW1 ↔ Charing Cross ☎ 020-7925-8900 Ⓕ 020-7930-1510 ◎ 8.45-12.45 ⊗ Sat, Sun

The Spanish Consulate 53-1B
20 Draycott Pl. London SW3 ↔ Sloane Square ☎ 09001-600123 Ⓗ www.spanishembassy.org.uk ◎ 9.15-12.00 ⊗ Sat, Sun

Embassy of Sweden 32-1A
11 Montagu Pl. London W1 ↔ Baker Street / Marble Arch ☎ 020-7724-2101/09901-600110 Ⓕ 020-7917-6475 Ⓗ www.swedish-embassy.org.uk/embassy ◎ 9.00-12.30 ⊗ Sat, Sun

Swiss Embassy 32-1A
16/18 Montagu Pl. London W1 ↔ Baker Street / Marble Arch ☎ 020-7616-6000 Ⓕ 020-7616-6040 Ⓗ www.swissembassy.org.uk ◎ 9.00-12.00 ⊗ Sat, Sun

EMBASSIES, CONSULATES, AIRLINES

The Royal Thai Embassy   45-2B
Basement, 29 Queen's Gate, London SW7 ↔ South Kensington ☎ 020-7589-2944/09001-600150 ◎ 9.30-12.30 ⊗ Sat, Sun

Turkish Consulate General   46-1B
Rutland Lodge, Rutland Gardens, London SW7 ↔ Knightsbridge ☎ 020-7589-0360 Ⓕ 020-7584-6235 Ⓗ www.turkishembassy-london.com ◎ 9.30-12.00 ⊗ Sat, Sun

American Embassy (U.S.A.)   27-1A
5 Upper Grosvenor St. London W1 ↔ Bond Street / Marble Arch ☎ 09061-500590 Ⓗ www.usembassy.org.uk ◎ 8.30-17.00 ⊗ Sat, Sun (All visitors need an appointment.)

AIRLINES

Aer Lingus [H1] [GS] [S] [C]   30-1B
64 Conduit St. London W1 ↔ Oxford Circus ☎Ⓡ 020-8899-4747 Ⓗ www.aerlingus.ie ◎ 9.30-17.30 ⊗ Sat, Sun

Aeroflot [H2] [GS]   30-2B
70 Piccadilly, London W1 ↔ Green Park ☎Ⓡ 020-7355-2233 Ⓕ 020-7493-1852 Ⓗ www.aeroflot.co.uk ◎ 9.30-17.30 ⊗ Sat, Sun

Air Canada [H3]   30-1B
Star Alliance Office, 7/8 Conduit St. London W1 ↔ Oxford Circus ☎Ⓡ 0870-524-7226 Ⓕ 020-8750-8415 Ⓡ 020-8750-8495 Ⓗ www.aircanada.ca ◎ 9.00-17.00 ⊗ Sat, Sun

Air France [H1] [H2] [GS] [C]   31-1A
1st Fl. 10 Warwick St. London W1 ↔ Piccadilly Circus ☎Ⓡ 0845-0845111 Ⓕ 020-8782-8115 Ⓗ www.airfrance.com ◎ 9.00-17.30 ⊗ Sat, Sun

Air India [H3]   27-1B
55 Berkeley Sq. London W1 ↔ Green Park ☎ 020-7495-7950 Ⓡ 020-8560-9996 Ⓕ 020-7495-1401 Ⓗ www.airindia.com ◎ 9.00-17.30 ⊗ Sat, Sun

Alitalia [H2] [GS] [S]   32-2B
4 Portman Sq. London W1 ↔ Marble Arch / Bond Street ☎ 020-7486-8432 Ⓡ 08705-448259 Ⓕ 01603-778-099 Ⓗ www.alitalia.co.uk ◎ 9.00-17.30 ⊗ Sat, Sun

All Nippon Airways [H3]   32-2B
100 George St. London W1 ↔ Baker Street / Marble Arch ☎ 020-7569-0900 Ⓡ 020-7224-8866 Ⓕ 020-7569-0921 Ⓗ www.ana.co.uk ◎ 9.00-17.30 ⊗ Sat, Sun

Austrian Airlines [H2]   29-1B
Swiss Centre, 10 Wardour St. London W1 ↔ Leicester Square / Piccadilly Circus ☎Ⓡ 020-7434-7350 Ⓕ 020-7434-7363 Ⓗ www.aua.com ◎ 9.00-18.00 ⊗ Sat, Sun

British Airways [H1] [H3] [H4] [GN] [S]   30-1B
156 Regent St. London W1 ↔ Piccadilly Circus / Oxford Circus ☎ 020-7434-4700 Ⓡ 034522-2111 Ⓕ 020-7434-4636 Ⓗ www.britishairways.com ◎ 9.30-18.00(Sat 10.00-16.00) ⊗ Sun

Cathay Pacific Airways [H3]   22-2A
Terminal 3, Heathrow Airport, London TW6 ↔ Heathrow Terminals 1, 2, 3 ☎Ⓡ 0845-7581581 Ⓕ 020-7925-0445 Ⓗ www.cathaypacific.com/uk/ ⊗ No

AIRLINES 195

CSA Czech Airlines H2 S   34-2B
72/73 Margaret St. London W1 ↔ Oxford Circus ☎ⓇR 020-7255-1898 Ⓕ 020-7323-1633 Ⓗ www.csa.cz Ⓞ 9.00-17.00 ⊗ Sat, Sun

easyJet L   —
London Luton Airport, Bedfordshire, LU2 ☎Ⓡ 0870-6000-000 Ⓗ www.easyjet.com

Egyptair H3   31-2A
29/31 Piccadilly, London W1 ↔ Piccadilly Circus ☎Ⓡ 020-7734-2395/7437-6309 Ⓕ 020-7287-1728 Ⓗ www.egyptair.com.eg Ⓞ 9.30-17.30(Sat 9.30-13.30) ⊗ Sun

Finnair H1 GN S   30-1A
14 Clifford St. London W1 ↔ Oxford Circus / Green Park ☎ 020-7514-2400 Ⓡ 020-7408-1222 Ⓕ 020-7629-7289 Ⓗ www.finnair.co.uk Ⓞ 9.00-17.00 ⊗ Sat, Sun

go S   —
Enterprise House, Stansted Airport, Essex, CM24 ☎Ⓡ 0845-60-54321 Ⓗ www.go-fly.com

Iberia Airlines H2 GS   31-1A
Venture House, 27/29 Glasshouse St. London W1 ↔ Piccadilly Circus ☎Ⓡ 020-7830-0011 Ⓕ 020-7413-1262 Ⓗ www.iberia.airlines.co.uk Ⓞ 10.30-16.30 ⊗ Sat, Sun

Japan Airlines H3   34-2A
Hanover Court, 5 Hanover Sq. London W1 ↔ Oxford Circus ☎ 020-7408-7770 Ⓡ 0845-774-7777 ⒻⓇ 020-7491-0969 Ⓗ www.jal-europe.com Ⓞ 9.00-17.30 ⊗ Sat, Sun

KLM-Royal Dutch Airlines H4 C S   22-2A
Terminal 4, Heathrow Airport, London TW6 ↔ Heathrow Terminal 4 ☎Ⓡ 0870-5074074 Ⓗ www.klmuk.com Ⓞ 5.00-21.00 (tel. Mon-Fri 8.00-19.00) ⊗ No

Korean Air H3   30-2B
66/68 Piccadilly, London W1 ↔ Green Park ☎ 020-7495-0077 / Ⓡ 0800-0656-2001 Ⓕ 020-7495-1616 Ⓗ www.koreanair.com Ⓞ 9.00-17.00 ⊗ Sat, Sun

LOT Polish Airlines H1 GN   34-1A
313 Regent St. London W1 ↔ Oxford Circus ☎Ⓡ 020-7500-5037 Ⓕ 020-7323-0774 Ⓞ 9.00-17.30 ⊗ Sat, Sun

Lufthansa German Airlines H2 C S   30-1B
Star Alliance Office, 7/8 Conduit St. London W1 ↔ Oxford Circus ☎ 020-8750-3500 Ⓡ 0345-737747 Ⓗ www.lufthansa.co.uk Ⓞ 9.00-17.30 ⊗ Sat, Sun

Malev Hungarian Airlines H2 GN   31-2A
1st Fl. 22/25A Sackville St. London W1 ↔ Piccadilly Circus ☎ 020-7439-0577 Ⓕ 020-7734-8116 Ⓗ www.malev.hu Ⓞ 9.30-17.30 ⊗ Sat, Sun

Northwest Airlines GS   22-2B
South Terminal, Gatwick Airport, West Sussex ⇌ Gatwick Airport ☎Ⓡ 0990-561000 Ⓗ www.nwa.com Ⓞ 5.30-21.00 ⊗ No

196 AIRLINES, TOURIST BOARDS

Olympic Airways H2 GS — 30-1A
11 Conduit St. London W1 ⊖ Oxford Circus ☎®087-0606-0460 Ⓕ 020-7493-0563 Ⓗ www.olympic-airways.co.uk ◎ 9.00-17.30 ⊗ Sat, Sun

Qantas Airways H4 — 37-2B
Arundel Great Court, 182 Strand, London WC2 ⊖ Temple ☎ 020-7497-2571 ® 0845-7747767 Ⓕ 020-8741-8669 Ⓗ www.qantas.com.au ◎ 9.00-17.00 ⊗ Sat, Sun

Ryanair GS L S — —
☎® 0870-156-9569 Ⓗ www.ryanair.com ◎ 8.00(Sat 9.00, Sun 11.00)-21.45(Fri 20.45, Sat, Sun 17.45) ⊗ No (Telephone enquiries only)

Sabena Belgian Airlines H1 GS S C — 34-1A
313 Regent St. London W1 ⊖ Oxford Circus ☎® 08456-010933 Ⓗ www.sabena.com ◎ 9.30-17.00 ⊗ Sat, Sun

SAS (Scandinavian Airlines System) H3 S — 30-1B
7/8 Conduit St. London W1 ⊖ Oxford Circus ☎® 0845-60727727 Ⓕ 020-8990-7127 Ⓗ www.scandinavian.net ◎ 9.00-17.00 ⊗ Sat, Sun

Singapore Airlines H3 — 30-1B
143/147 Regent St. London W1 ⊖ Oxford Circus / Piccadilly Circus ☎ 020-7439-8111 ® 0870-6088886 Ⓕ 020-7437-6856 Ⓗ www.singaporeair.com/uk/ ◎ 9.00-17.30 (Sat 12.45) ⊗ Sun

Swissair H2 S — 34-1A
313 Regent St. London W1 ⊖ Oxford Circus ☎ 020-8394-6000® 0870-601-0956 Ⓕ 020-8394-6001 Ⓗ www.swissair.co.uk ◎ 9.00-17.30 ⊗ Sat ,Sun

Thai Airways International H3 — 30-2B
41 Albemarle St. London W1 ⊖ Green Park ☎ 020-7491-7953 ® 0870-6060911 Ⓕ 020-7409-1463 Ⓗ www.thaiair.com ◎ 9.00-17.00 ⊗ Sat, Sun

Turkish Airlines H3 — 29-2B
125 Pall Mall, London SW1 ⊖ Piccadilly Circus / Charing Cross ☎® 020-7766-9300 Ⓕ 020-7976-1738 Ⓗ www.turkishairlines.com ◎ 9.00-17.30(Sat 13.00) ⊗ Sun

TWA (Trans World Airlines) GS — 29-2A
7 Regent St. London SW1 ⊖ Piccadilly Circus ☎® 0845-7333333 Ⓕ 020-7930-8354 Ⓗ www.twa.com ◎ 9.30-17.00 ⊗ Sat, Sun

United Airlines H3 — 30-1B
Star Alliance Office, 7/8 Conduit St. London W1 ⊖ Oxford Circus ☎® 0845-844-4777 Ⓗ www.uk.ual.com ◎ 9.00-17.15(Sat 16.45) ⊗ Sun

Virgin Atlantic Airways H2 H3 GS — 35-2B
Virgin Megastore, 14/16 Oxford St. London W1 ⊖ Tottenham Court Road ☎® 01293-747747 Ⓗ www.fly.virgin.com ◎ 9.30(Mon 9.00, Wed 10.00)-18.00 ⊗ Sun

TOURIST BOARDS

[BRITAIN]

Britain Visitor Centre — 29-2A
1 Regent St. London SW1 ⊖ Piccadilly Circus ☎ 020-8846-9000 ◎ 9.00-18.30(Sat, Sun 10.00-16.00) ⊗ No

TOURIST BOARDS 197

City of London Information Centre — 39-2A
St Paul's Churchyard, London EC4 ⊖ St Paul's ☎ 020-7332-1456 ◎ 9.30-17.00 ⊗ No

London Tourist Board — 49-2A
Tourist Information Centre, Victoria Station Forecourt, London SW1 ⊖ Victoria ☎ 020-7971-0026 ◎ 8.00-19.00(Nov-Mar: 18.00, Sun 9.00-16.00) ⊗ No

Scottish Tourist Board — 50-1A
19 Cockspur St. London SW1 ⊖ Charing Cross / Piccadilly Circus ☎ 0131-4722035 ⊕ www.visitscotland.com ◎ 9.00-18.00(Sat 10.00-17.00) ⊗ Sun

Wales Tourist Board — 29-2A
Britain Visitor Centre, 1 Regent St. London SW1 ⊖ Piccadilly Circus ☎ 020-7808-3838 ⓕ 020-7808-3830 ◎ 9.00-18.30 (Sat, Sun 10.00-16.00) ⊗ No

[OTHER COUNTRIES]

Australian Tourist Commission — 22-2B
Gemini House, 10/18 Putney Hill, London SW15 ⊖ East Putney ☎ 020-8780-2227 ⊕ www.australia.com ◎ 9.00-17.30 ⊗ Sat, Sun

Austrian National Tourist Office — —
14 Cork St. London W1 ☎ 020-7629-0461 ⓕ 020-7499-6058 ⊕ www.austria-tourism.at ◎ 9.30-13.00, 14.00-17.00 ⊗ Sat, Sun (Telephone or letter enquiries only)

Belgian Tourist Office/ Brussels & Ardennes — —
14 Cork St. London W1 ☎ 020-7629-0461 ⓕ 020-7499-6058 ⊕ www.visitbelgium.com ◎ 9.30-13.00, 14.00-17.00 ⊗ Sat, Sun (Telephone or letter enquiries only)

Tourism Flanders — 25-2B
31 Pepper St. London E14 ⊖ Crossharbour & London Arena ☎ 09001-887799/020-7867-0311 ⓕ 09001-669908 ⊕ www.visitflanders.com ◎ 9.00-17.00 ⊗ Sat, Sun

Visit Canada Centre — —
P.O.Box 5396, Northampton NN1 ☎ 0906-8715000 ⓕ 0127-9647139(Telephone or letter enquiries only) ⓔ visitcanada@dial.pipex.com ⊕ www.travelcanada.ca ◎ 8.00-17.00 ⊗ Sat, Sun

Czech Centre — 34-1A
95 Great Portland St. London W1 ⊖ Oxford Circus ☎ 020-7291-9920 ⓕ 020-7436-8300 ⊕ www.visitczech.cz ◎ 10.00-18.00 ⊗ Sat, Sun

Danish Tourist Board — 47-2B
55 Sloane St. London SW1 ⊖ Knightsbridge / Sloane Square ☎ 020-7259-5959/09001-600109 ⓕ 020-7259-5955 ⓔ dtb.london@dt.dk ⊕ www.visitdenmark.com ◎ 9.00-16.00 ⊗ Sat, Sun

Egyptian State Tourist Office — 30-2B
Egyptian House, 170 Piccadilly, London W1 ⊖ Green Park ☎ 020-7493-5283 ⓕ 020-7408-0295 ⊕ www.interoz.com/egypt ◎ 9.30-16.30 ⊗ Sat, Sun

Finnish Tourist Board — 29-2A
30/35 Pall Mall, London SW1 ⊖ Piccadilly Circus ☎ 020-7839-4048 ⓕ 020-7321-0696 ⊕ www.finland-tourism.com ◎ 9.00-18.00 ⊗ Sat, Sun

TOURIST BOARDS

Maison de la France — 31-2A
178 Piccadilly, London W1 ⊖ Green Park ☎ 0891-244123 Ⓕ 020-7493-6594
Ⓗ www.francetourism.com ◎ 10.00-18.00(Sat 17.00) ⊗ Sun

German National Tourist Office — —
P.O. Box 2695, London W1 ☎ 020-7317-0908/09001-600100 Ⓕ 020-7495-6129
Ⓗ www.germany-tourism.de (Telephone or letter enquiries only)

Greece: Hellenic Tourism Organisation — 30-1B
4 Conduit St. London W1 ⊖ Oxford Circus ☎ 020-7734-5997 Ⓕ 020-7287-1369
Ⓗ www.gnto.gr ◎ 9.30-17.00(Fri 16.30) ⊗ Sat, Sun

Hungarian National Tourist Office — 48-2A
46 Eaton Pl. London SW1 ⊖ Victoria ☎ 020-7823-1032/1055/0891-171200
Ⓕ 020-7823-1459 Ⓗ www.hungarytourism.hu ◎ 9.00-17.00

Irish Tourist Board — 30-1A
Ireland House, 150 New Bond St. London W1 ⊖ Green Park ☎ 020-7493-3201
Ⓕ 020-7493-9065 Ⓗ www.irland.travel.ie ◎ 9.15-17.15(Fri 17.00) ⊗ Sat, Sun

Italian State Tourist Board — 34-2A
1 Princes St. London W1 ⊖ Oxford Circus ☎ 020-7408-1254/09065-508925
Ⓕ 020-7493-6695 Ⓗ www.enit.it ◎ 9.00-17.00 ⊗ Sat, Sun

Japan National Tourist Organization — 30-1B
5th Fl. Heathcoat House, 20 Savile Row, London W1 ⊖ Oxford Circus / Piccadilly
Circus ☎ 020-7734-9638 Ⓕ 020-7734-4290 Ⓗ www.jnto.go.jp ◎ 9.30-17.30
⊗ Sat, Sun

Netherlands Board of Tourism — —
☎ 0891-717777 Ⓕ 020-7828-7941 Ⓗ www.holland.com/uk (Telephone enquiries
only)

New Zealand Tourism Board — 29-2B
New Zealand House, 80 Haymarket London SW1 ⊖ Piccadilly Circus ☎ 09069-
101010 Ⓕ 020-7839-8929 Ⓗ www.purenz.com ◎ 9.00-17.00 ⊗ Sat, Sun

Norwegian Tourist Board — 29-2A
Charles House, 5 Regent St. London SW1 ⊖ Piccadilly Circus ☎ 020-7839-6255
Ⓕ 020-7839-6014 Ⓗ www.visitnorway.com ◎ 9.00-13.00, 14.00-16.30
⊗ Sat, Sun

Polish National Tourist Office — 34-2A
Remo House, 310/312 Regent St. London W1 ⊖ Oxford Circus ☎ 020-7580-
8811 Ⓕ 020-7580-8866 Ⓗ www.pnto.com ◎ 9.00-17.00 ⊗ Sat, Sun

Portuguese Tourism Office — 31-2A
2nd Fl. 22/25A Sackville St. London W1 ⊖ Piccadilly Circus ☎ 020-7494-
1441/0900-1600370 Ⓕ 020-7494-1868 Ⓗ www.portugal-insite.pt ◎ 9.30-13.00
⊗ Sat, Sun

Spanish National Tourist Office — 33-2A
22/23 Manchester Sq. London W1 ⊖ Bond Street ☎ 020-7486-8077 / 09063-
640630 Ⓕ 020-7486-8034 Ⓗ www.tourspain.co.uk ◎ 9.15-16.15 ⊗ Sat, Sun

Swedish Travel & Tourism Council — 32-1A
11 Montagu Pl. London W1 ⊖ Baker Street / Marble Arch ☎ 020-7724-
5868/01476-578811 Ⓕ 020-7724-5872 Ⓗ www.visit-sweden.com ◎ 10.00-
15.00 ⊗ Sat, Sun

TOURIST BOARDS, USEFUL INFORMATION 199

Switzerland Travel Centre   29-1B
Swiss Centre, 10 Wardour St. London W1 ↔ *Leicester Square* ☎ *020-7734-1921*
Ⓕ *020-7437-4577* Ⓗ *www.myswitzerland.com* Ⓞ *9.00-17.00* ⊗ *Sat, Sun*

Tourism Authority of Thailand   30-2B
49 Albemarle St. London W1 ↔ *Green Park* ☎ *0870-900-2007/09063-640666*
Ⓕ *020-7629-5519* Ⓗ *www.tat.or.th* Ⓞ *9.30-17.00* ⊗ *Sat, Sun*

Turkish Tourist Office   30-2B
170/173 Piccadilly, London W1 ↔ *Green Park* ☎ *020-7629-7771/09001-887755*
Ⓕ *020-7491-0773* Ⓗ *www.tourist-offices.org.uk/turky* Ⓞ *9.30-17.30* ⊗ *Sat, Sun*

American Travel and Tourism Information   —
☎ *09065-508-972*   *(Telephone enquiries only)*

USEFUL INFORMATION

[LOST PROPERTY]

Heathrow Airport Lost Property Office   22-2A
Heathrow Express Terminals 1,2,3 Station, Heathrow Airport ↔ *Heatherow Terminals 1, 2, 3* ☎ *020-8745-7727/7750* Ⓞ *8.00-16.00* ⊗ *No*

London Transport Lost Property Office   32-1B
200 Baker St. London NW1 ↔ *Baker Street* ☎ *020-7486-2496* Ⓕ *020-7918-1028*
Ⓞ *9.30-14.00* ⊗ *Sat, Sun*

Taxi Lost Property Office   25-1A
Metropolitan Police, 15 Penton St. London N1 ↔ *Angel* ☎ *020-7833-0996*
Ⓞ *9.00-16.00* ⊗ *Sat, Sun*

[EMERGENCY]

Chelsea & Westminster Hospital   24-2A
369 Fulham Rd. London SW10 ↔ *Fulham Broadway /* ☎ *020-8746-8000*

Middlesex Hospital   34 1B
Mortimer St. London W1 ↔ *Goodge Street* ☎ *020-7636-8333*

St Mary's Hospital   24-1A
Praod St. London W2 ↔ *Paddington* ☎ *020-7725-6666*

St Thomas' Hospital   51-2A
Lambeth Palace Rd. London SE1 ↔ *Waterloo / Westminster* ☎ *020-7928-9292*

[LATE-OPENING CHEMISTS]

Boots   31-1B
44/46 Regent St. London W1 ↔ *Piccadilly Circus* ☎ *020-7734-6126* Ⓞ *8.30-20.00(Sat 9.00-19.00, Sun 12.00-18.00)* ⊗ *No*

[LATE-OPENING POST OFFICE]

Trafalgar Square Post Office   50-1A
24/28 William IV St. London WC2 ↔ *Charing Cross* ☎ *0345-223344* Ⓞ *8.00 (Fri 8.30, Sat 9.00)-20.00* ⊗ *Sun*

The Wimbledon Lawn Tennis Museum

The wide ranging displays tell the history of Lawn Tennis.
Attractions include:
Access to view the Centre Court.
Regular special exhibitions.
Victorian Garden Party,
Racket Makers' Workshop and other room sets.
Videos of some of the all time "greats"
from the 1920s to the present day.
Museum shop selling Wimbledon souvenirs.
Tea room. Free car park.

OPEN THROUGHOUT THE YEAR

Open
  Tuesday - Saturday
  10.30am - 5.00pm
  Sunday afternoon
  2.00pm - 5.00pm

Closed
  Mondays, Public Holidays,
  the middle Sunday of The Championships,
  and the Friday, Saturday and Sunday prior to The Championships.

Please telephone for Christmas and New Year opening times.

During The Championships the Museum is only open to people who are visiting the Tournament.

Admission : Adults £4.00
       O.A.P's, Children, Students £3.00

The All England Club, Church Road, Wimbledon, London SW19 5AE
TEL : 020-8946-6131

Index for
Red Directory

# INDEX A-B

22 Jermyn Street (H)	101
47 Park Street (H)	101
50 St James	172
100 Club	166
333	169
606 Club	166
925	123

A

À la mode	113
A La Reine Astrid	130,131
The Abbey Court (H)	100,101
ABC Shaftesbury Avenue	162
ABC Tottenham Court Road	162
Accademia Italiana	154
The Actor's Retreat	181
Adelphi Theatre	135
Aer Lingus	194
Aeroflot	194
Agnès B	113
Air Canada	194
Air France	194
Air India	194
AKA	169
Al Fawer	87
Al Sultan	87
Al-Casbah	63
Alain Figaret	116,117
The Albert	177
Albertine	181
Albery Theatre	135
The Albion	177
Aldwych Theatre	135
Alfie's Antique Market	177
Alfred	75
Ali Baba	87
Alitalia	194
All England Lawn Tennis & Croquet Club	189
All Nippon Airways	194
Alloro	79
Almeida Theatre	165
Alounak	63,87
Amato	184
Les Ambassadors	173
Anchor Bankside	177
Andrew Edmonds	182
Angela Hale	123
Annandale House (H)	100,101
Antiquarius	177
Anya Hindmarch	119
Apollo Victoria Theatre	135
Aquascutum	112,113
Archduke	182
Argyll Arms	177
Arirang	93
Army & Navy	173
Aroma	184
Aromatique	127
Art	136,145
Artigiano	65,79
Ascot Racecourse	190
Asprey	122,123
Assaggi	79
Astoria	167
Athenaeum (H)	101
The Atlas	177
Aubergine	77
Australian High Commission	192
Australian Tourist Commission	197
Austrian Airlines	194
Austrian Embassy	192
Austrian National Tourist Office	197
Ayoush	86,87

B

Baccarat	121
Ballantyne Cashmere	117
Balls Brothers Bishopsgate	182
Bank of England	149
Banqueting House	149
The Banqueting House	148
Bar des Amis	182
Bar Rumba	169
Baradero	81
Barbican Centre	164
Barbican Hall	164
Barkers	173
Barracuda Club	173
The Basil Street (H)	100,101
The Beaufort (H)	100,101
Belgian Embassy	192
Belgian Tourist Office/ Brussels & Ardennes	197
Belgium, Tourism Flanders	197
Benson & Hedges	129
Bentley's	54,74,75
The Berkeley (H)	101,102
Berkshire (H)	101
The Berners (H)	101
Berry Bros. & Rudd	131
Berwick Street Market	175
Bethnal Green Museum of Childhood	154
BFI London IMAX Cinema	163
Bhs	174
Bibendum	97
The Blackfriar	177
Blackheath Halls	164
Blakes (H)	101
El Blasson	81
Bleeding Heart	182
Blooms (H)	101
Blue Elephant	88,89
The Blue Jade	89
Blue Lagoon	89
Bluebird	131
Boisdale	166
Bombay Brasserie	65,84,85
Bombay Palace	84,85
Bonhams	125
Boots	199
Borderline	168
Borough Market	175
Borshtch'n Tears	83
Boulevard	184
Bow Wine Vaults	182
Bramah Tea & Coffee Museum	154
Brands Hatch Circuit	190
Break for the Border	168
Brent Cross Shopping Centre	175
Brick Lane Market	175
The Bridge (Restaurant)	57
The Bridge (Leather)	119
Bridgewater	121
Britain Visitor Centre	196
British Airways	194
British Airways London Eye	149
British Museum	154
Brixton Academy	168
Brown's (H)	101
Browns	112,113
Buckingham Palace	149
Buddy	134,140
Bug Bar	170
Builders Arms	177
Bull & Gate	168
Bull's Head	166
Bunch of Grapes	177
Buon Appetito	60

INDEX B-E

Burlington Arcade	175
Business Design Centre	190
Butlers Wharf Chop House	75
Buzzbar	186
Bvlgari	123

C

C R Frost & Son	123
Cabinet War Rooms	154
Cadogan (H)	103
Café Bagatelle	184
Café Bohème	184
Café de Paris	170
Café Delancey	184
Café Internet	187
Café Lazeez	85
Café Libre	184
Café Loco	81
Calabash	87
Cambridge Theatre	135
Camden Falcon	168
Camden Lock	176
Camden Palace	170
Camden Passage	176
Canada Centre, Visit	197
Canadian High Commission	192
The Capital (H)	103
Caravela	83
Carluccio's Caffè	184
Carlyle's House	149
Cartier Ltd	122,123
Cartoonist	178
The Cashmere Gallery	117
Cassia	97
Catford Stadium	190
Cathay Pacific Airways	194
Cats	134,141
Cavendish (H)	103
Caviar House	58,96,97,131
Celadon Art Gallery	124,125
Cellar Gascon	56,182
Ceramica Blue	121
The Chapel	178
Che	97
Chelsea & Westminster Hospital	199
Chelsea Cinema	162
Chelsea Green (H)	102,103
Cheshire Cheese	178
Chez Gerard	77
Chiang Mai	89
Chicago	134,142
China City Restaurant	90,91
China Rendezvous	90,91
Chinese Embassy	192
Chinoiserie	187
Chor Bizarre	85,110
Christian Dior	113
Christie's	125
Chung's	91
Church's	119
Churchill Inter-Continental (H)	102,103
Chutney Mary	72,84,85
Ciné Lumière	163
Circus	97
Cittie of York	178
City Littem Tree	182
City of London Information Centre	197
Clapham Picture House	162
Claridge's	188
Claridge's (H)	103
The Clinic	170
The Cliveden Town House (H)	102,103
Club Gascon	63
Coach	119
Coat & Badge	178
The Coffee Gallery	60,184
Coles	116,117
The Collection	97
Columbia Road Flower Market	176
Comme des Garçons	113
The Connaught (H)	103
Connoisseur Club	173
Conrad International (H)	103
The Conran Shop	127
The Conservatory	188
Contemporary Applied Arts	125
Contemporary Ceramics	120,121
Copthorne Tara (H)	103
Cork & Bottle	182
Corney & Barrow	182
Costa Dorada	80,81
Covent Garden	149
Cox & Power	123
The Cranley (H)	103,104
Crazy Larry's	170
The Crescent (Restaurant)	74,75
The Crescent (Wine Bar)	182
Criterion	77
Criterion Theatre	135
Crockfords Club	173
The Cross	170
Crowbar Coffee	184
The Crown	178
Crystal Palace National Sports Centre	189
CSA Czech Airlines	195
Curzon Mayfair	162
Curzon Soho	162
Cutty Sark	150
Cyberia Cyber Café	187
Czech & Slovak House	83
Czech Centre	197
The Czech Republic, Embassy of	192

D

D. R. Harris & Co	127
D.H. Evans	174
Da Paolo	78,79
Danish Embassy, Royal	192
Danish Tourist Board	197
Daquise	83
David Richards & Sons	121
Dawny Boys	178
Debenhams	174
The Delhi Brasserie	84,85
Design Museum	154
The Dickens House	150
Dickens Inn	178
Dickins & Jones	174
Dog & Duck	178
Dolce & Gabbana	113
Dôme	185
Don Pepe	81
Donna Karan	113
The Dorchester (H)	103
Dorset Square (H)	103
dot com	187
The Dove	178
Dover Street Restaurant & Bar	166
Dower & Hall	123
Dr Johnson's House	150
Dublin Castle	168
Duke of York	178
Dukes (H)	105
Dust	170

E

Earl's Court Exhibition Centre	190

INDEX E-H

easyEverything 146,187
easyJet 195
Eat 185
The Ebury Wine Bar 182
Egyptair 195
Egyptian Consulate 192
Egyptian State Tourist Office 197
Electric Ballroom 170
Elena's L'Etoile 78,79
Ellis Bringham 117
Emporio Armani caffè 79
The Emporium 170
The End 170
The Engineer 178
Epsom Racecourse 190
Equinox 170
The Everyman Cinema 163
Eye to Eye 127

F

Fabric 171
O' Fado 82,83
Fiction 71
The Fifth Floor 59
Fifth Floor Café 185
The Finca 81
Finchley Road Warner Village 162
Fine Art Society 125
Finland, Embassy of 192
Finnair 195
Finnish Tourist Board 197
Fish at 190 67
Flask 179
Flemings Mayfair (H) 105
Floris 127
Folli Follie 122,123
Food for Thought 71
Fortnum & Mason 131,174
Forum 168
The Fountain Restaurant 188
Four Seasons (H) 105
Fox & Anchor 179
France, Maison de la 198
Franco's 78,79
Frateilli Rosetti 119
French Consulate General 192
Frevd 127
The Fridge 171
Fung Shing 90,91
Furama 91

G

The Gainsborough (H) 104,105
Galerie Gaultier 113
The Gallery (H) 104,105
Garage 168
The Garden Café 185
Gate 162
The Gate 70
Gaudí 81
Le Gavroche 77
The Gay Hussar 82,83
Gaylord 85
Geeta 85
George Inn 179
German Embassy 192
German National Tourist Office 198
Gianfranco Ferre 112,113
Gianni Versace 113
Gielgud Theatre 135
Gieves & Hawkes 117
Giorgio Armani 113
Giraffe 185

Glesslin's 56
Global Café 187
Globe 97
go 195
Goethe Institut 163
Golden Dragon 91
Golden Nugget 173
Gordon Ramsay 58,77
Gordon's 183
The Gore (H) 105
Gossips 171
Goya 81
Gray's Antique Market 177
Greece, The Consulate General of 192
Greece: Hellenic Tourism Organisation 198
The Green Café 185
Green's 75
Greenhouse 75
Greenwich Cinema 162
The Grenadier 179
Grissini-london 79
Grosvenor Court (H) 105
Grosvenor House (H) 105
Grosvenor Victoria Casino 173
Guildhall 150
Guinea 179

H

H. R. Higgins 131
Hackett 113
Halcyon Days 128,129
The Halkin (H) 105
Hamleys 129
Hammersmith Apollo 168
Hammersmith Palais 171
Hampton Court Palace 150
Hanover Grand 171
The Hanover Square Wine Bar & Grill ...183
Harbour City 90,91
Hardy's 183
Harrods 174
Harvey Nichols 174
Harvey Nichols Foodmarket 130,131
Hay's Galleria 175
Hayward Gallery 155
Heathrow Airport Lost Property Office 199
Heaven 171
Hennel 123
Her Majesty's Theatre 135
Herbie Frogg 115
Hervie & Hudson 117
The Highlands 116,117
Hippodrome 171
HMS Belfast 150
Hobgoblin 129
Home 171
Hope & Anchor 168
House of Hanover 128,129
Houses of Parliament & Big Ben 151
The Howard (H) 105
Hoxton Furnace 66
Hungarian Embassy 192
Hungarian National Tourist Office 198
Hyatt Carlton Tower (H) 105

INDEX I-M 205

I

Iberia Airlines 195
ICA Café 185
ICA Cinema 163
ICA(Institute of Contemporary Arts) 164
Iceni 171
Ikeda 95
The Immortals 91
Imperial City 69
Imperial War Museum 155
Inter-Continental (H) 105
Intercafé 187
Internet Exchange 187
Ireland in London 129
Irish Embassy 192
The Irish Linen Company 126,127
Irish Tourist Board 198
Island Queen 179
Italian Consulate General 193
Italian State Tourist Board 198
Itsu 96,97

J

J.A.N. Fine Art 125
Jacob's 83
Jaeger 115
Jägerhütte 83
Jamaica Blue 185
James Smith & Sons 129
Jamie's 183
Jane Asher's Tea Room 188
Japan Airlines 195
Japan National Tourist Organization ... 198
Japan, Embassy of 193
Jazz After Dark 166
Jazz Café 166
Jerusalem Tavern 179
John Lewis 174
Jones 115
Joseph at Old Bond Street 115
Jubilee Market 176
Julie's Wine Bar 188

K

K.Mozer 122,123
Kai Mayfair 91
Kaya 93
Kempton Park Racecourse 190
Kensington Court (H) 105
Kensington Palace 151
Kenwood House 155
Kenya High Commission 193
Khan's 85,86
Kiku 95
Kirin Europo GmbH 132
KLM-Royal Dutch Airlines 195
Korea, Embassy of the Republic of 193
Korean Air 195
Kwan Thai 88,89

L

LA2 168
Lalibela 87
The Lamb 179
Lamb & Flag 179
Landmark London (H) 107
The Lanesborough (H) 104,107
Langan's Brasserie 96,97
Langham Hilton (H) 107
Lansdowne 179
Laura Ashley 112,115

Leather Lane Market 176
Legends 171
Leighton House 155
Leisure Lounge 168
Leith's 75
Lemonia 83
The Leonard (H) 106,107
Liberty 174
Lillywhite's 129
Limelight 171
The Linen Merchant 126,127
Lisboa Pâtisserie 185
Lisson Gallery 125
Livebait 97
The Lobster Pot 76,77
London Aquarium 151
The London Coliseum 165
London Dungeon 155
London Graphic Centre 128,129
London Palladium 135
London Park Tower Casino 173
London Tourist Board 197
London Transport Lost Property Office ... 199
London Transport Museum 155
London Zoo 151
Lord's Cricket Ground 189
The Los Locos Tejas 172
LOT Polish Airlines 195
The Lowndes Hyatt (H) 107
Lufthansa German Airlines 195
Lunch 185
Lux Cinema 163
Lyric Theatre 135

M

M.C.N. Antiques 124,125,138
Mackenzie's 114,115
Madame JoJo's 172
Madame Tussaud's 151
La Madeleine 185
Maison Bertaux 185
Maison Blanc 186
Maison Noveli 77
Malabar Junction 85
Malev Hungarian Airlines 195
La Mancha 80,81
Mandarin Oriental Hyde Park (H) 107
Manna 70
Manorom 88,89
Mansion House 151
Mappin & Webb 120,121
Marks & Spencer 174
Matsuri St James's 6,94,95
MaxMara 115
Mean Fiddler 169
Mokong River 93
La Meridien Piccadilly (H) 107
Mesclun 85
The Metro 164
Mezzo 96,97,166
Middlesex Hospital 199
Millennium Gloucester (H) 107
Ministry of Sound 172
The Mirabelle 77
Les Misérables 134,143
Mitsukoshi Restaurant 94,95
El Molino 81
Mon Plaisir 77
The Mongolian Barbecue 93
Monmouth Coffee Company 186
Montcalm Hotel Nikko London (H) ...106,107
The Monument 152
Motcombs 172
Mulberry 118,119

INDEX M-R

Museum of Garden History	156
Museum of London	156
Museum Tavern	179

N

Nag's Head	180
National Army Museum	156
National Gallery	156
National Maritime Museum	156
National Portrait Gallery	156
The Natural History Museum	157
The Neal Street	79
Neal's Yard Café Society	186
Neal's Yard Dairy	131
Neal's Yard Remedies	126,127
Nelson's Column	152
Netherlands Board of Tourism	198
Netherlands Embassy, Royal	193
New Caledonian Market	176
The New End	58
New Fook Lam Moon	91
New London Theatre	135
New Mayflower	91,160
New World	91
New Zealand High Commission	193
New Zealand Tourism Board	198
NFT (National Film Theatre)	164
Nico Central	76,77
Nikita's	83
No.77 Wine Bar	183
Nobu	95
Northwest Airlines	195
Norwegian Embassy, Royal	193
Norwegian Tourist Board	198
Noto Restaurant	94,95
Notting Hill Arts Club	172
Notting Hill Coronet	162

O

O'Hanlon	180
O's Bar	56
The Oak Room	77
Odeon Camden Town	162
Odeon Kensington	162
Odeon Leicester Square	162
Odeon Marble Arch	162
Odeon Swiss Cottage	162
Odette's Wine Bar	183
Old Vic Theatre	135
Olympia Exhibition Centre	190
Olympic Airways	196
The Orangery	186
Ordning & Reda	129
Oriel	183
Orient	91,92
Oriental City Food Court	92,93
Oriental Garden	93
Orrery	97
Osteria d'Isola	183
The Oval Cricket Ground	189
Oxo Tower Brasserie	57
Oxo Tower Restaurant	59
Ozer	83

P

Palace Theatre	135
Pallant	114,115
Palm Beach Casino Club	173
Palm Court	188
The Palm Court	188
Palm Court Lounge	188
Paraboot	118,119

Park Lane (H)	107
Patara	89
Pâtisserie Valerie (Cafe)	186
Pâtisserie Valerie (Tea Room)	188
Patogh	87
Patrick Cox	119
Paul Smith	114,115
Pavillon Christfle	121
Paxton & Whitfield	131
Peacock Theatre	165
Peasant	180
The Pelham (H)	107
Pembridge Court (H)	107
Penhaligon's	127
Pescatori	78,79
Peter Jones	174
Petticoat Lane Market	176
The Phantom of the Opera	136,144
Phillips	125
Phoenix	164
Phoenix Theatre	137
The Photographers' Gallery	157
Piccadilly Arcade	175
Pickett	119
Pin-Petch	89
Pineapple	180
El Pirata of Mayfair	80,81
Pizza Express	166
Pizza on the Park	167
Pizza Paradiso	66
The Place Below	71
The Place Theatre	165
Playhouse Theatre	137
Plaza	175
Poissonnerie de L'Avenue	76,77
Polish Consulate General	193
Polish National Tourist Office	198
Pollock's Toy Museum	157
La Porchetta	66
La Porte des Indes	85
Portmeirion	121
Portobello Road Market	176
Portrait Café	186
Portuguese Consulate General	193
Portuguese Tourism Office	198
Prestat	130,131
Primrose Pâtisserie	188
Prince Edward Theatre	137
Prince of Wales Theatre	137
Princess Louise	180
Printer's Devil	180
Prism	59
Prospect of Whitby	180
PU's Brasserie	89
Purcell Room	165

Q

Qantas Airways	196
Quaglino's	167
Quality Chop House	61
Queen Elizabeth Hall	165
Question Air	115

R

Radisson Mountbatten (H)	107
Ramen House Noto	95
Raoul's	186
Rasa	70,85
Rasa Samdra	67,85
Reiss	115
Rembrandt (H)	109
Los Remos	81
The Rendezvous Casino Club	173

INDEX R-T 207

The Rib Room 75
Richard James...117
Richoux..189
The Ritz, London (H) 106,109
Ritzy...163
Riverside Studios....................................164
Riverside Studios Cinema 164
The Roadhouse.......................................169
Roberson 131
Rock Garden 169
Romford Stadium....................................190
Ronnie Scott's 167
Royal Academy of Arts 157
Royal Air Force Museum 157
Royal Albert Hall 165
Royal Botanical Gardens Kew 152
Royal China 58,59,92,93
Royal College of Music 165
Royal Doulton..121
Royal Dragon..69
Royal Festival Hall 165
Royal Garden (H) 106,109
Royal Horseguards Thistle (H) 109
Royal Lancaster (H)................................109
The Royal Mews......................................152
Royal National Theatre..........................137
Royal Oak..180
Royal Opera House 166
Rugby Football Union Twickenham 189
Rules 62,75
Running Footman 180
Russell & Bromley 119
Russian Embassy....................................193
Ryanair 196
Ryo Noodle Bar 95

S

Sabena Belgian Airlines 196
Sadler's Wells Theatre 166
Saga 95
St George's (H).......................................109
St Giles Jazz Club 167
St James's Church Piccadilly 165
St James's Crafts Market 176
St James's Palace 152
St John 61,75
St John's Smith Square 165
St Margaret's Church..............................152
St Martin's Theatre 137
St Martin-in-the-Fields 165
St Mary's Hospital...................................199
St Paul's Cathedral.................................153
St Thomas' Hospital 199
St. Moritz Swiss Restaurant 82,83
The Salisbury..180
Salvador's El Bodegon 80,81
Samantha's..172
Sanderson 127
Sandown Park Racecourse 190
Sartoria 79
SAS (Scandinavian Airlines System)....196
Satay Bar...93
Satay House..93
Satsuma 57,95
The Savoy Group 98
The Savoy (H) 108,109
The Savoy Grill..75
Savoy Theatre 137
Scala..172
Science Museum....................................157
The Scotch House 117
Scottish Tourist Board 197
Screen on Baker Street 163
Screen on the Green 163

Screen on the Hill 163
Seashell...74,75
Selfridges..175
Serpentine Gallery..................................158
Seven Stars 180
Shakespeare's Globe Exhibition............158
Shakespeare's Globe Theatre...............137
Shellys...119
Shepherd's Bush Empire 169
Shepherd's Bush Market 176
Sheraton Belgravia (H)...........................109
Sherlock Holmes 181
The Sherlock Holmes Museum 158
Shiraz 183
Shirin Cashmere..............................116,117
Siam Square..89
The Silver Fund 124,125
Silverstone Circuit..................................190
Simpson's-in-the-Strand 74,75
Simpsons of cornhill 62
Singapore Airlines 196
Singapura 92,93
Sir John Soane's Museum.....................158
The Sloane (H) 108,109
Smollensky's on the Strand 167
The Social Bar...169
Sotheby's...124,125
Sotheby's Café 189
Souk 86,87
Sound Republic 169
South African High Commission 193
The South Bank Centre 164
Space NK Apothecary 126,127
Spaniard's Inn...181
The Spanish Consulate 193
Spanish National Tourist Office 198
Spiga 79
Spitalfields Market 176
The Spitz 167
Sportsman Club......................................173
Spread Eagle 181
Stair & Co. 125
Stanton House Hotel (H) 108,109
Star Tavern 181
Strand Palace (H) 109
Strand Theatre 137
Stream Bubble & Shell 67
Stringfellows 172
Subterania 172
Suntory 94,95
Swaine Adeney.......................................129
Sweden, Embassy of..............................193
Swedish Travel & Tourism Council......198
Swiss Embassy.......................................193
Swissair...196
Switzerland Travel Centre 199

T

Table Café...186
Tandori of Chelsea 87
Tanner Krolle 118,119
Tate Britain 158
Tate Modern 158
Tatsuso 95
Tattershall Castle....................................181
Taxi Lost Property Office.......................199
Le Tea Cosy 60
The Tea House 130,131
Terrace 76,77
Terrace Garden Restaurant...................189
Thai Airways International 196
Thai Embassy, The Royal 194
Thai Pavilion 88,89
Thai Pot 89

INDEX T-Z

Thai Square	88,89
Thailand, Tourism Authority of	199
Thames Foyer	189
Theatre Museum	159
Theatre Royal Drury Lane	137
Theatre Royal Haymarket	137
Thomas Goode & Co.	120,121
Thomas Neal's	175
Thomas Pink	117
The Tibetan	93
Tiffany & Co.	123
Tiles	183
Tin Tin Collectables	125
Tiroler Hut	82,83
Tokio	115
Top Curry Centre	87
Tower Bridge	153
The Tower of London	153
Trader Vic's	183
Trafalgar Square Post Office	199
Tricker's	118,119
Turkish Airlines	196
Turkish Consulate General	194
Turkish Tourist Office	199
Turnbull & Asser	117
TWA (Trans World Airlines)	196

U

UCI Whiteleys	163
UGC Chelsea	163
UGC Fulham Road	163
UGC Haymarket	163
United Airlines	196
United States of America, American Travel and Tourism Information	199
United States of America, American Embassy	194

V

Veeraswamy	86,87
La Ventura	61
Verbanella	79
Veronica's	62
The Vibe Bar	187
Victoria & Albert Museum	159
Victoria Palace Theatre	137
Victorian Oven	167
Victory Café	186
El Vino	183
Vinopolis Wine Wharf	184
The Vintage House	131
Virgin Atlantic Airways	196

Vivienne Westwood	114,115
Von Posch	120,121
Vong	97
Vortex Jazz Bar	167

W

WAG	169
Wales Tourist Board	197
The Wallace Collection	159
Walthamstow Market	176
Walthamstow Stadium	190
Warner Bros. Studio Stores	129
Warner Village West End	163
Washin Optical	127
Watches of Switzerland	123
Water Rats	169
Waterford Wedgewood	121
Webshack	187
Wellington Museum	159
Wembley Stadium	189
The Wenlock Arms	167
Westbury (H)	109
Westminster Abbey	153
Westminster Cathedral	153
Whistle Down the Wind	136
White Horse	181
Whitehall	153
Wigmore Hall	165
The Willett (H)	108,109
William Morris Gallery	159
Wimbledon Lawn Tennis Museum	159,200
Wimbledon Stadium	190
Windsor Castle	181
WKD Café	172
Wyndhams Theatre	137

Y

Ye Grapes	181
Ye Olde Mitre	181
Yo! Sushi	95
Young Cheng	93
Young England	129

Z

Zaika	87
Zelli	121
Zen Chelsea	93

RED DIRECTORY

EAT-LONDON
London's restaurants, hotels, shops, arts and entertainment

2001-2002 - Vol.5

Published by **Cross Media Ltd.**
4th Floor, 13 Berners Street, London W1T 3LH, UK
Tel: 020-7436-1960　Fax: 020-7436-1930
Managing Editor: Kazuhiro Marumo
Editor: Yoko Takechi
Restaurant Editorial: J.L.Rollinson
Editorial Assistants: Yumi Hiraide, Sachiko Sunaoka
Cover Design: Osamu Miyaki　　Cover Photo: Gina Boffa
DTP Production: Satchiko Ewing, Mutsumi Kawasaki
Printed in Japan
Copyright ©**Cross Media Ltd.** 2001

ISBN 1 897701 37 3